BEQUIA

Dive Bequia, P.O. Box 16,
Bequia, St Vincent, West Indies
Tel:809-458-3504
Fax:809-458-3886
VHF: 68

SPECIAL DISCOUNTS FOR PEOPLE ON
YACHTS SEE PAGE 204 FOR DETAILS

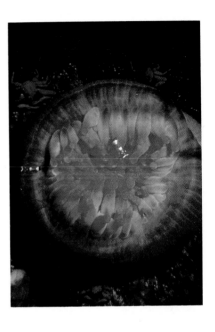

Bob works in close association with dive
shops in St. Vincent and in the Grenadines, so you can buy a dive package
good throughout the area, or start a full
certification course in Bequia and finish it
as you sail through the islands.
Sounds Good? Then call
"Dive Bequia"

SAILORS GUIDE TO THE

Text and charts

Chris Doyle

Illustrations

Sally Erdle

Technical chart consultant

Jesse Sheridan

Photos by:

Sally Erdle	Jeff Fisher
Kristina Lagerkvist	Bill Tewes
Virgina Barlow	Chris Doyle
John Douglas	

The cover map is by **Xandra Fisher** whose decorative maps and postcards are available at gift shops throughout the islands.

DISTRIBUTION

USA AND WORDWIDE
Cruising Guide Publications
P.O. Box 1017
Dunedin, Florida 34697-1017
Tel: 813-733-5322
Fax: 813-734-8179

ST. VINCENT AND THE
GRENADINES
Frances Punnett, Box 17
St. Vincent, W. I.
Tel: 809-458-4246
Fax: 809-456-2620

ST LUCIA
Cecil Baptiste, Box 1457
Castries, St. Lucia, W.I.
Tel: 809-452-8033

GRENADA
Tikal, Box 51, Young St.
St. George's, Grenada
Tel: 809-440-2310

PUBLISHED BY

CHRIS DOYLE PUBLISHING
in association with
CRUISING GUIDE PUBLICATIONS
ISBN 0-944428-28-2

First edition published........ 1980
Second edition published.... 1982
Third edition published...... 1984
Third edition revised..........1985
Third edition revised..........1986
Fourth edition published.....1988
Fifth edition published....... 1990
Sixth edition published....... 1992
Seventh edition published... 1994

OBEAH COPYRIGHT '94

LOOK OUT!

ANYONE *reprinting* ANYTHING *from this* book *without* the permission of th publishers is in **BIG TROUBLE.**

WINDWARD ISLANDS

NOTICE

The information in this guide was correct to the best of our knowledge at the time of going to press.

No warranty, expressed or implied, is made by the publishers for any errors or omissions in this publication. The skipper must use this guide together with U.S. Navy or Hydrographic charts or British Admiralty charts and other navigational aids and not place undue credence in the accuracy of this guide.

This guide should not
be used for navigation.

AUTHOR'S NOTES

In the text and in the directory at the back of the book we give the telephone numbers of business establishments and the credit cards they accept. We also give a very rough price guide to the restaurants. This is an estimate of what you might spend to eat out and have a drink:

$A is $50 U.S. or over
$B is $25 to $50 U.S.
$C is $12 to $25 U.S.
$D is under $12 U.S.

We use the following abbreviations:

F = Facsimile   T = Telephone
cc=Credit card
A = American Express
Dn = Diner's Club, Ds = Discover
V = Visa group, including MasterCard, Barclaycard and Eurocard.

On our sketch charts the main shoal areas are marked with a broken line; reefs which almost touch the surface are marked by squiggly lines; and rocks and deeper reefs are marked with crosses. We have colored danger areas yellow to make them stand out. These have been drawn for yachts drawing about 6.5 feet. Deeper draft yachts will have to refer to the depths on their charts. Depths where given are approximate and in feet. All bearings are magnetic; however, compass roses point to true north.

We are happy to include advertising. It gives extra information and keeps the price of the book reasonable. If you wish to help us keep it that way, tell all the restaurateurs and shopkeepers "I read about it in the Sailors Guide." It helps us no end.

If you like, tell us about your experiences, good or bad. We will consider your comments when writing the next edition.

Chris Doyle
Box 17
St. Vincent, W.I.

AUTHOR'S ACKNOWLEDGEMENTS

To everyone who helped: from those who sit me down in their bars and shops to explain what they are trying to achieve, to those who tap me on the shoulder and say "Hey you know what you should put in your guide?" and also to those who have written in with suggestions - a big thank you to all of you. The book would not be the same without your input. Special thanks to Virginia Barlow for hours of editing and support.

SAILORS
GUIDE
TO THE
WINDWARD
ISLANDS

7th Edition

TABLE OF CONTENTS

ANNANDALE FALLS, GRENADA

LOCATION OF SERVICES
(See details in "Services" section for each anchorage)

Symbols:
- ✓ - Usually
- S - Sometimes
- M - Most Necessities
- B - Basics only
- P - Proposed

Location	customs	ice	water	fuel	cooking gas	bank	telephone	provisioning	laundry*	restaurant	boutique	scuba station	chandlery	haul out	dockage	sail repair
MARTINIQUE																
St. Pierre	✓	✓	✓			✓	✓	✓	✓	✓	✓	✓				
Fort de France/Anse Mitan	✓	✓	✓	✓	✓	✓	✓	✓	✓	✓	✓	✓	✓	✓	✓	✓
St. Anne/Marin	✓	✓	✓			✓	✓	✓	✓	✓	✓	✓	✓	✓	✓	✓
ST. LUCIA																
Rodney Bay Lagoon	✓	✓	✓	✓		✓	✓	✓	✓	✓	✓	✓	✓	✓	✓	✓
Castries/Vigie	✓	✓	✓	✓		✓	✓	✓	✓	✓	✓	✓	B	✓	S	
Marigot Bay	✓	✓	✓	✓		P	✓	M	✓	✓	✓	✓			✓	
Soufriere		✓	✓	✓			✓	✓	✓		✓	✓			✓	
Vieux Fort	✓	✓				✓	✓	M	✓	✓		✓				
ST. VINCENT																
Kingstown/Ottley Hall	✓	✓	✓	✓		✓	✓	✓	✓	✓	✓		✓	✓	✓	
Wallilabou	✓	✓	✓				✓			✓	✓					
Young Island Cut		✓	✓		✓		✓	B	✓	✓	✓	✓				
Blue Lagoon		✓	✓	✓			✓		✓	✓	✓	✓	✓		✓	
GRENADINES																
Admiralty Bay	✓	✓	✓	✓	✓	✓	✓	✓	✓	✓	✓	✓		✓	✓	✓
Friendship Bay	✓	S	S				✓			✓	P	✓				
Mustique	✓	S					✓	B		✓	✓	✓				
Canouan	S	S								✓		✓				
Mayreau							✓	B		✓	✓					
Clifton, Union	✓	✓	✓			✓	✓	M	✓	✓	✓	✓		✓	✓	✓
Palm		S	✓				✓	B		✓	✓	✓				
P.S.V.		S	S	S			✓			✓	✓					
Petite Martinique		S	S	✓						✓						
Hillsborough	✓	✓				✓	✓	M		✓	✓	✓				
Tyrrel Bay		✓		✓			✓	M	✓	✓	✓			✓		✓
GRENADA																
St. George's	✓	✓	✓	✓	✓	✓	✓	✓	✓	✓			✓	✓	✓	✓
Grand Anse						✓	✓	✓		✓	✓	✓				
Prickly Bay	✓	S	✓	✓		✓	✓	M	✓	✓	✓	✓	✓	✓	✓	✓
Mt. Hartman Bay		✓	✓	✓		✓	✓	M	✓	✓	✓	✓			✓	✓

*One can find ladies to wash clothes by hand almost anywhere. Negotiate a fee in advance and specify "no bleach" if necessary.

MILEAGE CHART

From \ To	Ft. de France	Anse Mitan	Gd. A. D'Arlet	St. Anne	Rodney Bay	Castries	Marigot	Pitons	Vieux Fort	Wallilabou	Kingstown	Young Island	Admiralty B.	Friendship B.	Mustique	Canouan	Mayreau	Tobago Cays	Union I.	P.S.V.	Hillsborough	Tyrrel Bay	St. George's	Prickly Bay	Mt. Hartman B.
St. Pierre	12	14	16	30	42	45	47	56	67	90	97	99	105	109	115	122	127	127	130	133	136	139	166	172	173
Ft. de France		3	7	21	33	37	39	47	57	83	90	92	98	102	108	115	120	120	123	126	130	132	159	165	166
Anse Mitan			6	20	32	36	38	46	57	82	89	91	97	101	107	114	119	119	122	125	129	131	158	164	165
Gd. Anse D'Arlet				15	26	30	32	41	52	77	84	86	92	96	102	109	114	114	117	120	123	126	152	158	159
St. Anne					21	26	30	39	50	76	83	85	91	95	101	108	113	113	116	119	123	126	156	161	162
Rodney Bay						5	8	18	29	55	62	64	70	74	80	87	92	92	95	98	102	105	135	140	141
Castries							4	13	24	50	57	59	65	69	75	82	87	87	90	93	97	100	130	135	136
Marigot								10	21	46	53	55	61	65	71	78	83	83	86	89	93	96	126	131	132
Pitons									11	36	43	45	51	55	61	68	73	73	76	79	83	86	116	121	122
Vieux Fort										34	41	43	49	53	59	66	71	71	74	77	81	84	114	119	120
Wallilabou											7	9	15	19	25	32	37	37	40	43	47	50	80	85	85
Kingstown												2	9	11	16	27	32	32	35	38	42	45	75	80	81
Young Island													8	10	15	27	32	32	35	38	42	45	75	80	81
Admiralty Bay														7	12	20	26	24	29	33	35	38	68	73	74
Friendship Bay															7	18	24	24	27	31	33	36	66	71	72
Mustique																14	19	19	25	29	31	34	49	54	55
Canouan																	7	7	14	18	20	23	47	52	53
Mayreau (Saline Bay)																		4	6	10	14	16	45	50	51
Tobago Cays																			4	7	11	14	44	49	50
Union (Clifton)																				4	7	9	40	45	46
P.S.V.																					7	7	39	44	45
Hillsborough																						4	34	39	40
Tyrrel Bay																							30	35	36
St. George's																								7	8
Prickly Bay																									2

This table is approximate and offered as a guide to planning. Distances sailed are often in excess of those shown due to wind and current.

The islands of the Caribbean sweep southwards in a huge arc, making a bridge of giant sized stepping stones from Florida to Venezuela. On the eastern or windward side the Atlantic Ocean pounds the shore. On the leeward side the calmer Caribbean Sea lies tranquil, sparkling in the sun.

The Windward Islands are at the southern end of this chain, the last links before Trinidad and South America. They were called the Windwards by the British, because to get there from many of their other possessions you had to beat to windward.

They lie almost across the easterly trade winds which makes for easy passages north or south. They are just far enough apart to allow for some wild romps in the open ocean before tucking into the calm of the next lee shore.

The four main Windward Islands – Martinique, St. Lucia, St. Vincent and Grenada – are lush and richly tropical, with high mountains that trap the clouds and produce dense green vegetation. Here you can find excellent examples of tropical rain forest, easily accessible to those who like to hike.

Between St. Vincent and Grenada lie the Grenadines – a host of smaller islands, some with hills of a thousand feet, others no more than a reef-enclosed sand cay sprouting a few palms. Drier than the large islands, they all have perfect white beaches, crystal clear waters and colorful reefs.

Over 2000 years ago the islands were colonized by Arawaks, oriental looking people who were great navigators, artists and sportsmen. However, they were overtaken by a more warlike tribe called the Caribs who were in residence in the Windwards by the time Columbus sailed in. The Caribs resisted the Europeans and refused to be slaves. In Grenada the northern town of Sauteurs marks the spot where the last of the Grenada Caribs leapt to their deaths rather than be taken captive. They held out the longest in St. Vincent where the steep

12

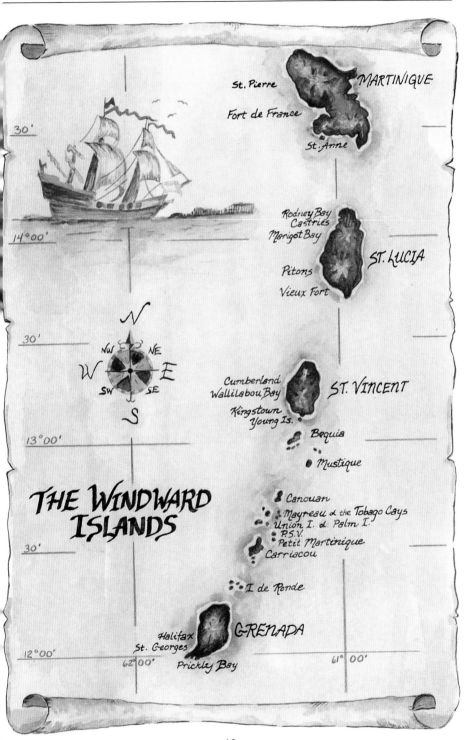

St. Pierre

MARTINIQUE

Fort de France

30'

St. Anne

Rodney Bay
Castries
Marigot Bay

14°00'

ST. LUCIA

Pitons

Vieux Fort

30'

N

NW   NE

W   E

SW   SE

S

Cumberland
Wallilabou Bay

ST. VINCENT

Kingstown
Young Is.

13°00'

Bequia

Mustique

Canouan

THE WINDWARD
ISLANDS

Mayreau & the Tobago Cays
Union I. & Palm I.
P.S.V.
Petit Martinique
Carriacou

30'

I. de Ronde

Halifax
St. Georges

GRENADA

12°00'

62°00'   Prickly Bay   61°00'

terrain made colonization harder. Even here they were eventually driven out by the European colonists. Today just a handful remain in the Windwards, on the north end of St. Vincent in a village called Fancy.

Years of colonization followed and the Windward Islands were fought over by the British and French. Plantation owners became rich from the production of sugar and slaves were brought from Africa to work in the fields. After slavery was abolished some East Indian laborers were imported to take over the field work.

Today, the intermingling of the races has produced an interesting blend of people who live in harmony together.

During its colonial history Martinique, the northernmost Windward Island, was nearly always in French hands. Today it is still part of France and therefore a member of the European Community. The language and ambience are French, and while not essential, it certainly helps to speak a few words of their language.

St. Lucia, St. Vincent and Grenada are now all independent nations with a British tradition; each has its own laws and customs. The official language is English, though the dialect can be hard to understand when locals talk fast among themselves. In St. Lucia, Patois, an Afro-anglicized French, is widely used, as well as English.

These countries are small nations by any standards, with populations of around 100,000 each. Recently there have been moves to form a union, but the process is in a very early stage and it is hard to foresee the outcome.

The Windwards are a joy for the sailor. Good trade winds ensure exhilarating passages and delightful anchorages abound. The weather is pleasant year round, the people friendly and there are few annoying regulations. You are free to sail and enjoy some of the most beautiful islands on earth.

Welcome to the Windwards!

ST. GEORGE'S, GRENADA

ALL ABOUT THE ISLANDS

Currency

In Martinique the currency is the French franc which varies widely in comparison with the U.S. dollar (between four and nine francs to the dollar). You get the best rates at the change places in Fort de France and Anse Mitan, rather than at the banks. Some tourist shops offer up to a 20% discount on purchases made with travelers checks.

In the other islands the currency is the Eastern Caribbean (E.C.) dollar at a fixed rate of 2.67 to one U.S. dollar. The banks usually give a better rate than the shops or taxi drivers, though most people are willing to take U.S. dollars. It seems like you get a lot of E.C. dollars for the U.S. ones, but they are much more quickly spent. Oh well, "EC come, EC go," or as Jimmy Buffet said: "It's much more fun to spend money with pictures of flowers and palm trees on it than money with pictures of green old men."

Tourist season

Charter and hotel rates vary with the time of year. Most people want to come down when it is cold up north, so the winter months (November to April) are the high (expensive) season; the rest of the year is low season. Restaurant and bar prices are generally the same year round. During the quietest months (September and October) some small hotels close down and go on holiday.

What to bring

Nearly all visitors bring too much luggage and do not realize that it is almost impossible to stow hard cases on a yacht. Only soft bags should be used. One of my charterers once arrived without luggage, the airline having spirited it away. Rather than wait, he bought a bathing suit, two pairs of shorts and a shirt and wondered why he had ever bothered packing anything else.

If you need prescription drugs, bring an ample supply and make sure they stay in your carry-on bag.

Life is very informal down here and even in the best of eating places men can get by with a pair of slacks and a sports shirt, women with a simple dress.

Local etiquette

Clothing. Unlike many other western seaside towns, people in the Caribbean will look somewhat askance at you if you wander away from the beach in a bathing suit or, perish the thought, a bikini. Away from the beach, even in that tiny waterfront village, people generally wear at least a shirt and pair of shorts or skirt. In the major towns people dress much as you would if you were going to your local town.

For women toplessness is accepted in some places, particularly in Martinique. I notice it occasionally now on the larger resort beaches in some of the other islands, but elsewhere it is frowned upon. The easiest thing is to see what other people are up to. Complete nudity is best confined to really secluded beaches or anchorages.

Greetings. Manners here are different and great store is set on greetings: "good morning" or "good afternoon" (or in Martinique "bon jour" or "bon nuit"). It is considered rude to approach people with a question or to transact business without beginning with the appropriate greeting.

Tipping. Everyone likes to be tipped, but it is not always expected. In restaurants where no service charge is added, a 10% tip is normal. If service has already been included, a little extra is appreciated but not essential. Taxi drivers do not normally expect to be tipped, but if they go out of their way to help you, you can add a few dollars to the fare to show your appreciation. If you get help from kids carrying your suitcases, they will expect an EC dollar or two.

Water skiing, jet skis

Local laws require that a water-ski vessel have at least two people on board. Water skiing or jet-skiing within 100 yards of a beach or in harbors where yachts are anchored is strictly forbidden. St. Vincent and the Grenadines has some enlightened environmental laws and jet skiing is strictly forbidden.

Drugs

Marijuana grows in the Windwards and is part of the local "Rasta" religion. It is, however, illegal, as are all other mind bending substances except alcohol and tobacco. Laws are very strict and those caught can expect yacht confiscation and up to life imprisonment (a longer vacation than you may have intended).

Suntanning

Whatever the season, the sun is intense and adequate protection is essential. It is advisable to bring down plenty of sunscreen (15+) and use it from the start, building up exposure slowly. The tops of your feet are vulnerable, so light cotton

socks are important. Loose long-sleeved cotton clothing, hats and sunglasses are essential. Heavy burning can still take place on cloudy days and in shade.

Markets

All the main islands have great open air fruit and vegetable markets. These are always colorful, but Saturday morning is the best and busiest time with the greatest selection (Friday in St. Lucia). Never be afraid to ask about things you do not recognize. The market ladies are helpful and will tell you how to cook different vegetables. Some things are not what they appear to be. For example many fruits which look like bananas to the untrained eye are starchier versions, known as plantains and bluggoes, which have to be cooked. (For more local food information, see our section on tropical food.)

Transport

If you don't like to hoof it, you have a choice between taxis, buses, communal taxis, and self-drive rent-a-cars.

Taxis are plentiful and come in all shapes and sizes. For long trips some bargaining is usually possible. In any case, always ask for the fare in E.C. dollars before you start. If you think you are being quoted too high a figure, try another driver.

Colorful, noisy and cheerful, the buses in the English speaking islands are the mainstay of the transport system. They often bear such names as "Trust no man," "De

bad ride," "In God we trust," and similar reflections. Not only is this an inexpensive way to travel, but you get to experience some local life. Some buses are huge custom-built wooden affairs, others are mini-buses. Whatever the type they are not for the claustrophobic, for there is always room for one more on a local bus. Just when you think the whole thing is packed to bursting, the driver's assistant manages to create a tiny square of spare air and, like a conjuror, he whips out yet another seat – a pull out piece of wood that is jammed in to take the extra person. Most buses have stereo systems and the drivers like to run them, like their buses, at full-bore. The buses are a wonderful example of the kind of service you can get with free enterprise. If you are carrying heavy shopping and wish to go off the normal route, this can be negotiated. They will stop to pick you up anywhere, so don't wait on a blind bend. Buses do get rather few and far between after dark, and may be very limited when going to a distant spot. Before taking off to the other end of an island, make sure there will be a bus coming back.

If you arrive by air at a reasonable hour, without too much luggage and can make it to the nearest main road, St. Lucia's Hewanorra Airport and the airport in St. Vincent are on bus routes, and Martinique's airport is on a communal taxi route.

BUGS, BEASTS AND PLANTS

Don't let the cockroaches bug you

Now, for the first time, we will discuss the unmentionable: the indomitable cockroach thrives. If you are on a yacht, the odds are that eventually you will find yourself face to face with one of these miniature, armor-plated monstrosities. No need to panic. Despite their off-putting appearance, they are quite harmless, make good pets, and in reasonable quantities are not a general reflection of the cleanliness of the boat. A good dose of spray will keep them

out of sight for a couple of days (this will be done automatically on a skippered yacht). If you are on a boat with a bad infestation, the permanent cure is as follows. First, give a good spray to reduce the numbers (not necessary if you only have one or two). Then, using a mortar and pestle, grind equal quantities of boric acid and white sugar together and distribute freely under drawers, in bottoms of lockers, etc. This will normally give at least six months of cockroach-free living. Some people prefer to mix the boric acid into a gooey mess with condensed milk because they can

At Doyle, we realize there are just as many different ways to use boats as there are different ways to rig them. So when you consult with us on a cruising inventory, we check more than the rig dimensions.

It's a practice that helped us succeed in building the right sails for mega-yachts like *Galileo* and *Freedom*. It's why so many owners of the world's finest custom and production boats trust Doyle when they head offshore.

 And it's led to the development of revolutionary products like the StackPack mainsail furling system and the Quicksilver roller furling genoa.

It's listening to our customers, and designing sails to meet their needs. If you need a cruising inventory, visit us at Doyle. But be prepared to roll out the charts before we roll out the cloth.

DOYLE
SAILMAKERS

Before we build a cruising inventory, we always check the sail plans.

Doyle Offshore Sails, Ltd
6 Crossroads, St. Philip
Barbados, West Indies
Phone: 423-4600 Fax: 423-4499

Agents:
Venezuela - 58-2-987-2357 **Trinidad** - 632-0559 **Grenada** - 444-4257/4342
St. Vincent - 456-9526 **St. Lucia** - 452-8648 **St. Maarten** - 5995-45231
Antigua - 460-1056 **Tortola** (loft) - 494-2569 **Puerto Rico** - 460-1433
Bermuda (loft) - 297-1008

Sails duty free into Caricom, French and Dutch islands

then stick it on walls and ceilings. I have also found some large versions of the "Sticky Box" to be very effective. Cockroaches generally arrive on board as stowaways in cardboard cartons or amid fruits and vegetables. It is essential to keep special "cockroach free" crates and boxes on board and transfer all incoming supplies into them. Examine local fruits and vegetables before you stow them. So much for the bad news. The good news is that the boat variety, known as the German cockroach, is relatively small, quite unlike the huge shore-side monsters that grow up to two inches long and are aptly called "mahogany birds."

Mosquitoes are not usually a problem on board because of the breeze, but jungly anchorages or enclosed lagoons on the lee of the large islands are occasionally buggy. If you find yourself in such a bay, you can always resort to the mosquito coil. This is not a contraceptive device for mosquitoes but a coil of incense-like material that burns slowly and puts the mosquitoes to sleep. It is effective, but you should be warned that it does not usually kill the bugs and, should the coil go out before you awake, they will be up first and you will be breakfast.

In the evening beaches can be buggy, especially on a still night in the rainy season (July to November). Worse than mosquitoes are the minute sand flies known as "no-see-ums." Any brand of bug repellent will help prevent your sunset barbecue from becoming a free-for-all slapping match.

Dangers

Perhaps we should start with the **rum punch**. This delicious concoction, a mixture of rum and fruit juice, is available in any waterside bar. It can be positively euphoric in small doses and lethal in large. Strongly recommended at sunset, but be warned that the potency is often stronger than the flavor would suggest.

There are poisonous **scorpions** and **centipedes** on the islands, but these are not generally deadly and luckily are rare. Still, take a good look at that old pile of twigs and leaves before you sit and take care

when picking up coconut husks to burn for your barbecue.

A real danger is the **manchineel tree** *(Hippomane mancinella)* which grows abundantly along some beaches. This pretty tree with yellow-green apples is toxic. The leaves can produce a rash like poison ivy. It is all right to take shade under the tree, but never stand under it in the rain and avoid using the branches for firewood, or that song "smoke gets in your eyes" may take on new meaning. If you eat the apples they will cause blisters from stem to stern

and are very dangerous. I once knew a couple who had a most romantic barbecue on the beach. They used the branches on their fire and lay on the leaves. The next morning they woke up with bunged-up red eyes and rashes in some unfortunate places. They had to stay in bed and delay their charter for two days. Seagrapes, which often grow near manchineels, are quite harmless.

Martinique and St. Lucia are also home to a deadly snake, the **fer de lance**, which

22

WE STOCK WHAT SAILORS WANT!

Before Budget Marine, cruising sailors found it difficult to find yachting parts in the Caribbean.

Robbie Ferron, a cruising yachtsman, set out to fill that need over a decade ago.

Today, Budget Marine in St. Maarten stocks a huge inventory of marine products from the U.S., England, France, Germany, Italy and Venezuela. Thanks to Sint Maarten's truly duty-free status, you get what you want at the best prices.

Each member of the Budget team has their own area of specialized knowledge in electronics, rigging, marine coatings, pumps, propulsion and steering systems.

In fact, our staff's knowledge is world-wide and chances are that the Budget team speaks your language, be it French, German, Dutch, Spanish, Swedish or English.

If you are looking for pump parts or a new inflatable, or a source for a complete refit, you can rely on Budget Marine to have in stock what you want.

 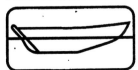

is thankfully very rare. St. Lucia has been listed as having a fresh water liver fluke. This is supposed to have been eradicated, but you might want to restrict your fresh water swimming to the fast streams well above habitations.

The main dangers in swimming and snorkeling are negligent and speeding fishermen, yacht tender drivers and water taxis. Lesser dangers include sea urchins. These are spiny creatures whose prickles penetrate and break off on contact. This is quite painful, especially for the first few hours. They are virtually impossible to pull out once embedded as they break into little pieces. It is best to leave them in and treat them with hot lime juice, as the acid helps dissolve them.

There are sharks and barracudas, but unlike their cousins in the movies, they have yet to attack anyone in these waters unless harassed and so are not considered dangerous here. There is no question that spearfishing can excite these fish. I have dived and snorkeled at night with no problem, but since so few people swim at night, it is impossible to assess how safe it is. Despite their reputations, moray eels are short sighted and timid, but it would be pushing your luck to stick your hand into holes in rock or coral. Some corals are poisonous, so it is safest to look and not touch. Coral scratches can become infected. If you get one, scrub it well with soap and fresh water. Stinging jellyfish are rare, but do exist, and occasionally the swimmer may feel a mild tingling from minute animals known as "sea ants."

A good book on dangerous marine animals would certainly list some more horrors, but the truth is that harm from any of these is extremely rare, and provided you watch where you put your hands and feet, and keep an eye on the sea conditions and current, snorkeling is safer than doing the weekly ironing and a lot more fun.

PEOPLE

Taxi drivers

Taxi drivers are often colorful characters, owners of highly individual cars, and they have a fund of local knowledge. In St. Vincent in particular, the taxi driver has come to reach beyond the normal bounds of his job. Here he often acts as a kind of commission agent as well, running around shopping for yachts or hotels, tracing and sending on lost luggage, obtaining hard to find parts, arranging and officiating at weddings, and even, if necessary, arrang-ing funerals. There is almost nothing a St. Vincent taxi driver won't attempt. In Martinique, only a few of the drivers speak English though they will bear with your French, sometimes with a sense of humor. (A friend once asked one in her best French if he was a taxi. "Oh, no" he replied, pointing at his car, "I am a driver; this is the taxi.") Unfortunately, among the good ones there are an overenthusiastic few who will bully or confuse the unwary passenger into going on a tour he really does not want.

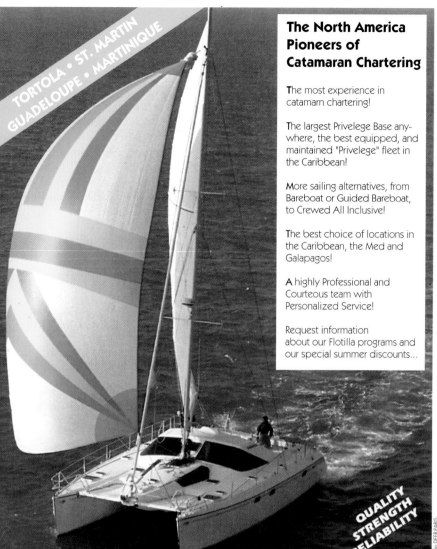

There is one basic rule: always discuss and agree on a price before you embark on a taxi ride and make sure you are both talking in EC dollars or, in Martinique, francs.

Boys in boats (girls, too)

At some point there will be a thump on your topsides and a voice shouting "Hey skip, want some limes? Any laundry then? How about a coconut boat? It sails very good." You are in islands with a great spirit of free enterprise – better get used to it. From the skipper's point of view the most harrowing thing is trying to persuade these vendors that you really do not want several hundred pounds of rough wood and exposed nail heads (a local dinghy) banging your topsides. The vendor's cheerful cry of "no problem, skip" does nothing to remove the scratch.

The problem is further exacerbated because in some areas the competition is so keen that you may be approached two miles from port. This most often occurs in the Soufriere/Pitons area in St. Lucia and the Cumberland/Wallilabou area in St. Vincent. In these areas it is necessary to tie to a palm tree, owing to the depth of water. Boats will approach you long before you arrive offering to "take a line ashore," which is quite a useful service. Whether powered by outboard, or high-powered oarsmen, boat boys have become highly skilled at working out trajectories, and even the most ruthless skipper with a powerful auxiliary finds it impossible to avoid them. They are quite capable of pulling alongside when you are going seven knots,

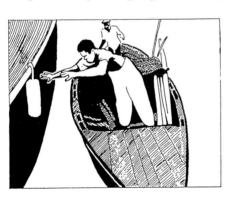

and the resultant crunch will hurt your topsides more than theirs. One skipper I knew used to keep a pile of coconuts which he used as missiles to deter those who came too close. But most of us are poor shots and want a quieter life, so I recommend the following which is very successful. When a local boat approaches manned by a oarsman whose determined strokes shows a keenness to do business at any cost, bring the boat to a complete stop and negotiate while he is still a few yards clear of you. (I offer a set fee of $7 EC on a "take it or leave it" basis.) If he accepts he will no doubt want a tow in, so take his line or tell him to hold onto your dinghy. When finally at anchor put out at least two big fenders and make sure any local boats coming alongside stay on them.

You will probably be offered, at various times, jewelry, fruit, scrimshaw, model boats, ice and live music. It is worthwhile looking at what is offered. All the jewelry is handmade and some items are attractive. No one minds if you do not buy. Some vendors can be a bit persistent, but usually a firm, confident and clear message that you are not interested is enough. Before you buy, please note that buying coral jewelry is unkind to the environment and most countries prohibit the import of turtle shell.

One service I would definitely avoid is the self-appointed "harbor pilots." Excellent though they may be in a small, "two bow" sailing boat, most of these youths have neither the training nor experience required to put them in charge of an expensive yacht. I have seen one charter boat put on a reef, and others anchored too close to other yachts or moorings. I am surprised at how many people will hand over the helm to youths who offer to "show dem de way." Better to trust your own judgment and charts and refuse the services of these youths, asking them to stand clear till you are anchored and have put fenders over the side. They may then prove quite helpful in taking out a second anchor.

Vendors are part of the local color and endemic to undeveloped countries with struggling economies. They are usually friendly, helpful and can add interest to your trip. Very rarely you might get one (either in Soufriere or Wallilabou) who is too pushy and boards the yacht uninvited. In such a case you should insist they get off, and if you have any further problems, try to get help on the VHF (in Soufriere call the Soufriere police station) and, if necessary, move.

Sometimes in the Soufriere and Cumberland anchorages kids use our dinghy as a swimming platform. I have given up trying to stop them; I give them a dollar to clean it instead.

Having someone watch your dinghy can be quite useful, especially at night with several boats moored to the same cleat, and where there is a chance that yours might get cast accidentally adrift. But no one is compelled to accept the service, especially after the fact, as when you leave your dinghy on a deserted dock and on your return a little six year old stumbles out of the bushes, hand outstretched, saying "I watched your dinghy." Dinghy watchers can have their uses and if asked will clean or bail it out for you. Payment is usually from one to three EC dollars, depending on the service given.

Some kids beg. "It's my birthday, what are you going to give me?" is a favorite line. It is important to bear in mind that wages for an unskilled adult may only be $10 to $20 EC a day. If young kids end up getting three times that much liming around the docks, begging from tourists, or getting grossly overpaid for watching dinghies, they skip school and it is hard for them to adjust later when they need to go out to work. Further, once you accept alms from someone you are no longer their equal, so by giving to normal healthy kids you are demeaning them, helping to build up future resentment. By all means employ kids and find something useful for them to do. That helps the economy, but just throwing money around is bad for everyone. For those who like to give away money, there are a few beggars who have handicaps. There are also local associations for the handicapped who are happy to accept donations.

"Tiefs"

Most islanders and yachtsmen are very honest, but obviously there are shady characters, too: thieves, con men and extortionists. Dinghies and outboards are sometimes stolen at night. It is hard to say how many, because no one wants to admit that his dinghy disappeared after that final rum punch because the "rabbit" lost its way while going through the "hole" to make the bowline. There have been cases when a dinghy is returned the next day and the finders demand huge sums for the "rescue." Occasionally some fisherman runs short of money for rope and gets tempted in Wallilabou or the Pitons by all those lines tied to a palm tree.

There are a few who will provide a service and then demand outrageous sums. Therefore always ask the price before accepting any service, including taxis. Make sure you are both referring to EC dollars. Many a delighted taxi driver has agreed, for example, that the fare is "twenty-five dollars" and been offered $25 US rather than EC. One can hardly blame him for accepting it. Worse though are those cases where you think they are talking EC and after the event you find they meant US.

When you are thinking of walking at night or hiking into remote places, it doesn't hurt to ask around first, especially if you are alone or with just one other person. Keep in mind that while the islands are generally safe, there are isolated incidents, as there are anywhere in the world. Occasionally someone turns bad and goes on a robbing spree, doing a "your money or life" bit with the aid of a cutlass. Usually they run amok for a month or two before they get well and truly nailed. Once they are put away everything reverts to normal.

PROTECT YOURSELF AGAINST PETTY THEFT
If you take the following precautions, you are unlikely to be affected.

Lock up when you leave the boat, and leave someone on board at night in St. George's, Kingstown, Castries and in Young Island Cut.

Lock your outboard onto your boat at night.

Lock your dinghy to the dock by day and onto your yacht by night.

Be cautious about inviting strangers onboard.

If anchored stern to a palm tree, use an old piece of line at the beach end. You can use your best anchor line to the edge of the beach, and have the older piece running from it to the tree.

Don't leave things unattended on the beach or in the dinghy in public places.

PHOTOGRAPHY

The light in the Windwards is so bright that colors often photograph better in the early morning or late afternoon. There is enough light for you to be able to use slow speed film (ASA 64 or 100). This changes if you venture into the rain forest where the light is poor and you need fast film. Film is sometimes hard to come by and expensive in the islands, so bring plenty with you. Sea shots will come out much better using a polarizing filter. If you don't have one, it is worth getting one for your trip. You can watch the colors change as you twist the filter. Keep an eye on the sky as well as the sea, as it will turn grey at some angles.

It is only polite to ask when you want to photograph someone. Local attitudes can be a little strange. People with cameras sometimes become a focal point for frustrations and feelings of being exploited. If you try to take a crowd scene, someone will often object, and funnily enough that person might not even be in the picture. Vendors who deal with tourists are usually happy to say "yes," especially if you are buying something. Those with a Polaroid "now for now" camera who are willing to give some prints will have the greatest success.

FISHING

Trolling for fish is fun, means free food and those you catch yourself always taste better. The simplest gear is adequate - about 150 yards of 80 to 100 lb. test line, a wire leader, swivel, hook and lure. Pink and white seem to be the fishes' "in" color recently. It is necessary to feel the line every few minutes to see if you have

How To Stay In Touch On Your Caribbean Vacation.

It's easy with your cellular phone and BOATPHONE, the most extensive cellular communications network in the Caribbean. Just one, simple toll-free phone call is all it takes to activate your cellular service. Charges are billed to your major credit card.

You never have to be out of touch with your family, friends and business interests back home. Because with BOATPHONE, you can stay in touch with everyone from just about anywhere in the Eastern Caribbean, Jamaica or the Cayman Islands.

And if you plan to charter a yacht, most are already equipped with cellular telephones. Many also have fax capability and access for your computer. But if your charter yacht lacks anything you need for your mobile floating office, inquire about BOATPHONE's attractive short-term rental program.

In fact, why not plan a longer vacation? With convenient, modern telecommunications, you can be just as productive — when you choose to be, that is — as you are back home. Most BOATPHONE locations even offer Voice/Fax Mail, so you'll never miss a call.

Call 1-800-BOATFON now to pre-register. That way, you'll have your Caribbean phone number to give to your family and business associates before you leave. Or, after your arrival in the Caribbean, just dial "O SND" (★ O SND in Jamaica) for instant over-the-phone registration. So even if you're indispensable, you can still take a vacation. Thanks to BOATPHONE!

1-800-BOATFON

(In Canada: **1-800-567-8366** Elsewhere: **809-462-5051**
Within the Windward Islands: **809-452-0361**)

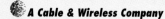 **A Cable & Wireless Company**

BOATPHONE™

The #1 Cellular Phone Company Of The Caribbean

caught anything (a clothes peg can be rigged as a telltale), and every 40 minutes or so it should be hauled in for a weed check. Fish never go for a weed lure. Fish are easily cleaned and scaled, but if you have never done it before, hire a local to show you how with your first fish.

Any fish you catch out in open water will almost certainly be good to eat. Fish poisoning, common farther north, is a rarity here. One might be suspicious of a really large barracuda who could be down from up north visiting relatives, but smaller barracuda (around five lbs.) are considered excellent eating. If you have no luck fishing, it is often possible to buy fish from the local fishermen. Do not be offended if they offer you dolphin. This is a delicious fish and no relative of Flipper.

The lobster season is usually from the first of October to the end of April. During this time lobsters may be bought from local fishermen and the most likely places to find them are Mustique, Union, the Tobago Cays and P.S.V.

It is against the law to buy lobster out of season, less than nine inches long, or lobsters bearing eggs at any time, and the fines are steep. You may be offered one, but please refuse.

MEDICAL CARE

There is adequate medical care for most ailments in all the larger islands and any of the hotels or charter companies will help you get in touch with a doctor. There is a doctor and a good little clinic in Port Elizabeth in Bequia. Mustique is a good place to get sick. There is an excellent small clinic, situated next to the airport in case you need further treatment. In emergencies remember that all cruise ships stand by on VHF: 16 and carry doctors on board. If you have a life threatening situation that needs hospitalization or includes serious head injuries, plan on immediate transport to Martinique or Barbados. You can call the Martinique hospital (596-55-20-00/51-51-52) for a helicopter ambulance. (See also the air charter companies in our directory.) For diving accidents needing decompression call: Martinique (596-50-20-00) or Barbados (809-436-6185) for immediate evacuation. For lesser emergencies:

Martinique: (clinic) 596-71-82-85

St. Lucia: Dr. Soni, surgery: 452-6002; home 452-8116; Rodney Bay Medical Clinic (Dr. Beaubrun) T:452-8621/0179

Grenada: Dr. Michael Radix, surgery 444-4850, 440-4379; home 443-5330; St. George's School of Medicine 444-4271

St. Vincent: Botanic Hospital 457-1747

Bequia Hospital: 458-3294

Mustique: (ask for clinic) 458-4621

ENTERTAINMENT AND SPECIAL EVENTS

Green flash

In the evenings, sunset brings an opportunity to look for the elusive "green flash." This happens as the sun disappears below the horizon. For about a second (blink and you've missed it) the very last bit of the sun to disappear turns bright green. To see this you need a clear horizon and the right atmospheric conditions. Some say rum punch helps. Binoculars make it a lot clearer. Photographers will need a big telephoto and an auto drive wouldn't hurt.

Entertainment

The most popular form of evening entertainment is the "jump up." This usually happens in one of the bars or hotels and takes the form of a dance, most often to a live band. If enough rum flows, everyone does indeed "jump up." Both Martinique and St. Vincent have casinos, but these are very low key. Most of the larger hotels offer evening dancing with a floor show. Some hotels serve Sunday lunch to the accompaniment of a steel band. One can dance, swim or just enjoy the music.

Special events

There are a variety of local occasions for entertainment and partying. If you happen to be down here at the right time, they will be worth investigating.

Carnival started as a riotous bacchanal before Lent. Carnivals feature costumed parades, calypso contests, steel bands and days of dancing in the street. Martinique and St. Lucia still have theirs before Lent, but St. Vincent and Grenada have switched. Check our information on holidays at the beginning of each island section.

Sailing Events. Martinique has an informal race early in April. It is called the Banana's Cup and you can ask about joining in at Puces Nautiques. If you happen to be here on their national holiday, July 14th,

you may see pirogue races around Fort de France. Pirogues also feature in each coastal village during celebrations for its patron saint. Anyone interested can get a list from the local tourist office.

St. Lucia's Pitons Regatta is in the second week of February and includes four days of racing out of Rodney Bay.

Bequia's Easter Regatta is well worth attending. It includes yacht races, local "two bow" fishing boat races, model boat races and cultural shows.

The Grenada Sailing Festival is held in January. It offers a program of race events backed by a well organized social program. All entrants are welcome, from serious racing boats to live-aboards.

The Carriacou Regatta (weekend before the first Monday in August) is a very local event featuring races for small fishing boats and the larger cargo carrying sloops. These are some of the finest sailing vessels made in the islands. Ashore there is plenty of fun.

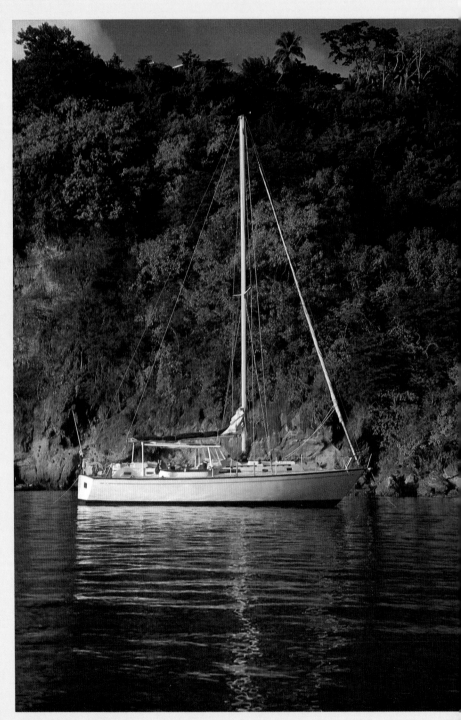

CRUISING INFORMATION

Continuous sunshine and balmy trade breezes, right? Well, not too far wrong.

There are two seasons, the dry and the wet, but they are not always well differentiated. During the dry season (February to June) there will often be weeks of clear sunny weather broken only by an occasional small rain shower. In the wet season (July until January) there will still be plenty of sunshine, but with more frequent showers and occasional rainy days with no sun. There is very little temperature difference between the seasons; you can expect 78 to 85 ° Fahrenheit year round.

The winds are nearly always from the northeast to southeast at 10 to 25 knots; calms are rare. The winds tend to strengthen around the northern ends of islands. Rain usually arrives in intense squalls which can be seen coming from afar. Sometimes these squalls have a lot of wind in them (40 knots or more); often they do not. There is no way to tell before they arrive. Infrequently, a squall or cold front can produce winds from the westerly quadrant, making the usual anchorages uncomfortable.

During the winter months cold front farther north sometimes produce swell that reach the Windwards. These northerl swells can make anchorages which ar open to the north or west rolly and occa sionally untenable.

Visibility varies from an exceptional lov of five miles to a high of over 50 miles. Th hazy days are caused by dust from Africa Sometimes reddish traces may be found o the cabin and decks. On hazy days w avoid dust stains when doing the laundr by wiping off the lifelines before hangin out the washing.

The hurricane season is from June unti October. The months of June, July an October only produce about one hurrican every three years for the whole wester Atlantic including the Caribbean Sea an Gulf of Mexico. During August and Sep tember the number is around five a yea Hurricanes frequently start well out in th Atlantic Ocean, often on the latitude of th

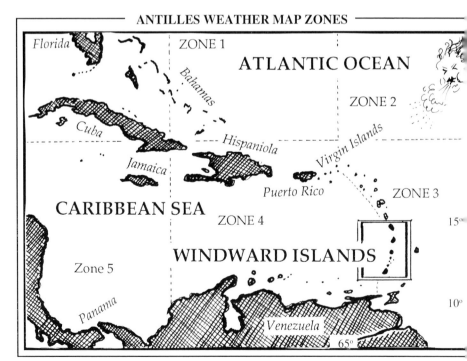

ANTILLES WEATHER MAP ZONES

Windwards, but then they usually swing north and pass through the Caribbean higher up. Very few hit the Windwards and sometimes years go by without one in this area, but it is essential to listen to the forecasts. Try Radio Antilles (930 AM) at 1820 after the local news and at about 0830, or Radio Barbados (900 AM) with a weather forecast after the 0700 morning news. If you are in Grenada, Radio Grenada (530 AM) has a forecast at about the same time. The Grenada Cruisers net puts out weather on VHF: 72 at 0800. Otherwise you can use your boatphone or a local phone and call a met office. (St. Lucia 545-6550, St. Vincent 458-4477. Mustique 458-4621 [ask for Mustique infomation services], Grenada 444-4142.)

Here are some terms you will hear on the radio and what they mean: "Intertropical Convergence Zone" affecting the area. This is not any kind of "low," but you may get some rain squalls or cloudy weather. "Tropical Disturbance," "Tropical Wave" and "Upper Level Trough" are poorly organized weather systems associated with rain squalls of varying intensity. A "Tropical Depression" is an organized weather system with sustained winds of up to 35 knots and rain. Sometimes these can be very nasty and other times they turn out to be nothing. A "Tropical Storm," on the other hand, is definitely something to be avoided as it has lots of rain and sustained winds of 35 to 63 knots. Once the sustained winds become more than 64 knots it is called a hurricane.

Hurricane winds can come from any direction, so be prepared to run for one of the hurricane holes: Cohe du Lamentin, Trois Ilet, or better still, Cul de Sac Marin in Martinique; Rodney Bay Lagoon or Marigot Bay in St. Lucia; the mangrove swamp in Tyrrel Bay, Carriacou, and in Grenada either in the Lagoon at St. George's or Port Egmont.

During one of the very few hurricanes that we did get, a charter party was advised by their company to make at once for a safe harbor to ride it out. "Oh no," they said "we have confirmed flights out and don't want to miss them - we will make it in time."

They sailed north from St. Vincent to St. Lucia, but by the time they reached Soufriere, it was raining cats and dogs, and the wind was howling, so they anchored and went ashore. The boat soon began to drag and the skipper, aided by a local fisherman, tried to re-anchor. They managed to get their anchor line caught in the prop so they could not use power, and it was blow-ing too hard to make sail. In the end they drifted all night through the hurricane, and were rescued, after the winds fell, by a French coast guard boat off Martinique. I suppose the moral of the tale is that it is amazing what you can get away with, but better not to try.

NAVIGATION

Charts

Those needing charts have a choice between British Admiralty (B.A.), U.S. Defense Mapping Agency (D.M.A) and Imray yachting charts. Some charts are more expensive down island than in the U.S. or U.K. U.K charts are much more expensive in the U.S. and vice versa. The new B.A. series of charts (marked by an asterisk on the list of charts we give in a box on the next page) are in full color and are based on W.G. 84 data so they can be used with Global positioning systems (GPS). They are the newest and most detailed charts of the area.

Charterers might like a general chart of the Windwards for plotting their cruise.

Buoyage

All the islands now use the IALA B buoyage system. Main channels are marked with red and green buoys or bea-cons with red to starboard when entering; in other words "Red Right Returning." Other shoals and channels are indicated by black and yellow buoys or beacons coded both with respect to color and triangulation (using cones) as shown in the diagram below.

Lights and buoys in the Windwards may be unreliable. Lights sometimes do not work, buoys can go adrift and beacons can lose color and cones. In short, treat navigational aids with great caution.

GPS

GPS is the biggest leap in navigational science since the invention of the chronometer. Now we can always know our precise position anywhere in the world. Accurate though this system is, there are limitations. I have noticed occasional inaccuracies up to a tenth of a mile, even when the GPS suggested the accuracy should

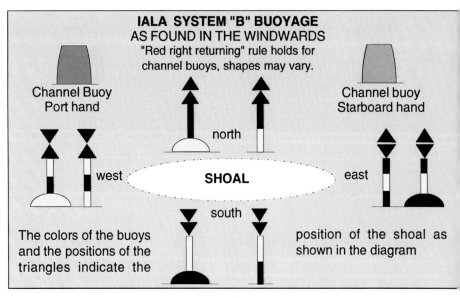

IALA SYSTEM "B" BUOYAGE
AS FOUND IN THE WINDWARDS
"Red right returning" rule holds for
channel buoys, shapes may vary.

Channel Buoy
Port hand

Channel buoy
Starboard hand

north

west   SHOAL   east

south

The colors of the buoys and the positions of the triangles indicate the

position of the shoal as shown in the diagram

have been better. Therefore I would not advise using a GPS to navigate reef-strewn passages at night or in poor visibility. Many available charts have been created on unspecified formats, and therefore sizeable inaccuracies (up to half a mile) may occur. The new British Admiralty charts are based on WG 84 data and work with GPS. The charts in this book are on GPS grids. These were created using a Garmin 50 on WG 84 data, using much interpolation. No guarantee is offered about their accuracy, but I would be happy to know how accurate readers find them. There is also a table of GPS positions for planning purposes. You cannot just punch these numbers in and sail safely there; land and shoals will probably be on your line of approach, depending on where you start.

CUSTOMS & IMMIGRATION

The Windwards contain four separate countries: Martinique; St. Lucia; St. Vincent, including the Grenadines to PSV; and Grenada, which includes Carriacou and Petite Martinique. Each has its own customs regulations and it is necessary to clear in and out of each country. On arrival you should anchor in a port of entry and hoist a yellow flag. After that you can go ashore in search of an officer. Three to four crew lists, passports and ship's papers are required. In Martinique, St. Lucia and St. Vincent the crew list forms are supplied and in St. Vincent there is a nominal fee for this. Grenada sometimes has them, but better take your own. Make three copies, include the yacht's name, tonnage and home port, along with the names of all crew members, their nationalities and passport numbers. When clearing, always take your previous clearance with you. Customs officers usually refuse to deal with anyone not wearing a shirt. Further details are given under island and harbor headings.

Dogs

So you've brought your pet all the way over the ocean and now you want to take it

CHARTS OF THE WINDWARDS

General Coverage
DMA 25001 Eastern Caribbean Sea
Imray B Martinique to Trinidad
Imray A4 Guadeloupe to St. Lucia
BA 956 Guadeloupe to Trinidad

Martinique
DMA 25524 Martinique
DMA 25525 Plans: St. Pierre, La Trinite
DMA 25526 North & West Coasts
DMA 25527 Fort de France
Imray A30 Martinique, incl. plans: Fort de France, Trinite, St. Pierre, Marin, Francois, Pte. du Bout
Imray A 301 East Coast of Martinique
BA 371 Northern Martinique (inc. plans)
BA 494   Southern Martinique (incl. plans)

St. Lucia
DMA 25521 St. Lucia
DMA 25528 Plans: Castries, Vieux Fort, Marigot, Rodney Bay.
Imray B1 St. Lucia, includes plans
BA 1273 St. Lucia
BA 197 Marigot to Pte. du Cap
BA 499 Plans: Vieux Fort, Castries, Marigot, etc.

St. Vincent and Bequia
DMA 25484 St. Vincent
DMA 25483 Plans: Kingstown to Calliaqua, Admiralty Bay.
Imray B30 St. Vincent, Bequia and Mustique, incl. plans of all major anchorages.
BA 791 St. Vincent
BA 799 Plans: Kingstown to Calliaqua, Admiralty Bay*

The Grenadines
DMA 25482 Bequia to Carriacou, incl. Tobago Cays plan
Imray B31 Bequia to Carriacou, inc. plans.
Imray B311 Canouan to Carriacou
BA 793 Bequia to Canouan, inc. plans*
BA 794 Canouan to Carriacou, inc. plans *
BA 795 Grenada to Carriacou, inc. plans*

Grenada
DMA 25481 Grenada, inc. plans
Imray B32 Carriacou and Grenada inc. plans
BA 797 Grenada*
BA 799 Plans: south coast & St. George's*

* On WG84 format for use with GPS

GPS POSITIONS

For locations see sketch charts, see also navigation text

MARTINIQUE	deg min (N)	deg min(W)
St Pierre	14 44.5	61 10.7
Case Pilot	14 38.4	61 08.5
Fort de France	14 35.7	61 04.5
Pointe du Bout	14 33.7	61 03.4
Grand Anse D'Arlet	14 30.0	61 06.0
Petit Anse D'Arlet	14 29.2	61 05.2
Cul de sac Marin (entrance)	14 26.7	60 54.0
St. Anne	14 26.2	60 53.2

ST LUCIA	deg min (N)	deg min(W)
Pigeon Island	14 05.5	60 58.2
Rodney Bay Lagoon (entrance)	14 04.7	60 57.4
Castries (entrance)	14 01.2	61 00.5
Marigot (entrance)	13 58.1	61 01.9
Anse Cochon	13 55.6	61 03.6
Off Anse Chastanet	13 51.5	61 05.2
Soufriere	13 51.2	61 03.8
Off Gros Piton	13 48.5	61 05.0
Off Vieux Fort	13 43.0	60 58.0

ST. VINCENT	deg min (N)	deg min(W)
Cumberland Bay	13 16.0	61 15.8
Wallilabou	13 14.9	61 16.5
Bottle & Glass	13 14.4	61 16.9
Petit Byahaut	13 10.9	61 16.2
Ottley Hall	13 09.5	61 14.9
Kingstown	13 09.0	61 14.0
Off Fort Duvernette	13 07.6	61 12.4

GRENADINES	deg min (N)	deg min(W)
Bequia, Devil's Table	13.00.7	61 15.1
Bequia, West Cay	12 59.5	61 17.6
Bequia, Friendship Bay	12 59.1	61 14.0
Mustique, Britannia Bay	12 52.8	61 11.5
Canouan, Charlestown Bay	12 42.7	61 20.2
Canouan, Glossy Hill	12 42.2	61 21.4
West of Baline Rocks	12 39.5	61 23.0
Tobago Cays	12 38.2	61 21.8
Mayreau, Salt Whistle Bay	12 39.0	61 23.7
Mayreau, Saline Bay	12 38.0	61 24.5
Union, Clifton	12 35.7	61 24.9
Union, west of Grand de Coi	12 35.0	61 25.0
Union, off Miss Irene Pt (Chatham B).	12 35.5	61 28.0
PSV, Mopion Channel	12 32.9	61 24.1
PSV	12 32.0	61 23.5
Carriacou , off north end	12 32.0	61 27.0
Tyrrel Bay	12 27.5	61 30.0

GRENADA	deg min (N)	deg min(W)
Off north end	12 15.0	61 40.0
Halifax Harbour, entrance	12 06.7	61 45.0
Dragons Bay	12 05.2	61 45.9
St. George's, entrance	12 02.7	61 45.7
Point Saline	12 00.2	61 48.3
True Blue	11 59.6	61 46.2
Prickly Bay, entrance	11 59.3	61 46.0
West of Porpoises rocks	11 58.6	61 45.9

for a walk? Well, here is what you can expect from the local authorities. In Martinique and Grenada you should have a rabies vaccination certificate handy when you clear in, and you can walk your dog ashore. St. Vincent and St. Lucia are both rabies free and animals are not allowed ashore under any circumstances.

Few people realize that dogs in the Caribbean are subject to a deadly little heart worm. Check with a vet for appropriate counter measures before leaving, or as soon as you get here.

PROTECTING THE ENVIRONMENT

People can easily harm the environment, but we say "thank you" to most visitors who have been courteous and well behaved. With the increasing volume of yachts in the area, it definitely helps if people are considerate. This area has been wonderfully free of loud noises, whether from drunken raucous laughter, stereo equipment, endlessly running generators, or loudly clanking halyards. Luckily, there is plenty of room in most anchorages, so those who want to make noise or need to run generators for much of the time, can just stay well away from everyone else. Most of us have to run our engines at sometime during the day, but let us at least leave the hour around sunset free so everyone can enjoy it in peace. One disturbing exception to this has been the increase in windmills. Most of these are quiet and unobtrusive, but many two bladed varieties can be heard well over 100 yards away. They can destroy the natural peace of many a quiet anchorage. Further, the people who own them seem to think that, because they are not using fossil fuels, they are on the side of the angels and can do no wrong. They run them 24 hours a day without giving any consideration to those who might find the noise irritating. If you have not yet bought a windmill, I suggest you consider buying a quiet one, or better still, try solar panels. If you already own a noisy one, please try to anchor to the back of the fleet, and when your batteries are charged up, stop the blades.

Right now you can don a mask and snorkel and dive over the side anywhere in the Windwards and find the seabed pretty clean. Let's keep it that way.

Fishing and hunting

The days have now gone when we could jump over the side, bristling with knives and festooned with spearguns long enough to be sold by the yard, to decimate the local fish population. Spearfishing has proved too damaging and new laws have been passed to control it. By the time this guide comes out it will be illegal to spearfish almost anywhere from St. Lucia to Grenada. It is worth noting that compliance not only helps the environment, but that illegal fishing fines exceeded $100,000 during the first couple of years they were enacted in St. Vincent and the Grenadines. Hunters should note that all cows, goats and sheep, even on remote uninhabited islands, are privately owned. They are often put out to graze and left for months on end. They should not be harmed.

Garbage

Unfortunately yacht garbage has totally overwhelmed the land facilities of the Grenadine islands, and we have to cut down on what we bring ashore. The best way to do this is to buy things with as little packing as possible and use returnable bottles. Always take along your own shopping bags and avoid all those plastic ones.

Food waste in all its forms should be dumped at sea in deep water. Carrying organic food matter from one island to another as garbage is a dangerous practice. Fruit flies, cockroaches, fungi and other potentially dangerous pests can be inadvertently transported from one island to another, with devastating results. At present Grenada can trade fruit with the U.S.A. because it does not have the Mediterranean fruit fly. Other islands do, and fruit peelings or other organic garbage brought into Grenada could contain fruit fly eggs. Should this happen it would cost Grenada millions of dollars in lost trade. Conversely, Grenada has palm and banana diseases not present in the islands further north. So take care when transporting and disposing of fresh fruit and vegetable matter. In addition, it is unwise to transport things like palm woven hats and baskets

MARTINQUE (France)

ST. LUCIA

ST. VINCENT and the Grenadines

GRENADA

between islands.

No plastics, including bags and bottled water containers, must ever be thrown at sea. Leatherback turtles eat jellyfish and many have been found dead, their stomachs filled with plastic bags. Take the plastic bags ashore and let the turtles eat the jellyfish. Smelly bags can be rinsed in the ocean before storing. Other items that should never be thrown out at sea include string and fishing line which might be eaten, or which might form a tangle trap somewhere, wax lined cardboard cartons (juice cartons, etc.) and tin foil. These can all be rinsed in seawater before stowing. Similarly, anything that could be in the least bit toxic, including aerosol sprays and chemicals, should never be dumped at sea.

Most of our garbage consists of paper, cardboard, cans and bottles. Should we throw these at sea? Ideally, no. The ocean is not a dumping ground, and if we are not very careful where we dump such garbage we can damage reef structures. On the other hand we should not take these items ashore and dump them in the Grenadines where the facilities are totally inadequate.

So what to do? As far as possible keep the garbage for an adequate refuse facility in one of the larger islands. Martinique has plenty of places to put garbage and you will find adequate facilities in Rodney Bay and Marigot Bay in St. Lucia, and in GYS, Spice Island Marine and Secret Harbour in Grenada. Dirty cans and other food containers should be rinsed before stowing so they do not stink up your boat.

If you are unable to do this then it is probably marginally better to dump nonreturnable bottles, cans, shredded paper and cardboard out far from land, with no islands or reefs in the lee, in water over 600 feet deep than it is to pile them in a heap on land where they are not being collected.

CUMBERLAND BAY

Paper and cardboard will eventually dissolve (though we do not know about the toxicity of the inks printed on them). Cans and bottles will sink and sit on the sea bed which, in deep water, is mainly sand or mud. Nothing should ever be dumped near a reef or in an anchorage.

Never give garbage to vendors. Some will offer to dispose of it for a fee. However, the person offering to take your garbage has no proper means of disposing of it. The good ones try to burn it, but combustion is never complete and the remains are left strewn around. Others dump your garbage in holes in the bushes and the worst take it to the nearest beach, rummage through for items of interest, and abandon it. Tougher garbage laws are coming in. You are responsible for your own garbage. If you give it to someone else for a fee, they are considered your employee, and if they litter with your garbage, you are legally liable.

Eco-purchasing

Few people realize how powerfully their dollars speak and one of the very best things you can do for the environment is to spend wisely.

Dollars spent on such items as wood carvings, jewelry made from decorative local seeds, banana craft, straw goods, woven grasses and anything made from coconut shells will really help the economy and the environment. Jewelry made from conch shells is also okay as these are caught for their meat, and the shell is just thrown away.

Avoid buying any coral and turtleshell products. Coral grows very slowly and considerable damage to reef structures is done by youths who take corals to sell to the jewelry makers. The hawksbill turtle, most often killed for its shell, is an endangered species, and importation of turtle shell is forbidden in most countries. Most of these items are sold mainly to yachts, so let us say no to the vendors and support the turtles and reefs. If you visit during the lobster season and are buying lobsters, always turn them over to see if they have eggs underneath (easily seen as a red caviar). If they do, refuse to buy them.

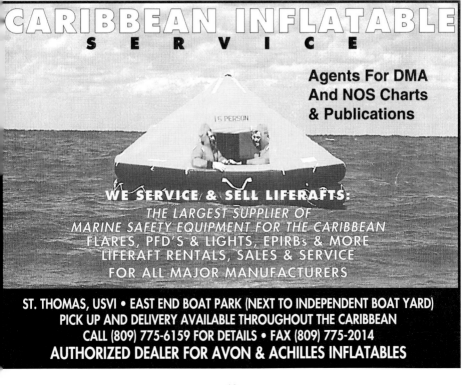

"It's fantastic. I could breathe underwater just like a fish, and fish swam up and looked at me. What an incredible feeling."

"It's the greatest sensation I've ever felt. When we swam back with the current it was just like gliding through a beautiful garden!"

These are typical comments from first-time divers who find that diving is the most exciting thing they have ever done. No wonder: it is the closest most of us will ever come to visiting a strange planet. But not only that, underwater we are weightless, and seem to fly. Rather like birds we can soar, hover and dive down to see anything of interest.

The underwater world is full of wonders – tall soft waving "plants" that are really colonies of tiny animals, or sponges which look like ancient urns, in colors ranging from yellow to a psychedelic luminous blue. Huge schools of fish swim by, unconcerned about your presence. Little squids move by a kind of jet propulsion, turtles and gentle giant rays glide with elegant ease.

Yet many people are put off diving because they are under the impression it is complicated and difficult. Nothing could be further from the truth. With modern equipment diving is very simple, and with one of the popular "resort courses" you can be diving in half a day. In fact the problem most divers have is to avoid boring their non-diving friends to distraction with tales of undersea adventure.

Equipment

Experienced divers will want to bring their own masks, fins and regulators. A really good comfortable B.C. (buoyancy compensator) might be worth bringing, too; as for the rest, forget it. There is no point in humping tanks and weight belts. Far better to rent them here. Those without any equipment don't need to worry. The dive shops will supply everything and it is usually excellent up-to-date gear. In many parts of the world you have to wear a protective "wet suit" against the cold, but in the Windwards the water is warm enough that for most of us this isn't necessary.

Courses for learners

Anyone who just wants to give diving a go can do so very quickly with a "resort course." It will take one whole morning or afternoon. First you get a one hour talk which tells you in simple language what it is all about. Then you try out the equipment in shallow water and, lastly, you go for your first dive. A resort course only qualifies you to dive under the close supervision of an instructor. If you are staying in the same place, you can keep going on dives with the instructor without further training but what if you move locations? If you keep a log book of your dives, you may find another instructor on another island willing to take you down, but many will want you to redo the resort course. Once you go home and stop diving, you must take another course before starting again. If you take to diving, it is much better to become fully qualified.

First dive

Wherever you take a resort course the instructors will choose a site which is easy but interesting enough to attract aficiona-

dos. A typical example is Devil's Table in Bequia. The rocks and coral start at 12 feet and slope down to about 35 feet deep. You enter the water and feel a bit nervous, but you breathe out and gently sink. Soon your attention turns outwards. Large pillar corals rise from among the rocks. They look fuzzy but if you brush them ever so lightly with your hand, the tentacles withdraw, leaving them looking like rocks. You stop to examine some pretty shells clinging to a waving sea fan and to your surprise a tiny damsel fish shoots up and tries to chase you away. He's protecting his patch, and you don't scare him; it's then you learn that you can even laugh through your regulator. There is a great deal more to see: brightly colored parrotfish and angelfish, moray eels staring at you from their holes, strange looking arrow crabs and brightly banded coral shrimp. You enjoyed it? Good! It can count as your first dive toward full certification.

Certification

If you've ever thought about getting certified, or if you try a dive and like it, then it makes sense to get certified on your holiday. If you get certified at home, the chances are that it will be in a swimming pool with nothing more interesting to look at than white walls. Your open water dives are likely to be in some grey frigid lake. Furthermore you will probably have to buy or rent equipment which is normally included in the course price down island. In the Caribbean you can train at a cost not much greater than the dives alone. The course includes all equipment, you do everything in open water, the dives are fantastic, and you can take home a diving certificate as

well as your memories. There are several diving associations which have accredited diving instructors who can train you and give you a certificate. These include Padi and Naui which are equally good. A full diving course in the islands takes about four or five days, and includes a couple of hours instruction each day followed by a dive, during which you increase your practical skills.

You do not have to stay in one place for the time it takes to get certified. Dive St. Vincent, (which includes Dive Canouan and Grenadines Dive) and Dive Bequia work together so you can start a certification course in any of their locations and continue it as you sail through the islands.

For qualified divers

Some people, especially those chartering yachts, prefer to rent gear and go off diving by themselves. Others prefer to join a dive with professional instructors. At least for your first few dives, I recommend going with the dive instructors. They know all the good sites, the hidden caves, the special ledge where angel fish live, and maybe they know where there is a tame octopus, seahorse or frogfish. A good instructor is also a good guide and can often point out many things that would otherwise be missed, which can add interest to your dive. Perhaps the most important reason is that many good dive sites are in places that can only be reached with a powerful dive boat rather than a dinghy. I have worked with many charterers who have tried it both ways and noticed that those who went with dive instructors had a much better time than those who went on their own.

The diving in the Windwards varies mark-

edly from island to island, and from one dive site to the next, so enthusiasts will want to try diving in several different spots. We will mention the good sites and their accessibility in the text under each anchorage section.

DIVE STATIONS OF THE WINDWARDS

MARTINIQUE, (area code:596)

Trois Ilets
Lichee T:66 05 26
Blue Passion Caraibe 66 04 90
Planet Bleu 66 08 79
Meridien hotel T:66 01 79
Case Pilote
Case Pilote Diving Club T:78 73 75
St Pierre
Tropicasud, T:78 38 03, cc:A,V.
St. Anne
Histoires D'Eau, T:76 92 98

Also Polymar [T:70 62 88], Ship Shop [71 43 40] and Sub Evasion [T&F:66 11 25], fill Scuba tanks.

ST. LUCIA (area code:809)

Vigie and Rodney Bay
Buddies Scuba, T:452-5288/452-7044
Dolphin Divers T:452-9485, F:452 0802
Windjammer Landings
Windjammer Diving, T:452-2311
Marigot Bay,
Dolphin Divers T452-9485/451-4357, F:452-0802, VHF:16
Anse Chastenet, Soufriere
Scuba St. Lucia, T:454-7354/5, VHF:16

ST. VINCENT (area code: 809)

Young Island Cut
Dive St. Vincent, T:457-4928/4714, Fax:457-4948, VHF:68
Petit Byahaut
Petit Byahaut T:457-7008, VHF:68, cc:V,
Blue Lagoon
St. Vincent Dive Experience, T:456-9741, F:457-2768, VHF:68

BEQUIA (area code: 809)

Admiralty Bay
Dive Bequia, T:458-3504, F:458-3886, VHF:68
Sunsports, T:458-3577, Fax:458-3907, VHF:68
Friendship Bay
Paradise Diving, T:458-3222,

MUSTIQUE (area code: 809)

Mustique Watersports, T:456-4777, ext-426, F:456-4565, VHF:68.

CANOUAN (area code: 809)

Dive Canouan, T:458-8648, F:457-4948, VHF:68, 16

UNION ISLAND (area code: 809)

Grenadines Dive, T&F:458-8138, VHF:68,16

PALM (area code: 809)

Scuba Shack, T:458-8804, VHF:68,

CARRIACOU (Area Code: 809)

Hillsborough
Silver Beach Diving, T:443-7337, VHF:16, cc:V, Instructors.
Paradise Dive Shop T:443 8406, 443 8391, VHF:16,

GRENADA (Area Code: 809)

Grand Anse
Grenada Aquatics, T:444-4129, F:444-4808, VHF:16
Dive Grenada, T: 444-5875/4334, F:444-4875, VHF:16
Mt Hartman Bay
Scuba World, T:809-444-3333 ext 584. (also in Rex Grenadian).

TRINITY YACHT FACILITIES

WELCOMES YOU TO OUR OUTHAUL AND STORAGE FACILITY AT CHAGUARAMAS BAY, TRINIDAD.

VERY ATTRACTIVE RATES ON WORK AND STORAGE

THE FACILITIES:
- 50 Ton ACME Marine Hoist
- Telephone and FAX services
- Free Water and Electricity
- Mast Removal
- Laundramat, Toilets, Showers, Grocery, Supply Store
- Bona fide crews are allowed to work on own boats free of charge

THE WORK:
- Skilled and semi-skilled labour available for painting/fibreglassing/welding/wood-working/engine repairs
- Sail and rigging repairs
- Very comprehensive machine shop work for propeller repair and all Aluminum, Stainless Steel and Bronze repairs

AND REMEMBER:
- Trinidad is out of the main hurricane belt!
- Teak is grown in Trinidad and is readily available at excellent prices!

VHF: CH. 72 "Trinity Yachts" (call sign)
VHF: CH. 68 "Power Boats" (call sign)
Address: P.O. Box 3163, Carenage, Trinidad & Tobago
TEL: 1 (809) 634-4303   Fax: 1 (809) 634-4327

MARTINIQUE

When in Martinique everyone stocks up on wine, beer, soft drinks, spirits, cigarettes & cigars at:

PHILIPPE

DISTRIBUTION SARL

- We sell by the case and the bottle
- Easy selection from our lists
- **Duty free prices**
- Delivered to the Abri Cotier dock or pick up from Quai de Tourelles

We supply to private yachts, charter yachts, hotels, bars and restaurants throughout the islands. Visit us or call for more information:

Phone: (596)-70-11-39, Fax: (596)-60-00-00

Quai des Tourelles Port de Fort de France, 97200, Fort de France, Martinique

We have now moved to Quai des Tourelles
Visit our new 500 sq meter premises:-
by road (12 minutes walk),
by Dinghy, or come by yacht*
*Before approaching by yacht get permission from the Port Authority - Call them on channel 16 and switch to channel 12.

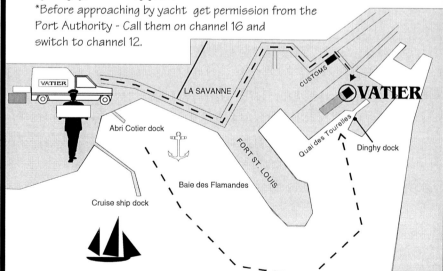

Regulations

The main customs office is in Fort de France, but clearance may be found in Marin and St. Pierre. Martinique is free to many countries, including the U.K. and the U.S., but some countries are charged on a per day per ton basis. Yachts present in Martinique waters over six months in one year are liable to import duty. (You might avoid this by special permission if you want leave your yacht in Martinique while you fly abroad.) Visas are not currently necessary for EEC members or U.S. citizens. Other nationals should check to see if they need a visa. Customs in each port has its own opening times which are given in the harbor sections. There are no overtime fees.

Shopping Hours

Shops are normally open 0800-1200 then 1500-1730, Monday to Saturday. Many offices are closed on Saturday. The large supermarkets (and many smaller ones) open at 0800 or 0900 and stay open till 1900.

Holidays

Jan 1st - New Year's Day
Jan 2nd - Recovery Day
Carnival - Monday and Tuesday 40
  days before Easter
Easter Friday through Monday
May 1st - Labor Day
May 8th - Victory Day (1945)
May 22nd - Abolition of slavery
May 28th - Ascencion Day
July 14th - National Day
August 15th - Virgin Mary Day
Nov 1st - Honoring the dead
Nov 11th - Victory Day (1918)
Dec 25th - Christmas Day

Telephones

Card telephones are placed all around Martinique. You need a card to make a call; they are available at post offices, change houses, and most newspaper stands. You need a card to get the operator for a reverse charge (PCV. – pronounced "Pay Say Vay") or credit card call, but the card is not charged. The latest working numbers were 19 00 11 and 19 596 11. If these do not work, you can get the current number through directory enquiries. Otherwise you can use your card. Dial 19 to get out of the country and then the country code and number you want. If you are calling Martinique from abroad the area code is 596.

Transport

Martinique has a few suburban buses. For other places you can take a communal taxi "TC". They are found on most town squares and run on fixed routes, mainly to and from Fort de France. They are reasonably priced. There are also taxis. Typical taxi rates in French francs are:

Airport - Fort de France................ 80
Airport - Anse Mitan................. 160
Anse Mitan - Golf course.............. 50
Fort de France - Euromarche......... 60
Short ride............................ 50
Full day Tour........................ 1500
By the hour........................ · 200

Rental cars are available (check our directory). You can use your own license. Drive on the right.

MARTINIQUE

Martinique is the largest of the Windwards, and apart from a few short spells under the British, has been French since it was colonized. It is a part of France and feels it, with excellent roads, expanding industry and a thriving economy. Fort de France is a busy city, bustling with shoppers and cars. The smaller towns are quieter and sometimes look so clean they could have just been scrubbed. That typically French smell - a blend of Gitane smoke, pastis and well-percolated coffee - wafts out from the bars and cafes. You can get almost anything done in Martinique - from galvanizing your boat to having stainless steel tanks made. The sailmakers are first rate, the chandlery stores are magnificently stocked, restaurants and boutiques abound. In short, when you have had enough deserted beaches and raw nature, Martinique is the place for a breath of civilization. But more than this, Martinique has enough excellent and varied anchorages for a week or two of exploring: not only fashionable resorts, but sleepy waterfront villages and deserted bays with excellent snorkeling.

The Empress Josephine grew up in Martinique on a 200-acre, 150-slave estate near Trois Ilets. A strange quirk of fate links Josephine and Martinique to the Battle of Trafalgar. In 1804 Napoleon was master of Europe, but the British still had naval supremacy and largely controlled Caribbean waters. However, ships were always scarce and some bright spark noticed that Diamond Rock on the south coast of Martinique was just about where they would station another British vessel if they had one, so they decided to commission the rock as a ship. In those days it was quite a feat to climb this steep, barren snake-infested pinnacle, and equip it with cannons and enough supplies and water for a full crew of men. But they succeeded and for some 18 months H.M.S. Diamond Rock was a highly unpleasant surprise for unsuspecting ships sailing into Martinique. Napoleon was incensed; this was after all the birthplace of his beloved Josephine. Napoleon, brilliant though he was on land, never really understood his navy or its problems, and considered them feeble shirkers. So he ordered them to sea under Admiral Villeneuve, to free the rock and destroy Nelson while they were about it. Villeneuve slipped out under the British blockade and headed straight for Martinique. Lord Nelson with his well trained and battle-ready fleet smelled blood and bounty and hurtled off in hot pursuit. However, poor information sent him on a wild goose chase to Trinidad and Villeneuve liberated the rock and returned to France, prudently keeping well clear of Nelson. Napoleon was none too pleased with Villeneuve as the British fleet was still in control of the high seas, so he was ordered to report in disgrace. Villeneuve preferred death to dishonor so he put his ill prepared fleet to sea to fight Nelson at the Battle of Trafalgar. Ironically, Villeneuve, who wished to die, survived the battle, while Nelson died.

This guide covers all the most frequently used anchorages. However, it does not include Martinique's east coast which is not for the average visitor. Martinique's east coast is pleasant and interesting, but it is also tricky with many reefs and shoals in water that is often difficult to read. The charts that are available have scant detail in areas of interest. Over the years it has claimed more than its fair share of hulls. Adventurous cruisers who wish to visit should buy the Trois Rivières guide to Martinique by Jerome Nouel. It is in French and English with excellent color photographs. It is the only guide that covers this area well.

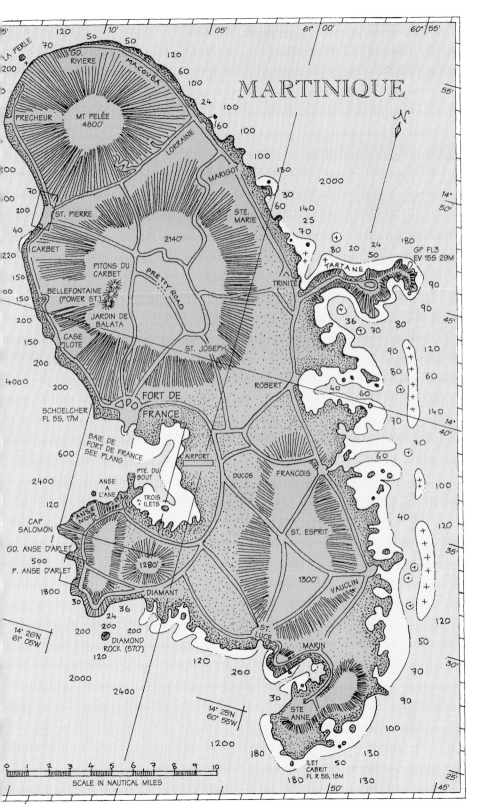

MARTINIQUE

Navigation

The south coast of Martinique between Ste. Anne and Diamond Rock has several shoals extending up to half a mile offshore. Fish traps are plentiful and two or three are often tied together. It is best to stay in several hundred feet of water outside the shallows. The current here usually runs to the west and can be strong. Therefore, if you are cruising to Martinique from St. Lucia, it makes sense to go first to Marin and Ste. Anne, leaving an easy downwind trip to Fort de France. However, if you do visit Fort de France first, the beat to Marin is in protected water and can be exhilarating.

The west coast (excluding the Bay of Fort de France) up to St. Pierre is mainly steep-to, and a quarter of a mile offshore clears any dangers.

The bay of Fort de France has many shoals, especially at its eastern end. Check the charts and instructions given under the appropriate section.

ST. PIERRE

St. Pierre lies at the foot of Mt. Pelée volcano, not far from where European settlers finally wiped out the Carib residents in 1658. It is said that before the last ones died they uttered horrible curses invoking the fiery mountain to take its revenge. Mt. Pelée, in true Caribbean fashion took its own sweet time – until 1902.

At this time St. Pierre was the cultural and social center of Martinique with a population of 30,000, many of them elegant and well educated. It was the center of fashion and the arts and known as the Paris of the Caribbean. It was a great post for the governor who was coming up for reelection, so when Mt. Pelée started rumbling, he hired a scientist to say there was no danger and did his best to keep voters in town. He prevented the people from fleeing but could not stop the volcano which erupted, wiping out the entire town, including the governor, in a cloud of super-heated gas. The sole survivor was the inmate of the local prison who escaped with bad burns.

Today St. Pierre is fascinating. The ruins have been left largely intact. Post-disaster buildings were added onto old structures so nearly every new building shares at least one wall with the past. Ruins also form garden walls, and many have been tidied up as historical corners. There is a museum in a modern building up a small hill, depicting those earlier days and the tragedy. It stands on top of old walls that are artistically lit up at night, making an enchanting backdrop for those anchored below.

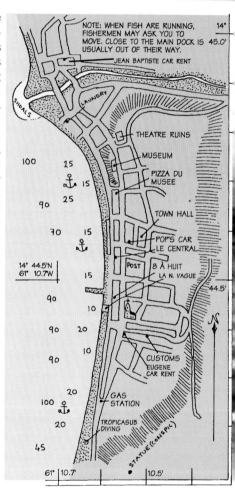

Navigation

St. Pierre makes a good overnight anchorage except in heavy northerly swells. There is an adequate shelf on which to

ST. PIERRE

nchor, about 25 feet deep, on either side of the town dock. The dropoff is very steep, so make sure you are well hooked. Sometimes you have to move for local fishermen who have been known to move unattended yachts. There is a conspicuous statue on the hill at the southern end of the beach which is lit at night.

Regulations

You can clear in and out here. The customs officer is nearly always in his office on Wednesday mornings and often around other mornings. If you fail to find an officer you can catch a communal taxi to Fort de France (about 40 minutes) and clear there.

Ashore

St. Pierre has a beautiful new dock for tying your dinghy. There is a water tap on the dock (get permission to use it from the town hall) and the gas station at its foot sells cube ice. If you need to get things cleaned, try the laundry and dry cleaner called L'auxiliaire [T:78 16 64, fax:78 16 92]. There are a couple of banks, a pharmacy, several boutiques and a good little 8 à Huit supermarket [T:77 20 96] which closes for lunch and half an hour earlier than its name suggests. It also opens Sunday mornings. On Saturday morning there is an active market.

The museum gives a historical perspective and it is open daily 0900-1200 and 1500-1700. There is a small admission charge. Among the most interesting places to visit are the theater ruins beyond the museum and the prison, where Cyparus, the sole survivor, was jailed, which is just below the theater. Before you go into the theater ruins you should pay a visit to Jenny Marie-Olive-Carnier's Au Plateau du Theater [T:78 11 52], a delightful patisserie. Jenny's father narrowly missed the volcano. He was 12 years old at the time and lived in St. Pierre. A few hours before the eruption he had left for Fort de France, where his grandmother lived, to meet an uncle off a ship. Not only was his family destroyed, but so were all the deeds to his family property. Consequently, when he grew up he had to go to France to make enough money to buy back his inheritance. Jenny's shop has delicious patisseries, ice creams, coffee and lunchtime specials. Before you leave, ask for their visiting card (carte de visite). On the card is a picture which shows the theater as it looked from this spot before the tragedy.

Tours around the town are available in an imitation train called the Cyparis Express.

St. Pierre sits amid the most magnificent scenery in Martinique, so if you are thinking of sightseeing, this is an excellent place to start. Rental cars are available from Eugene Garage [T:77 13 21/77 15 89], or Pop's Rentals [T:78 14 46], a short walk from the dock. Eugene also sells car parts and has some good buys on batteries. If you have no luck there, try Jean Baptiste's garage at the northern end of town [T:77 22 91]. On a clear day there is a magnificent drive half way up the volcano where you can eat lunch at the Auberge de Mt. Pelée. However, if Pelée is in cloud it would be better to go to Plantation Leyritz on the northeast coast. The Gorges de la Falaise offers a hike for a couple of hours in wild mountain scenery leading to tropical waterfalls. Guides are available. It is closed to tourists from the beginning of October until just before Christmas because of falling rocks.

There are a few choices for an evening meal out. Anastase and Martine cook superb pizzas on their old wood-fired oven at Pizzeria du Musée [T:78 31 13, $C-D, closed Sunday]. You can sit inside, or there is one outside table where you can watch life go by on the road and smell the pizzas cook. For those who prefer, creole specialities are available. The pizzeria opens for lunch, then reopens for dinner at 1900.

Lyvia and Simon's Le Central [T:78 12 54, $C] is a small restaurant serving first rate creole food. You should check them out during the day and look at the menu. While mainly a lunch time restaurant, you can arrange dinner by reservation. La Vague [T:78 14 34, $B-C, cc:A,V] has an impressive waterfront location and busloads arrive for lunch; it is quieter for

dinner. Other restaurants include Roya Bellevue [T:78 10 69, $C, cc:V] on th road to the museum which serves Chines food, and for creole food Chez Hugo [7 11 00, $C-D, cc:V] near Le Central, and L Mouillage [78 15 09, $B-C, cc:V] near th gas station. Chez Hugo and La Mouillag only serve food in the evening by reserva tion.

Water sport

There are 12 wrecks that sank in th tragedy of 1902 and most are within din ghy range of the anchorage. The best wa to find them is to watch the local dive boa which visit them frequently. The mos popular are out from the town dock and ar buoyed. They vary in depth from 30 to 15 feet. Tropicasub Diving [T:77 15 02/78 3 03, VHF:16, cc:A,V, closed Monday] i based right on the beach. Owner Françoise and Lionel Lafont know th wrecks well and you can arrange a div with them. They dive twice daily, at 093 and 1500. Since the number of places i limited call up in advance on the VHF Françoise speaks good English.

If you are diving on your own, there is a easy dive right off the beach in front of th big wall under the museum. There is good reef with a dropoff from 40 to 90 fee old anchors, a huge old chain draped ove the coral and plenty of fish.

CASE PILOTE

58

CASE PILOTE

Case Pilote is a delightful small fishing own whose pretty church is one of the oldest in Martinique. There is a picturesque little fishing port with an active fish processing plant which buys fish from boats that come from as far away as Venezuela. One charm of this place is that it is unspoiled and the locals have no intention of becoming another yacht haven. Anchorage outside the port is limited by the needs of the active fishing fleet which seine nets at about 0500 hours and will wake anyone they feel to be in their way. To avoid this, anchor well inshore over on the northwest side of the bay (see our sketch chart). Go in as close as you dare, drop your hook, then back down and use a second anchor to keep your stern to any swells and to stop you from riding up on the beach. Otherwise you can anchor just round the headland off the next small bay in about 25 feet of water. When you want to go ashore you can dinghy into the port.

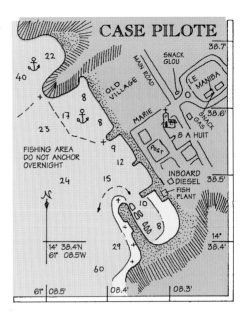

Regulations

There are currently no customs in Case Pilote, so you must clear in at a port of entry. If you are staying here for more than a few hours, you should visit the police station with your ship's papers, including your inward clearance.

Services

Right at the entrance to the port you will find Frank Ågren's Inboard Diesel [T:78 71 96]. Frank also stands by on VHF:16, but the range is limited by the hills. Frank is the main Volvo Penta dealer for the Windwards. He does warranty work and can supply spares somewhat more cheaply than you may pay in other islands. He has a hot line to the factory and, being Swedish, he speaks the same language as the engine. Anyone having Volvo Penta problems should give him a call. Those visiting Frank can come inside the port where he has a couple of reserved spaces. Frank speaks perfect English and is happy to work on other brands of inboard diesel.

Expansion of the fishing port is under way, and fuel pumps, customs and immi-

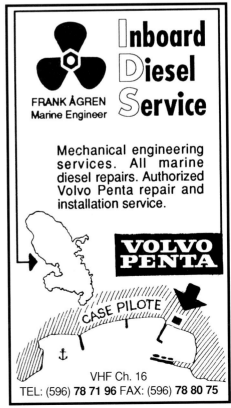

gration are planned. Meanwhile you can fetch diesel from the gas station in jugs.

Ashore

Case Pilote is charming and quiet. The church is worth a visit and it is pleasant to stroll around the town. For topping up provisions visit 8 à Huit [T:78 80 09], whose name gives you their weekday hours. For a breakfast of fresh French bread and croissants, visit Snack Bar de La Plage [T:78 81 36] right on the waterfront. Manager Bertrand will greet you with a big smile. They serve sandwiches and local dishes for lunch, and have a barbecue Friday and Saturday nights.

Celeste's Village [T:78 80 41, $B-D, cc:A, V] is a congenial little cafe, bar and restaurant in the town square. It is run by Celeste Champeaux and her husband Jean Philippe. You can sit outside in true French fashion and watch life go by. Reasonably priced snacks and full meals are availabl

For dinner there is also Le Maniba [78 7 89, $B-C, cc:V, closed Sunday and Mor day]. It is small and a little formal (wea long trousers). Owner Monique Rango specializes in first rate French/creole foo at reasonable prices. Her filet of fish i maracudja (passion fruit) sauce is exce lent. The Maitre D speaks English.

Water sport

Diving and snorkeling off the headlan just south of the marina are very goo Huge rocks rise from 70 feet and the who area is filled with brightly colore sponges, corals and fish. If you don't hav your own gear, contact the Case Pilo Diving Club [T:78 73 75/61 60 01]. F those interested in wildlife there is a b cave in the cliffs behind the snorkelin area.

FORT DE FRANC

When approaching Fort de France from Cap Salomon it is hard to see at a glance exactly where the harbor is, as the whole surrounding area is built up, including a huge hotel and some apartment blocks at Schoelcher, a couple of miles to its west.

As you approach, you can identify th main yacht anchorage by the promine slab-sided fort wall and all the yachts anchor.

Fort de France is the largest and livelie city in the Windwards. It is fun to sho

here, and you are in the center of many yacht services.

The Government has built a large new cruise ship dock costing many millions of dollars. Most captains find it unsuitably placed to take cruise ships. It has turned into an excellent, if somewhat expensive, platform from which to fish or eat lunch-time sandwiches. There is an adjoining compound which was planned for a duty free shopping area. The customs and immigration now have their permanent premises here.

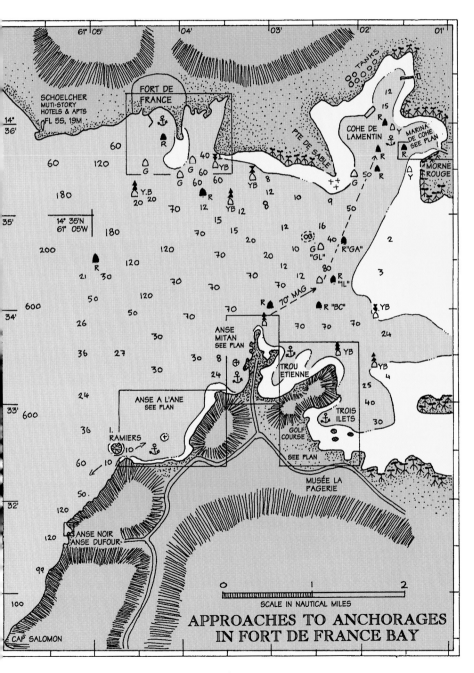

APPROACHES TO ANCHORAGES
IN FORT DE FRANCE BAY

SCALE IN NAUTICAL MILES

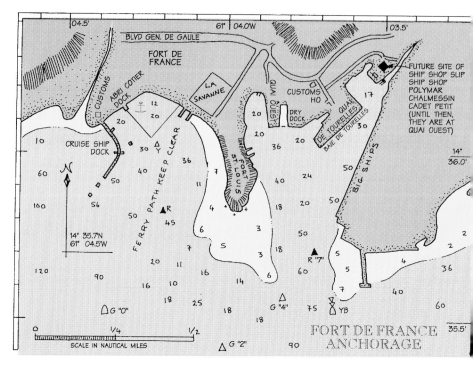

One or two cruise ships have managed to use the dock and more may follow. To make room for these ships the police came round and chased every yacht out of Fort de France. Now the government has allowed a small anchorage area which we show on our sketch chart. This will be totally inadequate during the busy season. Meanwhile, yachts anchor everywhere else as before, but occasionally the police come and chase them away.

Holding in the bay is fair in soft mud. Ferries can make the anchorage rolly. Those who prefer a quieter spot can clear in here and then sail over to Anse Mitan, Anse a L'Ane or Trois Ilets which are connected to town by an efficient ferry service.

Those seeking repairs can find a work berth down in Quai Ouest, though this is now a ferry terminal and yachts are often chased out. If you are heading east (or southeastwards toward Anse Mitan), keep well clear of the shoals off the fort. It is possible to cut somewhat inside the green buoys, but to be on the safe side, go around them.

Regulations

The customs and immigration office is in the new cruise ship compound. If the gate right on the waterfront is closed, there is another round the back near La Grande Voile Restaurant. (I have noticed that those adverse to walking edge their way into the compound round the rocks past the fence). Customs open daily 0800-1100, 1500-1700, including holidays and there are no overtime charges.

Services

There is a good dinghy tie-up at the Abri Cotier dock. Block ice can be bought at the Abri Cotier restaurant right on the dock. For cooking gas go to Sea Services. There are bins for garbage. As part of the new port planning the government took away the fuel pumps at the Abri Cotier dock. There is no immediate plan to replace them.

Helenon [T:60 22 05, F:63 17 63] is a good and reliable sailmaker with many years of experience in Martinique. He will repair your sails or make you new ones, along with awnings and biminis. He is conveniently located and easily found upstairs next to Littoral at 32 Blvd. Allègre (the canal road). You can dinghy up the canal to outside his shop where there is a adder going up the wall. He will help hoist your sails over the wall, or he will come and collect your sails from anywhere in Fort de France. He will also come collect your sails or measure you up for a new sail in Marin. Helenon has a monster machine that can sew any thickness of cloth, even a cruise ship sail.

Barnacles bugging you? The main slipping facility in town is the Ship Shop travel lift [T:73 73 99, cc:V] in Quai Ouest. They have a 30-ton travel lift and they are experienced, efficient and employ a night guard. Their standard rate includes five days, but you can get a discount for shorter periods. They have a full paint shop for your complete refit. Philippe is very helpful and if you have a major problem they will help you send faxes. They also run a

larger slipping facility at Marin.

There are plans to move this facility and all the others in Quai Ouest, except Multicap Caraibes, over to Basin Thibeault in Baie de Tourelles. The new facility will include a fuel dock with water and ice, a restaurant and a branch of Ship Shop chandlery. (See our Fort de France anchorage chart.) Bassin Thibeault is easily visited by foot, by dinghy or in your yacht. The walk to Quai de Tourelles is about 10 minutes from town. You head out past Quai Ouest on the main road out of town. Turn right immediately after the big customs (douanes) building which is on the right side of the road. Follow the road and turn left at the junction. This leads you to the new basin. However, don't go too soon. The move was supposed to happen

T DE FRANCE

by the end of 1994, but no work has started yet. The move could be long delayed and may or may not happen during the life of this guide.

Meanwhile, in Quai Ouest you will find everything you might need done in the way of work. Language is not a problem as most people speak fair English. If you have trouble finding anyone, go to Max at Polymar and he will help. Polymar [T:70 62 88, F:60 10 97] is a complete fiberglass shop. They will do anything from repairing your hull or refinishing it with a top quality spray paint job, to custom building hard tops or tanks. Polymar builds a good line of dinghies and they also sell marine ply, resins, paints and foam. They can fill diving tanks and they sell Scubapro gear.

Jean Pierre and François Chalmessin [T:60 03 75 F:63 49 67] can work wonders with stainless and aluminum, including argon welding, bending, building and machining. Whatever your problem, from a broken winch to needing a new pulpit or water tank, they can do it. You can also ask here about contacting QTS which specializes in chroming, galvanizing and cadmium plating.

Troublesome engine or gearbox, or want to upgrade your machinery with new equipment? Go talk to Pierre and his wife Nichol at Madia Boat [T:63 10 61, F:63 48 70]. They can help sort out your problems. Pierre is an agent for BMW, Yanmar, Perkins, and Ford and works on all other makes of motor (both normal and turbo charged) including Volvo, Holset, Garrett and KKK. They are also agents for Hurth, Borg Warner and Twin Disk gear boxes and will work on any other type. Pierre is a boating man himself with a high speed jet motor boat he uses for fishing and trips down to the Grenadines.

Alain Belat is the man to visit for electronic equipment or repair. His company is called Carib Electronic Engineering [60 07 00, F:63 60 14]. He keeps a lot of Navico and President electronic gear in stock.

Cadet Petit [T:63 79 18] will fix all your electrical problems, be it starter motor, generator or alternator. He repairs and when necessary rewinds all manner of

electrical motors.

If you want to fix your own Perkins, spares may be available from Madia Boat, Mecanique Plaisance (see Anse Mitan) or at Croquet [T:71 91 50, cc:V,A], out by Euromarche. Look for the big Caterpillar sign. Manager Jean Trudo speaks perfect English.

If you are too long, wide, heavy or ugly to haul elsewhere, you can arrange to be slipped alongside a ship in the huge Martinique dry dock [T:72 69 40/72 67 48, F:63 17 69] which will take anything up to a cruise ship. Many really large yachts haul here. You have to fit in with their schedule.

While on dry land, you can arrange to buy your bottom paint through Ship Shop, Camaco [T:73 70 45] or Polymar. Sea Services also sells bottom paint and will deliver to your boat.

In Quai Ouest (and staying there) Multicap Caraibes [T:71 41 81, F:71 41 83] builds all kinds of boats. You see their ferries crossing Fort de France Bay, and their fast catamaran yachts chartering up and down the islands. They also build a variety of custom dive boats, fishing boats and racing yachts. Multicap Caraibes build in foam core, wood/epoxy, aluminum or steel to the French Bureau Veritas standard. They are also the main repair station for large multihulls, and they have their own 60 ton crane to bring them out on the quay. They regularly repair aluminum masts. Christian Hernandez runs the yard and as part of their repair service they have a good mechanical workshop, but they will only work on Volvo, Lombardini, or Beaudouin inboards and Suzuki outboards. They keep a good range of new inboard engines and outboards in stock. Multicap Caraibes also has a chandlery shop. Here you will find a good selection of the materials and fittings used in construction. There are lots of resins and cloths and marine hardware, including Anderson and Fredericksen winches, electrical panels, anchor winches, light fittings and all the technical hardware that goes into building a yacht.

Injectors or injection pumps need ser-

icing? Christian Liard's Martinique Diesel [T:51 16 13/51 34 33], out by the airport, is the place to take them. He services all kinds except Caterpillar and Cummins and has a vast stock of filters, separators, and other parts. In addition he has a full scuba shop called Nautica Antilles [T:51 69 72] with everything from inflatable boats to compressors.

Those with inflatables will be delighted to know La Survy [T:79 70 66] offers a first class repair service. It is run by Maurice Phillias, Pascal and the rest of his family and they have over 30 years of experience. Their modern shop is temperature and humidity controlled and they will fix any kind of inflatable. They also repair and are warranty agents for Zodiac, Bombard and Plastimo. Their shop is out of town and difficult to find, but you can contact them through Jerome at the Captain's Shop or check out their new office in Marin.

If you need something trans-shipped through customs, check with Jean Marc Berte over at Quai de Tourelles.

Laveries Valgom [T:63 32 49] is a laun-

dry that is in a small pathway behind Le Bogedon Restaurant.

Ashore

(See our Fort de France plan and Fort de France anchorage chart.)

Changing money in Fort de France is now easy at the best rates, thanks to efficient little change places like Change Caraibes [T:60 28 40/73 06 16], which is at the Savanne end of Rue Ernest Déproge and opens weekdays 0800-1730, Saturdays 0800-1230. There is also another called Martinque Change [63 80 33] at the Blvd. Allègre end of Rue Victor Hugo.

The yacht shops in Fort de France are wonderful, and even if you have no pressing needs, they are fun to peruse. Most have hidden stocks as well, so ask if you don't see what you want. Ship Shop [T:71 43 40, F:70 13 02, cc:A,V], now on Rue Ernest Déproge will eventually move over to the new Basin Thibeault in the Baie de Tourelles when it comes on line. Ship Shop has been around for years and is a long-standing friend to yachtspeople. You can have your mail sent to the new location (c/o Ship Shop, Baie de Tourelles, Fort de France, Martinique, FWI). However, since the move has not yet happened you should to call them on the phone to confirm the new address before using it. Ship Shop is an excellent chandlery with everything from anchors, chain and dinghies to electronics, and electric/gas refrigerators They usually keep a few outboards in stock. They have expanded to include water sports, with a full range of diving gear, fishing gear (with an emphasis on trolling) and a complete sailboarding shop. Elina, who is usually behind the cash desk, speaks good English and will help you in any way she can, including sending faxes.

Sea Services [T:70 26 69, F:70 26 69, cc:V,D], on the opposite side of the road, is a first class chandlery with a wide range of products, including International Paints, Avon inflatable dinghies, 316 stainless fasteners, Plastimo liferafts, charts and guides. There is a good range of electrical equipment from wire and connectors to

FORT DE FRANCE
PLAN

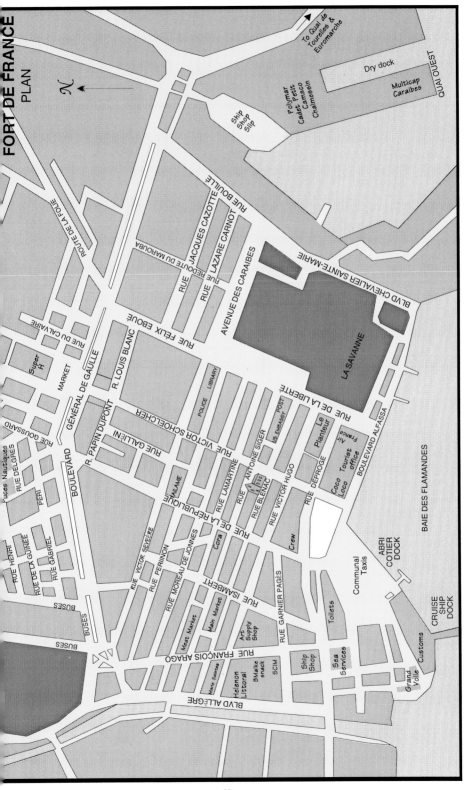

solar panels, Ampair wind generators, diesel generators, fridges, watermakers and batteries. They have now doubled the size of their shop and have expanded to include deck shoes, a little nautical clothing and many nautical furniture and decor items. Owners Jacques and Ciarla speak perfect English (Ciarla is English Canadian), so people having problems with French come by to seek advice on anything and everything. Jacques loves to do rigging and they have a full rigging service, with a machine in the shop to do swage fittings for two to 12 mm wire and they do larger diameters by order. Sea Services is open weekdays right through from 0800-1800 and on Saturdays from 0800-1300.

Bricogite [T:63 61 20/61 20, F:60 05 19, cc:V], next door, is a useful hardware and do-it-yourself shop. It stocks a big range of tools, materials, electrical wire and fittings. In addition they keep a stock of interior and exterior grade ply, and a little marine ply which they will cut into squares and sell by the meter. This can vastly speed up building projects.

There are also two excellent fishin stores/chandleries, well worth visiting Littoral, 32-34 Blvd. Allègre [T:70 28 7(cc:V], next to the canal, has a wonderfu selection of fishing gear, probably the larg est in Martinique, along with snorkelin, gear, ropes and some yacht chandler SCIM, down Rue François Arago [T:73 5. 00/60 63 03, F:71 38 13, cc:V], has a equal balance between fishing gear an yacht hardware. For a look at their ful range of stock, go out to their huge new store near Euromarche at Dillon.

Puces Nautique [T:60 58 48, F:63 73 3] cc:V] is a sort of second hand and "end o line" new shop. It is totally irresistible t poke around looking for bargains, and th range is immense. Shackles, second han sails, "pack away" motor bikes, snorkelin; gear, old pulpits, bits of teak, pumps, div ing gear, ancient looking stoves and bran new stainless fittings are all on show. Yo can leave unwanted gear here for sale o commission. Prices vary considerably de pending on the owner's own evaluation Sorting out the best bargains is part of th

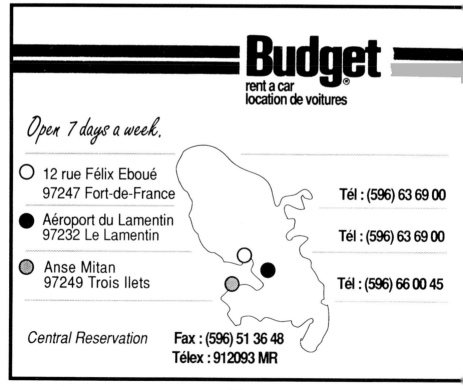

n. To find it, walk right down Rue de la
épublique till you cross the big Blvd. du
énéral de Gaulle. The road soon comes to
T-junction. You turn left down the road
efore the T-junction and look out on your
ft-hand side.

Anyone need personal protection?
rmes Levalois [T:73 11 96, cc:V] on Rue
éproge sells small spray cans of CS gas.

Provisioning in Martinique is a pleasure.
Vhen you are ready to stock up on duty
ee drinks, walk or dinghy down to
atier's new, large, air conditioned office
a Quai de Tourelles [T:70 11 39, F:60 00
0] where you will find Philippe Vatier
ho speaks excellent English. The walk to
uai de Tourelles is about 10 minutes from
wn. You head out past Quai Ouest on the
ain road out of town. Turn right immedi-
tely after the big customs (douanes)
uilding which is on the right side of the
ad. Follow the road down and Vatier is in
e large building on the Quai. Vatier will
ive you a computerized print out of their
tock so you can order all your duty free

wines, spirits, beers, soft drinks, and cigarettes. They deliver right to the Abri Cotier
dock, but you must have outward clearance for the day they deliver. Vatier can
fax you his price list in advance and have
everything ready when you arrive, a good
service for charter yachts on a tight turn
around. If you prefer you can now also
arrange to pick up your drinks by yacht or
dinghy alongside Quai de Tourelles

One of the easiest ways to provision is to
walk down to Super H [T:63 69 69, cc:V],
the biggest supermarket in Fort de France,
with excellent cheese, pate, meat and produce sections. They are interested enough
in the yacht trade to offer free delivery to
Abri Cotier Dock or Quai Ouest. Make
arrangements with the "Chef Caissier."
They only deliver once a day, but if you
arrive too late they will store your frozen
foods in the freezer for delivery the next
day. There is also a local produce market in
the square just outside Super H. The other
big supermarket in town is Cora, which is
upstairs in a department store. They cur-

RESTAURANT

Le Planteur

*Open every day
for lunch and dinner
Closed for lunch
on Sundays*

1er étage
1 rue de la Liberté
97200 Fort-de-France
Tél : 63.17.45

*French and Creole
cuisine*

rently deliver orders of more than 1500 francs.

There are several gargantuan and very modern supermarkets outside town, aptly called hypermarches which are worth visiting, either for fun or when you have a really huge provisioning to do. Buses go to all these from Blvd. du Général de Gaulle and from around the cemetery, or you can take a taxi from in front of La Savanne. You can ask the supermarket staff to call a return taxi for you.

Cluny, to the west of town, has the least traffic and you can ask to be put off near Cora, a huge supermarket surrounded by many other boutiques and shops. In the same direction, but much closer to town (just five minutes by taxi), La Ronde Pointe supermarket should be completely rebuilt by the time this guide comes out.

Euromarche is in the other direction, at Dillon, on the road to the airport. This vast market tends to be a little more expensive than the others but they offer a 5% discount to charter yachts. Considerably farther down the same road is La Galleria, a mall with a Hyper U supermarket and about 16 other shops.

For a first rate butcher, try Tailame [T:71 87 57, cc:V]. They will vacuum pack and freeze your purchases for you.

There are some good restaurants in Fort de France for a French meal out. Le Planteur [T:63 17 45, $C, cc:V, closed for Monday lunch], is upstairs on Rue de la Liberté with pleasant views over both La Savanne and the anchorage. It has an artistic atmosphere in traditional Caribbean

style. Owner Patrick de Reynal is a sympathetic host who will greet you when you arrive and ensure you are well taken care of. His creole food is first rate and the prices are reasonable. Le Planteur open for both lunch and dinner. At noon the a conditioning is a blessed contrast from the midday heat.

Below Le Planteur, the budget minded can get coffee, sandwiches, pastries and ice cream, as well as bread, at Pain, Buerr et Chocolat. Coco Loco [T:63 19 62/63 6 77, $C, cc:V, closed Sundays], is a pleasan bar and ice cream parlor which also serve lunch. It is one of the few places in Fort d France where you can sit comfortably out side and watch life go by. They do no serve dinner, but they do continue to serv snacks and ice creams in the evening an they have live music several times a week

Le Mayflower [T:70 54 45, $D, close Monday evening and all day Sunday] is pleasant bar that has musical entertain ment several nights a week. They also ope for lunch when they serve just a couple o "plats du jour" which are good value.

The Crew [T:33 04 14, $B-C, cc:V closed Saturday and Sunday evenings] i reliable, easy to find and relatively inex pensive. It serves good French food, an while it is crowded with businessmen fo lunch, it is usually easy to find space a dinner.

Going up market, L'Ami Fritz used to be an excellent restaurant in Petite Anse D'arlet. It then moved to the east coast and then closed for a while. We have just heard it has reopened on Rue République.

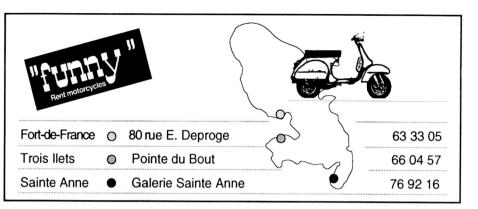

Fort-de-France	◎	80 rue E. Deproge	63 33 05
Trois Ilets	◉	Pointe du Bout	66 04 57
Sainte Anne	●	Galerie Sainte Anne	76 92 16

La Grand Voile [T:70 29 29, $A, cc:V] overlooks the bay near the new cruise ship complex. It has been going for a long time and the food is generally very good.

Several other places are open only for lunch. Marie Saintes [T:70 00 81, $C] is a small but fine creole restaurant which is very popular with the locals, so go early. Another less crowded lunch spot is Bmalke Snack [T:63 03 10, $C-D] which serves food with a Syrian flavor. Abri Cotier [T:63 66 46, $B-C, cc:V], right on the dock, makes a convenient beer stop and serves an inexpensive lunch. La Chacuterie [T:63 45 96] is on Rue Lazare Carnot, behind La Savanne. It is a traiture where you can get a large variety of ready made foods. Just across the road they have a sitting area and you can make up your own lunch from their display or sit and choose from their menu. On the same street El Racor is ($A-B) a top quality restaurant which opens for lunch from Monday to Friday and for dinner from Tuesday to Saturday. Beware of those little green peppers when eating out in Martinique. They are often used for decoration, or put beside the food. They are the hottest of hot.

Fort de France is the place for both fashionable shopping and souvenir hunting. There are two handicraft markets, one right on The Savanne and the other on Rue de la République near Rue Moreau de Jonnes. You can buy anything from jewelry to varnished palm fruits. Half the artists and carvers in Haiti must be kept busy whipping out an overwhelming number of coconut trees, banana plants, fruits and models in balsa wood. These are available all over town, though the easiest place to find them is in Carombole [T:63 80 00, cc:V] just opposite Coco Loco.

When it comes to fashion, there are plenty of stylish boutiques, most of them along Rue Victor Hugo. Salines Shop [T:70 28 28, cc:V,A], 66 Rue Victor Hugo, has some particularly elegant bathing and casual wear, ideal for lounging around on the afterdeck of the fancier yacht. Ah!Nanas [T:73 60 94, cc:V,A], 61 Rue Victor Hugo, has elegant clothing for both men and women, from casual to lightweight formal wear. Crazy [T:73 26 68, cc:V,A], 17 Rue Victor Hugo, has stylish women's wear. Green [63 27 96, cc:V,A] is at 12 Rue Antoine Siger, not far from La Savanne. It has very good quality clothing for both men and women including the Polo and Ralph Lauren lines. Some other boutiques seem a little odd to some of us. You see a well dressed window when inside a few completely different clothes are hanging up and the rest are hidden away. As a welcome break from all this you can visit Au Printemps [T:71 89 50, cc:V,A,Dn] which takes up the corner between Rue Antoine Siger and Rue Schoelcher. This is a first rate French department store, where everything is laid out so that it is easy to see and try on. They have men's, women's and children's departments as well as perfume, linens, luggage and accessories.

If you are spending a while in Martinique, pay an early visit to the tourist office. They will not only answer your questions but will fill your arms with informative maps, books and brochures. Make sure you ask for their dining guide.

Do you have photos to develop? Photo First develops both print film and E6 slide processing (Fujicolor and Ectachrome). Their quality is normally good.

History buffs should visit the little pre-Columbian museum on Rue La Liberté, architecture buffs the Schoelcher Library.

Fort de France is a convenient starting point to see the island as there are buses and communal taxis that go to all major towns and villages. Currently most of them start right outside the Abri Cotier, though this may change if the second stage of the planned port ever works out. If you are going to the airport, take the "Ducos" car. The charge is less than 10 francs. Most of the suburban buses go from around Avenue Général de Gaulle. These include buses to Dillon, Balata and Didier. Taxis may be found by La Savanne.

The Caribs called Martinique "Madinina" (Island of Flowers). To see a superb collection of these flowers, I highly recommend a trip to Jardin de Balata, a privately-owned and perfectly maintained garden high in the mountains behind Fort de France near the Pitons de Carbet. These gardens are the result of over 20 years of work by their owner Jean Philippe Those, aided by a team of gardeners. There are acres of carefully laid out tropical plants with a small stream and ponds. The views southwards toward St. Lucia and St. Vincent and northwards into the rain forest are excellent. There are several small seating areas for enjoying the peace. The entrance fee is about 30 francs per person, but it is the kind of place where you could happily spend an hour or two. You can get there on the bus to Balata which goes from around the western end of Blvd. Général de Gaulle. Now that there is a by-pass around Fort de France, Le Jardin de Balata is also accessible by rental car from Anse Mitan or Fort de France. This makes it possible to continue your exploration through the rain forest and back by a coast road.

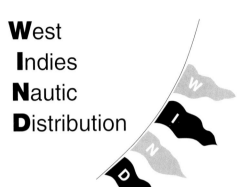

If you are in Martinique during the first week of April and would like to get to know some locals, join in for the big race and party time of the Banana's Cup. It is sponsored by Multicap Caraibes and Puces Nautiques and arranged by the yacht club. Either can give you details.

Rivière Sallée

Rivière Sallée is an industrial area back from the sea. However, there are two businesses here that work with yachts. West Indies Nautic Distribution (Wind) [T:68 21 28, F:68 21 38] is run by Bruno and Isabelle Marmousez. They specialize in just a few items and offer these at excellent prices. Their main products are Surette batteries, especially the larger sizes used on yachts, Seajet antifouling, an effective Japanese co-polymar concoction produced in the States, and fiberglass materials. These include epoxy system 3, polyester resins and cloth. You don't have to visit Rivière Sallée personally. You can call Bruno on the phone (he speaks excellent English) and he will deliver to your boat.

North Sails has changed management and is represented by Gianni Bruno at Tech Sails Voilerie [T:68 03 34]. It is a small one man operation run by Bruno who is very pleasant to deal with. Bruno speaks just enough English if you speak slowly. He will collect your sails for repair from anywhere in Martinique. He is also hooked into North Sails Caraibes in Guadeloupe and can order your new North sails.

COHE DE LAMENTIN

(See also our "Approaches to Anchorages in Fort de France Bay," page 61)

This murky backwater is only of interest if you need to get close to the airport, are hiding from a hurricane, or need somewhere to leave your boat while you go away.

To approach from Anse Mitan, start by the black and yellow buoy just off the point and head about 70 degrees magnetic which joins you into the main channel. Leave all the red buoys to starboard and the green ones to port. Your course will change to about 40 degrees at the red buoy "1L".

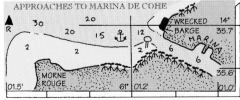

From Fort de France go outside the green buoys marking the shoals off the fort, then head about 130 degrees magnetic until you join up with the main channel from Anse Mitan. The troublesome shoal is the one extending from Pte. des Sable. The water on this route is mainly 10 to 12 feet deep but watch out for any unmarked wrecks or obstructions. Last time I passed there was a large wooden structure sticking out of the mud, probably designed to attract fish.

Marina de Cohe is a somewhat strange, quiet, hot backwater tucked in the mangroves. It should be generally safe as the grounds are patrolled by dogs that make the hound of the Baskervilles look like a playful puppy. As you approach, be sure to leave the red buoy off Morne Rouge to starboard. The entrance to the Marina is hidden down a small creek which is marked by a wrecked barge. Stay center channel and do not cut the corner on the southern shore, which is where most people go aground. Yachts of around six-foot draft can get in.

There is another dock (usually full of local boats) tucked up in the top corner of Cohe de Lamentin.

TROIS ILETS

TROIS ILETS

This is a pleasant area with scenic and quiet places to anchor, some of which are protected enough to ride out a hurricane.

Approach from Anse Mitan by leaving the black and yellow buoys off Pte. du Bout and Pte. de la Rose to starboard. Give the shoals along the coast between Pte. de la Rose and Pte. Angboeuf reasonable clearance. You can anchor off the golf course or farther up in the bay. You can also anchor off the town of Trois Ilets. The approach to town is between the islands. It is narrow and the shoals are hard to spot which makes it difficult. It helps if you come on a line between Pte. Angboeuf and the town dock, just edging west a shade as you come by the island (see chart). Nowadays, yachts usually obstruct the view of the dock, but you can see the yacht masts on the dock.

Ashore

Trois Ilets is a small town untouched by tourism with plenty of peaceful charm. Most houses are old with fish-scale tile roofs. There is a handsome square between the church and the town hall. Close by you will find most essentials: a local market (open every day), a post office, a butcher, boulangerie and patisserie, pharmacy and a couple of general stores. A good restaurant is currently missing, though you can find snacks in some rum shops.

More yachts use this port now that there is a ferry to Fort de France. It runs from the town dock at quarter past the hour between 0615 and 0915 and in the afternoon it runs hourly at quarter to the hour between 1245 and 1645. It returns from Fort de France half an hour after it leaves Trois Ilets.

This is one of the few places in the islands where you can play golf overlooking your yacht in the bay below.

TROU ETIENNE

Just occasionally the weather goes crazy and storms from afar create huge swells which make both Fort de France and Anse Mitan untenable. If this happens you can pop round to the other side of Pte. du Bout and anchor in Trou Etienne. As you come from the west, leave both yellow and black buoys to starboard and as you enter the bay, do not go too close to shore. The water is either rather deep or too shallow, so if you are anchoring on chain, choose your spot carefully. Docks and roads are private, but there is a small public access path just to the north of the hotel. The hotel is quite conspicuous.

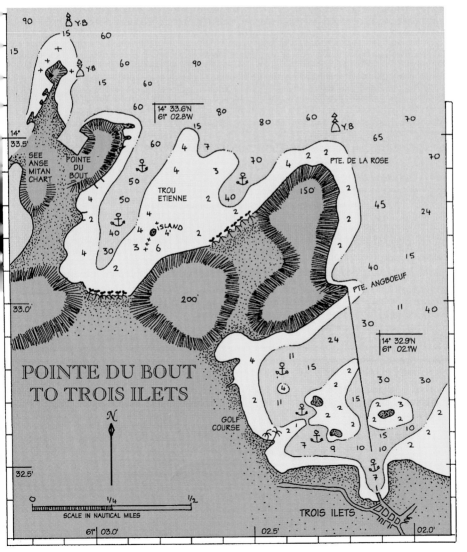

77

Anse Mitan is the main tourist area in Martinique. It is part of the Trois Ilets district, and the head of the peninsula is called Pointe du Bout. There are beaches, boutiques, restaurants and two excellent ferry services to Fort de France. One operates out of the marina at Pointe du Bout, the other at the Langouste Dock on Anse Mitan. (this one also services Anse A L'Ane). Both use high speed ferries.

FERRY TIMES
Marina Ferry

Leaves Anse Mitan 0610, 0715, 0830, 0930, 1030, 1130, 1245, 1430, 1530, 1630 1730, 1830 1930, 2345. It returns from Fort de France at 0630, 0800, 0900, 1000, 1100, 1215, 1315, 1500, 1600, 1700, 1800, 1900, 2000, 0010. Extra ferries run most days so check the board at the terminal

The Langouste Dock Ferry

Be ready to catch the ferry at Anse Mitan or Anse a L'Ane at 10 to the hour, although you may have to wait 10 minutes if it calls at the other station first; this varies. It returns from Fort de France at half past the hour (except 1320 which is ten minutes early for lunch). During the season several supplementary ferries also run so check on the dock when you arrive.

All this makes Anse Mitan very attractive to live-aboards, many of whom commute to town, and there are often over 100 yachts here.

When approaching Anse Mitan, the main danger is the reef lying 200 yards to the west of the Bakoua Dock where

SEMB sells fuel. Yachts are often anchored all around it. It is marked by a small red and black buoy. The mayor has also spread around many yellow buoys whose purpose is known only to him.

Anchor anywhere among the other yachts. Holding is good in sand, poor on patches of coral. Leave a couple of hundred feet in front of the beach clear for swimmers (occasionally marked by yellow buoys) and a channel for the ferry.

On those very rare occasions when there is a bad northwesterly swell, go around the other side of Pointe du Bout to Trou Etienne, or on down to Trois Ilets.

Services

The Ponton du Bakoua [T:66 05 45, Fax:66 09 50, VHF:16,cc:V] is a good service oriented mini marina. It is a single dock with berthing space along both sides. Yachts of any size can come along the outside; the inside is limited to yachts drawing less than 2-meters. You have to take some care on the approach to the inside as rocks come out a fair way from shore. There is one rock in particular that makes one of the spaces suitable only for catamarans. Manager Olivier Carniaux speaks English and if you call on the VHF he will help you in.

At the end of the dock there is an octagonal fuel dock designed so several yachts can come alongside at once.

Diesel fuel (duty free for French charter yachts which have cleared out), cube ice,

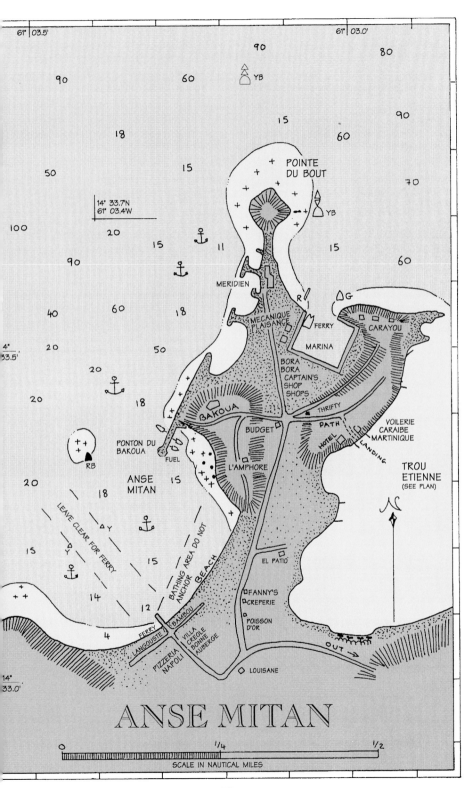

ANSE MITAN

SCALE IN NAUTICAL MILES

gasoline and water are all available; an ice cream bar is planned.

Along the dock there is water and 220 volts, 50-cycle electricity. They offer full communications and a laundry service. There are showers and toilets, a shop selling wine, beer, soft drinks, and chandlery basics.

Ponton du Bakoua is particularly well organized to help charter yachts get turned around fast. Besides the services mentioned above, they work with a service company called Alphamar [T:66 00 89, 66 07 03, F:66 03 29] run by Vincent and Lucile Reichert, both of whom speak English. They run a full provisioning service and put out a complete provisioning list booklet and order form with all the prices. To make life easy for charter cooks they include a series of menus in their publication with the cost per head. It is possible to order by the meal and all the ingredients will be delivered. Provisioning with Alphamar is probably a little less than you will pay in a big supermarkets as they get all their food wholesale.

Apart from provisioning, Alphamar is geared up to organize a quick solution to any technical problems, including mechanics, electronics and refrigeration. They are also a charter and crew agency.

Somatras Marina (Marina Pte. du Bout) [T:66 07 74, F:66 00 50, VHF:9] is a small marina offering stern-to berthing with water and electricity. Short and long term berths are now often available. There is no fuel dock. Behind the marina, Laveries Valgom (T:66 04 00) runs a small laundry.

Patrice Caillot's Mecanique Plaisance [T:66 05 40, cc:V] is a complete shop and repair facility for everything to do with diesel engines on pleasure boats. They are agents for Perkins and Yanmar and keep a full line of yacht engines for both makes in stock, as well as Yanmar generators. Their shop also sells everything from cutlass bearings, shaft materials and stern glands to plumbing bits, alternators, electrical parts, gaskets, engine spares and a complete range of Racor filters. Patrice can fix any make of diesel, guarantees his work and has contacts for air-expressing any parts he does not have. He also stocks refrigeration systems and repairs all makes. They usually have a small stock of second hand engines available. Both Patrice and his wife Viviane speak good English.

Herve Lepault's Voilerie Caraibe Martinique [T:66 07 24, F:66 09 98, VHF:16] is a full sail loft where you can get anything built or repaired from a new main to bimini or a sailboard cover. Herve builds sails with the well known French Incidences label and guarantee. The sails are computer designed in France with the latest technology and built in Herve's loft. Herve speaks English and if you call him from Anse Mitan on your radio, he will come by your boat and pick up your sail and deliver it back later. You can also visit his loft in Trou Etienne by foot or dinghy. (Look for the only dock with dinghies tied to it.)

Jerome and Dominique's Captain's Shop [T:66 06 77, F:66 01 03, cc:V] is a great chandlery where the stock ranges from technical parts such as impellers, Mariner outboards and watermakers right through to cushions and cutlery, taking in the full range of stainless fittings, electrical equipment and general chandlery on the way. They stock electronics and are agents for Boatphone. Captain's Shop also has a full service department. They fix all brands of motors both diesel and outboard, electrical and electronic equipment, air-conditioning, refrigeration and water-makers. Both Jerome and Dominique speak good English and will help with any kind of problem, from sending faxes to flying you parts when you get stuck in the Grenadines.

In the marina the 3 S organization [T:68 40 79, F:68 40 88] sells Caribe dinghies and helps with technical services.

There is an Austrian family on a yacht called Sheba [VHF:16] who call themselves Nonstop Marine Service. They do mechanical, electric and electronic repairs and will come any time.

You can change money at Martinique Change [T:66 04 44] by the marina. They also sell telephone cards and are agents for DHL.

Ashore

The Bora Bora [T:66 01 68, cc:V] Supermarket is compact but complete. It is open all day every day, except Sundays and holidays when it is open mornings only. If you are buying a large amount they will deliver it to the water front. It is the cheapest place to have a cold beer. Albert, the manager, speaks English. For fresh produce go to Jardin Creole [T:66 06 78], a greengrocer down by the beach. For a really huge provisioning it is best to rent a car for a day and drive to one of the giants.

One of the delights of Anse Mitan is to stroll over to Deli France [T:66 04 09] or Boule de Neige next door [T:66 05 60, cc:V] and have a breakfast of French coffee, fresh croissants and pain de chocolat. You can pick up your bread at Deli France and it is well worth returning to Boule de Neige later in the day for one of their wonderfully decadent ice cream specials. They also serve crêpes and are open till 2200.

The whole of Pointe du Bout is full of trendy little boutiques with enough variety to keep everyone happy. There is also a massage parlour/beauty salon and two hairdressers. Looking for a gift? You can find something even for someone who has everything at Phileas Fogg [T:66 07 17, cc:A,V]. This small shop is crammed with elegant curios, brass telescopes, models and more. For clothing your best bet is Cannelle [T:66 05 33, cc:V,A], well stocked with the best brands of bathing suits, casual and smart formal wear. The traditional costumes make great gifts for kids and there are locally printed t-shirts, souvenirs and Martiniquan dolls. Calypso [T:66 08 96, cc:V], which you will find in the concrete jungle behind the Marina, has some very stylish handicrafts and household items. Galerie D'Art T:[66 09 89, cc:V] features local and Haitian art and locally made objets d'art. Citron Vert carries some fancy souvenirs, ornaments and t-shirts.

Anse Mitan is devoted to satisfying those on holiday, so there is plenty to do. This is a great place to rent a car and explore the island. Budget [T:63 69 00, F:63 51 35,

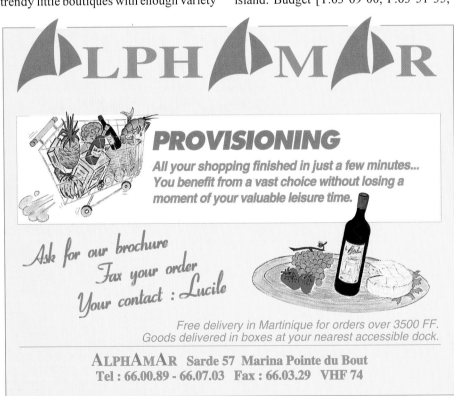

ANSE MITAN

cc:V,A,Dn] is the biggest, with everything from a small car to a van or minibus for large groups. Their subsidiary, Funny, rents scooters. There is also Thrifty [T:66 09 59, cc:V,A].

Once you hit the road there are plenty of roadside attractions. Not far away is a scenic 18-hole golf course where you can rent the gear you need. Opposite is La Pagerie Museum, the original home of Empress Josephine. Most of the old estate house burned down when she was three years old, but you can still see the old kitchen and the remains of the sugar mill on the plantation where she lived until she was 16 and left for France. Farther down the road, past Trois Ilets village, are a sugar cane museum and some potteries.

For a pleasant English speaking taxi driver (he's a St. Lucian) call Julien Alexander [T:41 22 41/76 45 10]. There is also a taxi stand near the marina. For a light lunch right on the beach, check out the snack bars Le Tam Tam [T:66 06 29, $C-D] or Co Co [T:66 07 88, $C-D].

A pleasant place to start the evening is at Le Marine [T:66 02 32, $B-D cc:V] or Davidiana [T:66 00 54, $B cc:A,V] where you get a marina front view.

Yachties seem to have a flair for finding the best buy in food, and in Anse Mitan it is definitely Fanny's [T:66 04 34, $C-D, cc:V], a creole restaurant with a menu that changes daily posted outside which might include anything from chicken to filet mignon and fresh water crayfish (ecrevisse). Fanny's creole food is both excellent and very inexpensive. Shorts are acceptable

and the outside tables are pleasant enough, though during lunch on a hot day the inside air conditioning is a boon. It is currently open for lunch and dinner every day except Sunday (it opens for dinner at 1900). To get there from La Langouste dock, walk down the beach until you see the road on your right. It is right across the road. Do not mistake it for Corosol Creperie which is next door. Corosol Creperie sets a very similar menu for about the same price, but is not the same. If you do not understand the menu, Fanny and some of her staff speak English.

If you want to go a little more up market without breaking the bank, try Pizzeria Napoli [T:66 03 79, $C-D, cc:V] which has an attractive outside dining room. Their speciality is pizza which makes a very inexpensive meal. But they have quite an extensive alternate menu which reflects the Italian, French and Dutch influences of its owner, Mr. Smeets. Their veal Florentine is excellent and chocolate lovers should finish with Negresco or profiterolles. Shorts are acceptable here, but they do appreciate shoes.

Otherwise you can just wander round and look at menus. Aux Poisson D'Or [T:66 01 80, $B-C, cc:V] has a pleasant atmosphere and is a little less expensive than most of the others which include: La Villa creole [T:66 05 53, $A-B, cc:V,Dn], L'Amphore [T:66 03 09, $A-B, cc:V,Dn], and Le Perroquet [T:66 06 98, $A-B, cc:V]. Several restaurants have changed and newcomers include La Grilladerie [T:66 11 44, $B, cc:V]. They plan an ice

cream parlor and upstairs piano bar. El Patio [T:66 02 70, $B, cc:V] specializes in Spanish food, including tapas and paella and they offer light lunches. La Petite Louisiane, [T:66 05 36,$B, cc:A,V] serves French and creole meals with nightly live music.

There is plenty of entertainment in Anse Mitan, though cover charges are often 100 to 200 francs. There are some quite elegant floor shows depicting local life that are often performed at the major hotels. Get a copy of "Choubouloute," available everywhere, for the latest schedule. Both the Carayou and the Meridien have discos. One of the cheapest places for entertainment is the Bambou, a rough and ready beach hotel. They have entertainment here most nights and you can just go in and buy a drink.

Water sports

There are no good diving sites near Anse Mitan, but dive boats take groups farther afield daily from the marina. Walk around the docks till you find Lichee run by Thierry Poisard [T:66 05 26], Mr. Berttin's Blue Passion Caraibe [T:66 04 90] or Planet Bleu run by Michel Pivette [T:66 08 79]. Also, Philippe Negrel runs a Padi shop at the Meridien Hotel [T:66 0179]. Best of all, wander into the small dive shop called Sub Evasion [T&F:66 11 25, cc:V]. Jean Jacques Aleci and his friend both speak English and are very helpful. They sell and rent all kinds of diving gear and fill tanks. They do not take people on dives but will happily advise you who to go with or tell you about the dive sites should you wish to go on your own.

ANSE A L'ANE

Just around the corner from Anse Mitan is Anse a L'Ane, a sweet little bay with a pretty beach. It makes a pleasant anchorage except in a northerly swell and is a lot quieter than Anse Mitan. It is well serviced by the high speed ferry to Fort de France which runs once an hour. Check the times on their notice board.

Right in the middle of the bay, about one third of a mile offshore, there is a reef about four feet deep which is hard to spot. You can pass on either side to anchor in about 12 feet, sand bottom. Make sure your anchor is well dug in and leave plenty of

room for the ferries which come into the long main dock. When approaching from Anse Mitan give the first bit of coast a really wide clearance as it is all rocky and at one point shoals stick out 270 yards (see chart). When heading toward Cap Salomon from Anse a L'Ane, there is about 10 to 14 feet of water between Ilet a Ramiers and the mainland, enough for most yachts to pass.

Ashore

Anse a L'Ane is a sort of mixed rent holiday area where the smart new Frantour Hotel rubs shoulders with some cheap and

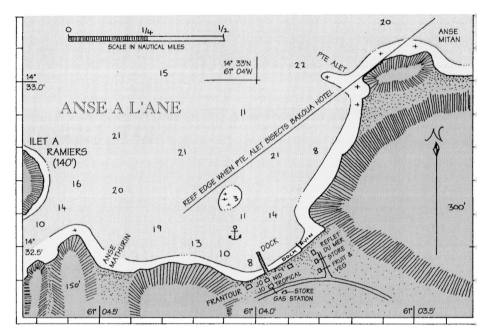

cheerful chalets and camping sites. You can leave your dinghy on the inner end of the ferry dock and there are garbage bins ashore. There is a gas station on the main road and two small food stores, one opposite the gas station and the other on the road behind Reflet de Mer. Farther down the same road is a greengrocer.

Ready for a meal out? Pignon sur Mer [T:68 38 37, $A-B] serves fine creole food. The Calalou [T:68 31 67, $B-C, cc:V,A, Dn,Ds] at the Frantour Hotel offers good lunchtime buffets, elaborate dinners and entertainment most nights of the week. Anyone with children should check out the quaint, hand carved, wooden merry-go-round in the garden. Chez Jo Jo [T:68 37

43, $C, cc:V] is an inexpensive restaurant and the local hot-spot, with live Zouk music most nights. It is very informal and shorts are fine. There is an inexpensive snack bar, Le Nid Tropical [T:68 31 30 $D], which also sells pastries. Across the bridge Reflet de la Mer [T:68 32 14, $C] is cute and inexpensive. Not far away, opposite the gas station, there is also Ti-Calebasse [T:68 38 77, $B, cc:V,A] which is good for fish especially on Fridays.

If you need a doctor, Dr. Jacquesson [T:68 42 41] has a clinic opposite the supermarket behind Reflet de la Mer. Dr. Jacquesson speaks English and spent some years skippering charter yachts.

ANSE NOIRE

Anse Noire is a tiny, deeply indented bay about half way between Ilet a Ramiers and Cap Salomon. It should be avoided in northerly swells, but it is otherwise well protected. Small colorful cliffs rise on the southern headland and there is a steep hill on the northern one. Palms back the black sand beach at the head of the bay. Behind the beach a steep jungly valley rises into the mountains. There is a dilapidated dock in the middle of the beach. Anse Noire is a

popular day time anchorage, especially on the weekends. It is usually deserted and peaceful at night. The wind swings in all directions. Just south of Anse Noire is a small fishing village called Anse Dufours with a white sand beach.

Ashore
It is pleasant just to sit and watch the kingfishers and other birds on the cliffs. There is an interesting hike up the river behind the beach (river bed in the dry

season). The strip of lush riverine forest is very different from the dry scrub that covers the hill sides.

Hidden behind the vegetation, Restaurant Anse Noire [T:68 62 82, $B-C, closed Mondays] has more the feeling of the Pacific than the Caribbean with its tall thatched roof and wooden benches. Owners Viviane Eglantine and Claude Castex have a simple menu of fish or lobster. The fish is grilled and served whole covered in herbs with a separate sauce. It is delicious. They add to the Pacific feeling by serving it on a breadfruit leaf. They are only open for lunch.

If you want a larger menu, there is another local lunch restaurant, Desir's Sable D'Or [T:68 62 97, $C-D, closed Tuesday], which overlooks Anse du Fours. This restaurant specializes in fresh seafood, but also offers creole meat dishes at reasonable prices. To get there, climb the steps up the cliff and walk a short way up the road.

Water sports

The snorkeling along the southern edge

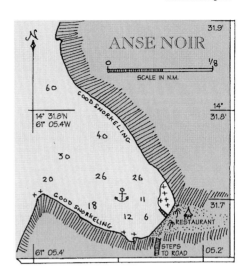

of the bay right round the headland is excellent. There are small walls, crevices and rocks decorated with sponges, tube worms and anemones which provide habitat for a large variety of smaller fish. Electric rays, octopuses, squid and a variety of sea cucumbers are often found here.

GRAND ANSE D'ARLET

Grand Anse D'Arlet is a picturesque fishing village set on a white sand beach which houses a fleet of dug out fishing pirogues. It is becoming popular with tourists and the northern corner has a touch of the Riviera with brightly colored beach umbrellas. Anse D'Arlet is a popular weekend spot for yachts based in Fort de France. Yachts should anchor on either side of the bay to leave the center free for the fishermen. (This area may be marked by yellow buoys.) Avoid sailing too close to the center of the village as a shoal area extends seaward several hundred feet. The best spot is in the southeastern corner of the bay which has a sand bottom 8-30 feet deep.

Ashore

There are several small food stores ashore. Go to the main road behind Gaby's and turn right for the two closest, or left for the Epicerie Delroy which also sells ice. There is a small boutique called Solal which sells local art and handicrafts.

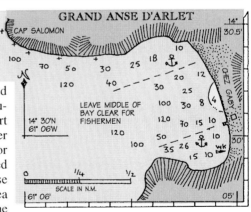

Something to look forward to in this bay is a meal at Chez Gaby [T:68 65 04, F:68 60 42, $C, cc:V, closed Sunday night and all Monday], a small, informal and clean restaurant just behind the main dock. It is run by Gabrielle, originally from Germany, and her husband, Marcel, who spent many years working there. Their food is both good and inexpensive with local seafood always featured. If that doesn't suit, there

GRAND ANSE D'ARLET

are many others, including L'Amandier [$C, cc:A], Delices des Anses [T:68 68 33, $C], Tamarin Plage [$C, cc:V] and L'Abre a Pain [$C-D]. Down at the northern end of the beach, behind all the fancy Mediterranean style sunshades, is Quai Sud [T:68 66 30, $B-C, cc:V], open lunchtime only and Ti Sable [T:68 62 44, $B-C, cc:V]. Motor scooters can be rented from the beach and the coast road from Petite Anse D'Arlet and over the hills to Diamant offers spectacular views.

Water Sports

Snorkeling is interesting all along the headland between Grand Anse D'Arlet and Petite Anse D'Arlet. This is a popular area for diving and you can dive with Plongée Passion [T:76 27 39] on either of their two daily dives at 1000 or 1430.

You can rent small craft, including Hobie cats, from the northern end of the beach by Ti Sable.

PETITE ANSE D'ARLET

The village of Petite Anse D'Arlet is photogenic with a picturesque church right near the waterfront. It makes an acceptable overnight anchorage in settled conditions. When approaching the town look out for the rocks to the west of the dock. Some are visible but others extend some yards seaward. Look for a patch of sand to anchor in off the town dock.

There is also an anchorage at Anse Chadière in the southeastern corner of the bay which is suitable for a quick dip or snorkel. Approach with caution as isolated rocks extend about 100 feet offshore. Anchor in the sand bottom at 10 to 12 feet.

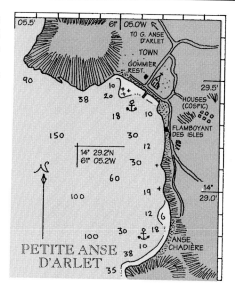

Ashore

Ashore you will find a couple of tiny shops, a post office and a pharmacy. There is a quaint and entertaining restaurant set in an old house in the town (just follow the road that runs back a bit to the west of the church). It is called Le Gommier des Caraibes [68 62 79, $C]. The proprietor Bruno Perrier specializes in local creole cooking. For a fancier restaurant, turn right off the dock and walk along the coast road. Mme. Rose Elouise's Le Flamboyant des Isles [T:68 67 75, $B, cc:V, closed Sunday night and Tuesday] has a splendid view across the anchorage and is a short way uphill. In town there is also an inexpensive snack bar called Chez Desert [T:68 61 86, $C, lunchtime only].

Water sports

The snorkeling is good in the southeastern corner of the bay. It may be worth giving scuba a go here also.

THE SOUTH COAST OF MARTINIQUE

There are no good anchorages along Martinique's south coast until you get to Ste. Anne. There are some shoals along this coast that extend up to half a mile. There is deep water (over a hundred feet) some way outside these shoals. It is best to stay in this deep water, as there are numerous fish traps at lesser depths.

As long as you don't get too far offshore, the sail eastwards to Ste. Anne is usually an exhilarating brisk beat to windward in protected water.

STE. ANNE

The photogenic white buildings of Ste. Anne stand out clearly against the surrounding green hills. Above the town is a prominent shrine with a walled path leading up to it. Anchor anywhere off the town. The buoyed area off the beach is reserved for swimming and dinghy sailing. You can also eyeball your way south and anchor off the Caritan Hotel. The water depth is 10 to 20 feet and holding is good in sand. There are shoals close to shore between Ste. Anne and Anse Caritan. If you are arriving here from abroad you should first go up to Marin and clear customs.

Ashore

Ste. Anne is a delightful seaside town,

small and peaceful, yet just big enough to have a town square. It has two small supermarkets, several boutiques, a pharmacy, a bank and a bookstore (down the back street). Several local handicraft stores have now opened. You can get fresh bread and Danish early in the morning from the boulangerie. Turn right off the dock and walk past the market. Look for an unmarked hole in the wall just before the T-junction. Let your nose be your guide. L'Epi Soleil, the boulangerie/patisserie opposite the supermarket, opens later in the day. It includes a congenial beachside sitting area for a lunchtime sandwich. There are card phones and a post office. If the lines are too long to buy a phone card at the post office, the quincaillerie by the market sells them.

There is a great walk up to the shrine on the top of the hill. The path starts just behind the church and the view is ample reward.

There are enough restaurants in Ste.

Anne to suit every budget. At the lower end of the scale, Restaurant Anthor [T:76 72 93, $C-D, cc:V] on the front street and L'Outre Mer, [T:76 91 51, $C-D, cc:V] on the back street both turn out good Creole meals at a reasonable price, and in addition they cook pizzas. Getting fancier, Les Tameriniers [T:76 75 62, $B closed Tuesday evening and all day Wednesday] is a cute restaurant with a picturesque exterior of flowers. Jean Claude Edmond cooks tasty French/creole food and adds artful touches to his more expensive dishes by decorating them with flowers. Poi et Virginie [$A-B, cc:A,V, closed Monday] has a pleasant dining room overlooking the bay and offers first rate seafood. La Dunette [T:76 73 90, $C, cc:V] has an open dining room under a blue striped awning,

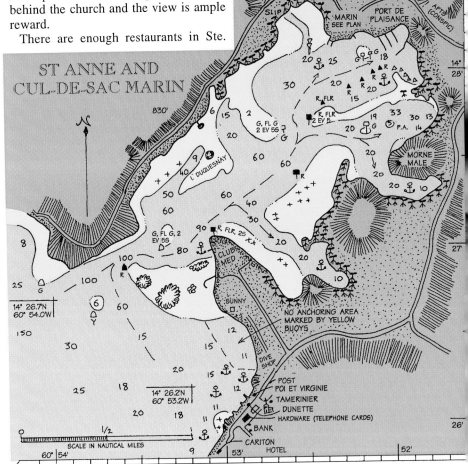

and is a pleasant place to stop for a beer or ice cream.

There are more restaurants and snack bars behind the long beach which stretches from Ste. Anne to the Club Med. One particularly charming one is Philippe and Brigitte's Sunny [T:76 76 74, $B-C, cc:V] where you eat outside in the garden under a big tree overlooking the beach. Philippe and Sunny have been yachtspeople themselves and used to have a restaurant in Union Island.

Water Sports

There are several shallow reefs for snorkeling and in some spots the reefs drop off steeply enough to make scuba diving pleasant. A good place to start snorkeling or scuba is out at the first red buoy in the channel toward Marin. Snorkelers can follow the shallow part of the reef in and scuba divers can head south into deeper water. Pierre Cadiou is the friendly and cheerful owner of Histoires D'Eau [T:76 92 98], the local dive shop at the Ste. Anne end of the beach. They dive twice daily at 0930 and 1430.

Small sailing catamarans and sailboards are available for rent on the beach. The area is generally breezy enough to be fun but is well protected from waves.

MARIN

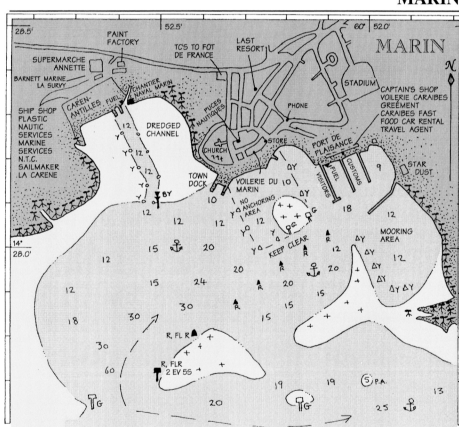

Marin is a pleasant small town, an important yachting center, and the main base for the Martinique charter industry. The Moorings, Stardust, Sunsail, Star Voyage, Catana, Tropical Yacht Services, Chimere Yachting and Petit Breton all have bases here. There is a large marina, a haul-out facility and many other yacht services.

Navigation

Cul-de-Sac du Marin is a vast, deeply indented bay, surrounded by hills and

lined with mangroves. It is full of shoals that are often visible in good light. The whole area is a gunkholer's dream and the best place to be in Martinique in a hurricane.

Before the entrance is a small reef about six feet deep. It has been marked by a yellow buoy. There is plenty of water on either side of the shoal and you can usually see it. Give the buoy plenty of clearance.

There is a long reef extending to the west of the southern part of Club Med. This is marked by a red buoy which must be left to starboard when entering. A reef due west of the north part of Club Med is marked by a green buoy which should be left well to port when entering. After that head for the apartment buildings behind the forest of masts until you see the pair of red and green beacons in the middle of the bay. Pass between them, leaving the red one to starboard and the green one to port. Now you must head toward Marin and go at least half way there before turning up toward the marina, leaving all the red buoys to starboard. The last little shoal off the town is

marked by two green beacons whic should both be left to port as you enter th marina area.

Regulation

Marin is a port of entry, and a custom officer is available at his office in th marina every morning. He usually arrive about 0730. He is occasionally there in th afternoon.

Anchoring is forbidden in the swimmin area in front of the beach. It is marked b yellow buoys.

Service

SAEPP [T:74 85 33, F:74 74 30, VHF:9 cc:V], generally known as the Port d Plaisance Marin, operates a large marina You can get fuel and water here, and dock age is available with 220-volt, 60-cycl electricity (110 volt transformers are als available). There is space for yachts up t 80 tons and 140 feet long. The marin management can introduce anyone want ing to leave their boats to people who loo after yachts.

CarenAntilles [T:74 77 70, F:74 78 22

VHF:16/73, cc:V] is a large haul-out facility and fuel station. They can take boats up to 23-foot beam with a 65-ton travel lift. The dredged channel to the lift and fuel dock is about 11.5 feet deep and marked by yellow buoys to port and very faded red buoys to starboard as you go in. The storage area is large enough to take about 120 boats, and they can always make more room. Rates are in line with the other islands, and it is a good place to leave your yacht in dry storage. Rates depend on how long you need to be ashore and the current parity between the franc and other currencies. You can fax them for a rate sheet. You can do your own work on the slip, or if you prefer, there are workshops that can do it for you. Facilities include toilets, showers and a restaurant. There is a convenient dinghy dock by the fuel station for those wanting to visit the chandlery or any of the other facilities. The yard manager speaks good English.

Ship Shop [T:74 78 22] is an excellent chandlery, well stocked with everything from electronics to dinghies, including a whole range of yacht hardware, fishing equipment and diving gear. They are helpful and happy to act as a mail drop: c/o Ship Shop, CarenAntilles, Ancien Usine du Marin, Marin 97290, Martinique. Michel De Holland speaks good English.

Talba Gaston's Nautic Services [T:74 70 45, F:74 70 52] right in the CarenAntilles compound is the place to get your boat's antifouling redone. Gaston also ships yachts long distance and makes the cradles for them. He does all the antifouling and shipping for The Moorings in Martinique. Gaston does commercial diving and rents scuba gear, usually to yachts going on charter.

Also in the compound, Plastic Services [T:74 70 37, F:74 70 43] does all kinds of fiberglass repairs, osmosis treatment and topside paint jobs.

If your engine is giving troubles, you will be safe with Yves Icare at Antilles Marine Services [T:74 70 78, 76 97 93, F:76 78 28], just behind CarenAntilles. Yves is a competent mechanic who speaks English and is a diesel specialist. He will work on

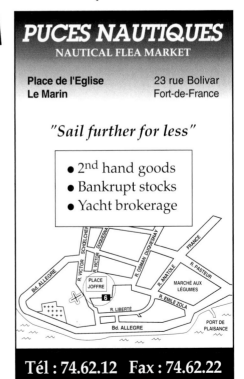

any engine, though he is agent for Nannidiesel and Man, and keeps new Nannidiesel engines in stock. Yves is also an agent for watermakers and will work on any brand, and he is agent for Zeise generators. There are plans for a new outboard shop to set up next to Antilles Marine Services, and refrigeration repairs can be arranged.

Right behind the new CarenAntilles is Barnett Marine [T&F:70 26 69, cc:V], a marine hardware store directed at maintenance. You can get a full range of International paints and antifoulings are also available from other manufacturers such as Rule, Nautic and Petit. They also sell pumps, batteries, stainless fasteners, foam and marine tapes, anchors and chain. Barnett Marine offers a full rigging service. Since Barnett Marine is associated with Sea Services in Fort de France, they can quickly bring down any hardware that is not in the store.

In the same building La Survy, the inflat-

able repair people, is opening an office.

In the same area you can also check ou the Marine Paint Factory [T:74 84 14, F:74 99 46], which carries French brands a competitive prices.

There are three sailmakers experienced at both making sails, biminis and covers and at fast repairs for charter turn-arounds. They are all conveniently placed for close approach by dinghy.

At CarenAntilles, Vladimir Owlig, a friendly young man of Russian extraction owns Nautic Tech Care [T:74 74 64, F:74 61 46]. He has a large loft upstairs by the restaurant and can make or repair any kind of sail you might need. In addition he does covers, biminis, awnings, cushions and anything else that is made by sewing.

In the marina you will find a branch o Voilerie Caraibe Martinique owned by Herve Lepault [T:74 88 09], whose main shop is in Pointe du Bout. New sails are by Incidence, the well known French sailmaker. They are computer designed in

France and made locally. If the shop gets overwhelmed by work, they can truck sails needing repair to Pointe du Bout.

La Voilerie du Marin [T:74 73 10, F:74 72 22, VHF:67] is easily found in the blue and white building facing the waterfront. A convenient dinghy dock is just across the road. Guylaine and Robert run a first rate sail loft and can build new sails, awnings, biminis or cushions or repair your old ones. They also have a laundry service, and offer a mail drop (4, Rue de la Liberte, 97290 Marin, Martinique, FWI), and will send and receive faxes. They can also help with boat watching should you wish to leave your boat at anchor while you go away. Guylaine speaks English and can direct you to other services you may need.

Caraibes Greement [T:74 80 33] is a full rigging service run by Philippe LeConte. He can handle any rigging problem you may have, from replacing a stay to a complete re-rig of your yacht including a new mast. They are agents for FranceSpar and Harken, and keep a good supply of new fittings in stock. Anything they do not have can be shipped in at short order. They are happy to work on your yacht and make repairs aloft.

Chantier Naval du Marin [T:74 89 42], next to CarenAntilles, is owned by Endrik Hozinger from Germany. He does custom fiberglass and wood epoxy construction. He will build anything from a water tank to a power cruiser. You can also ask him about repairs and he is happy to come and sort out your electrics.

Ashore

In the marina you will find a branch of the Captain's Shop [T:74 87 55, F:74 96 71, cc:V]. This well stocked chandlery has almost anything in it you might need, but should you need something not on show, ask as there is another even bigger branch of this shop in Pointe du Bout. Less well known is the Captain's Shop Service Department, available by asking at the Captain's Shop. Their service department fixes just about anything, including mo-

tors, refrigeration, electrics and electronics.

If you need to get some fishing gear together before setting sail, visit Caraibes Plaisance [T:74 85 73], the tackle shop. They will even set you up with a rig with live bait on it – a sure way to increase your chances of a catch.

In the marina you will also find M Voyages [T:74 71 07, cc:A,V], a travel agent, Pop's Car Rental [T:51 02 72, cc:V] and Le Kaoma [T:74 83 62, $C-D], a bar and fast food pizza place with a pleasant view over the marina.

Up in town, in the main square opposite the church, is a branch of Puces Nautiques [T:74 62 12, F:74 62 22], the bargain basement and nearly new shop of the marine industry. You can find great bargains here on all kinds of marine hardware. Puces Nautiques is open weekdays 0900-1300 and 1430-1730 and on Saturday mornings.

Provisioning in Marin is good. The Annette family runs three supermarkets called Supermarche Annette [T:74 92 73, F:74 90 96, cc:V]. The biggest and best of these is just behind the new slip, next to Azurel. They have just rebuilt this supermarket, doubling its size and it is ample for provisioning with good meat, cheese and wine sections. It is the only large supermarket in Martinique within walking distance of your boat. Better yet, the prices are lower than most other markets on many items.

It is a fairly long walk to Supermarche Annette from the marina, or you can dinghy to CarenAntilles and walk up. There is also a little local Marin bus which goes round and round the town and passes by. They are happy to deliver large orders (one thousand francs or more) back to the waterfront in Marin. You can arrange this with Jean-Michelle Annette in the office at the back of the store. When they deliver the food back they will take you with them so you can show them where your boat is, but local laws only allow them to take back one person with the food. So any others in the group must walk or take a taxi or bus. Jean-Michelle Annette will happily organize a full provisioning for charter yachts on a turn around. You can fax through your order two days in advance, and he will have it ready when you arrive. Anything they do not stock in their shop they will bring in from outside. Should you prefer to shop without leaving the marina, Annette has a little office in the marina [T:74 71 01, F:74 70 98]. Chancel Mina will give you their provisioning list in English or French, complete with prices. You can tick off what you want and have it delivered to you.

Marin offers three good restaurants for eating out. The Last Resort [T:74 83 88, $C-D, cc:V] up in town is quaint and entertaining with lots of atmosphere. They offer good French style family cooking at a reasonable price. The Last Resort is open every night and most days for lunch. They are very popular in the evenings so it is best to call, or pop up and make a reservation.

On the waterfront, the Lagon Bleu, above the yacht club [T:74 80 10, $A-B, cc:V, closed Monday night and all day

Tuesday], is a smarter restaurant with a perfect location looking out over the bay. They offer first rate French cooking with a variety of both meat and seafood dishes.

La Carene [T:74 70 22, $C-D, cc:V] is right in the CarenAntilles compound upstairs with a good view over the harbor. There is easy approach by dinghy to the dinghy dock. It offers some of the best

value for money with very inexpensive creole fare such as fish court buillon, stewed lambi and shrimps. They do a good steak and chips. In addition they have daily specials. Happy hour is 1900-2000 every night. It is currently inexpensive enough to eat any time you cannot be bothered to cook.

· PIGEON ISLAND ·

PASSAGE BETWEEN MARTINIQUE AND ST. LUCIA

Northbound

The passage between St. Lucia and Fort de France is usually a fast reach. A course of due north from Rodney Bay generally gets you close to the lee coast. It doesn't hurt to be a little way offshore when you arrive as the wind tends to follow you along the coast and is flukey close in. If Martinique is visible at the outset, it will appear as two islands, as the lower-lying and in the center is not visible from St. Lucia. As you approach Martinique, Diamond Rock stands out as a clear landmark.

If you are heading for Ste. Anne you can often make it in one tack, but be sure to head up a bit to allow for current as you cross.

Southbound

The southerly passage from Anse D'Arlet is sometimes a pleasant reach. At other times it can be hard on the wind. As the wind flows round the land, you will be pointing high as you follow the coast. It often pays to motor sail to stay reasonably close to the shore before setting off across the channel. If sailing, it may pay to sail fast on the southerly tack and hope to play lifts later. When you see St. Lucia, head for the highest (rather rounded) mountain in the north end of the island until you begin to make out the distinct shape of Pigeon Island, a clear double peak joined by a slope. The higher twin mounds of Mt. Pinard and Mt. Flambeau (see Rodney Bay

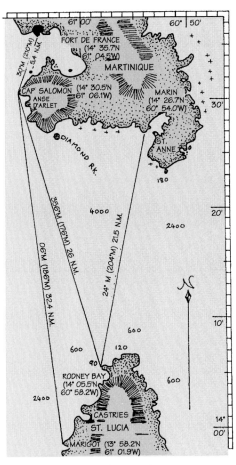

chart) also sometimes stand out.

The sail from Ste. Anne to St. Lucia is generally an easy reach.

Regulations

St. Lucia has customs offices in Vieux Fort, Marigot Bay, Castries and Rodney Bay. The entry charges in $ EC are as follows. All yachts pay $15 navigational aids, $10 pratique (up to 100 tons) and clearance fees according to length; $5 for under 40 feet and $15 for over 40 feet. In addition, yachts on charter which are less than 40 feet pay $20; between 40 and 70 feet, $30 and over 70 feet, $40. For stays of less than three days, you can clear in and out on arrival. You can get permission for stays up to 2 months (with a further one month extension) from the customs officer on arrival. Longer stays have to be arranged with the main customs in town. Do not underestimate your stay as extensions involve a trip to town and a charge of $25 EC a head. You cannot clear into Soufriere, but you can get a temporary permit to moor from the police station for $25 EC. This allows you to stay one night before clearing in. When you clear out, you can pay $25 EC for a permit to stay in the Pitons on your way out. Those clearing out of normal office hours (weekdays 0800-1215, 1330-1545) will be charged a reasonable overtime fee. St. Lucia has strict environmental laws. Most coastal areas are now protected and spearfishing, damaging corals, buying coral products or buying lobsters out of season (lobstering season is 31st October to 31st April) are strictly forbidden. Pets are not allowed ashore. If you wish to report your arrival or departure to Vigie Light, they keep a safety log.

Holidays

Jan 1st and 2nd
Monday and Tuesday 40 days before Easter - Carnival
Easter Friday through Monday
Feb 22 - Independence Day
May 1 - Labor day
Whit Monday (7 weeks after Easter)
Corpus Christi (Thursday, 10 days after Whit Monday)
First Monday in August
October 5th - Thanksgiving
December 13th - National day
Dec 25th and Dec 26th

Shopping hours

In St. Lucia shops are normally open 0830-1230, then 1330-1600. Saturday is half day and most places are closed by noon. Banks normally open weekdays till 1300, and on Fridays from 1500 to 1700, though some banks are now open in the afternoon as well.

Telephones

There are card phones all over the island. You buy phone cards in selected shops. For USA dial 1+10 digits, For other overseas calls dial 011+country code+number. For collect and credit card calls dial 0+10 digits (USA), 01+country code+number (other countries). There are some USA direct phones in Rodney Bay Marina. When dialing from overseas the area code is 809 followed by a 7 digit number.

Transport

In St. Lucia there are inexpensive ($1.50-6 EC) buses running to most towns and villages. If you are going a long way check on the time of the last returning bus. Taxis are plentiful. Sample taxi rates are:

	$EC
Rodney Bay - Vigie	35
Rodney Bay - Castries	35
Rodney Bay - Hewanorra	130
Castries - Hewanorra	120
Castries - Marigot	55
By the hour	52
Short ride	10

Rental cars are available (check our directory). You will need to buy a local licence which costs $30 EC. Drive on the left.

ST. LUCIA

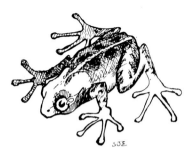

St. Lucia, the largest of the English speaking Windwards, is mountainous and lush, with many beautiful white sand beaches. Tropical rain forest covers the steep slopes of the center and gives way to cultivated agricultural land around the more moderately sloping coastal fringe. Bananas are the principal crop. For sheer physical beauty, the area around Soufriere and the Pitons is outstanding.

St. Lucia offers excellent sightseeing and hiking. You can see most of it by bus or a rental car. Adventurous travelers willing to combine driving with hiking will want to rent a four-wheel drive vehicle and explore some far away corners like Grand Anse or Anse Louvet on the windward shore. Organized tours are available through most travel agents and this is an easy way to see St. Lucia. All day tours cost in the region of $40 US and include lunch, drinks and transport from your nearest dock. Popular tours are round the island tours, plantation tours, where you get to see the backbone of the St. Lucia economy at work, and the rainforest tour which involves hiking across the middle of the island. For those really interested in local nature, the National Trust runs tours to Frigate Island and the Maria Islands.

St. Lucia has been developing at an amazing rate over the last few years and offers not only the newest and best full service marina in the Windwards, but also a large choice of restaurants. St. Lucia is a major charter center, with large charter companies in Rodney Bay and Marigot Bay.

Navigation west coast

Between the northern tip of St. Lucia and Rodney Bay there are several shoals and no anchorages, so it is best to keep clear. Rodney Bay offers several anchorages which are dealt with in detail below.

Barrel of Beef is a low lying rock about a quarter of a mile off the southern side of the entrance to Rodney Bay. It is marked by a white light which flashes every five seconds. The water is deep enough (about 18 feet) for most yachts to pass inside it.

Between Barrel of Beef and Castries, the coast sweeps back in a large bay containing Rat Island. This bay is full of reefs and shoals and best avoided. On leaving Rodney Bay the normal route is to pass inside Barrel of Beef and head directly toward Castries Harbor.

Tapion Rock forms the southern entrance to Castries Harbor. There are some rocks close by, so give it a reasonable clearance. Two miles south of Castries, Cul De Sac Bay is a huge depot for Hess Oil. It is well lit and makes an obvious landmark by day or night. There is a buoy in the middle of the entrance to this bay which flashes at night.

From Cul de Sac Bay to the Pitons the island is mainly steep-to and a quarter of a mile offshore clears all dangers. There are a few rock hazards lying up to 100 yards or more offshore. The worst is a sizable rock patch off the southern end of Anse Chastanet which should be given a wide clearance.

RODNEY BAY

Rodney Bay is over a mile long. At the northern end an artificial causeway connects Pigeon Island to the mainland, providing the whole bay with protection. In the old days, when Europeans used to entertain themselves by sailing around in wooden boats taking potshots at each other, Pigeon Island was the main base for

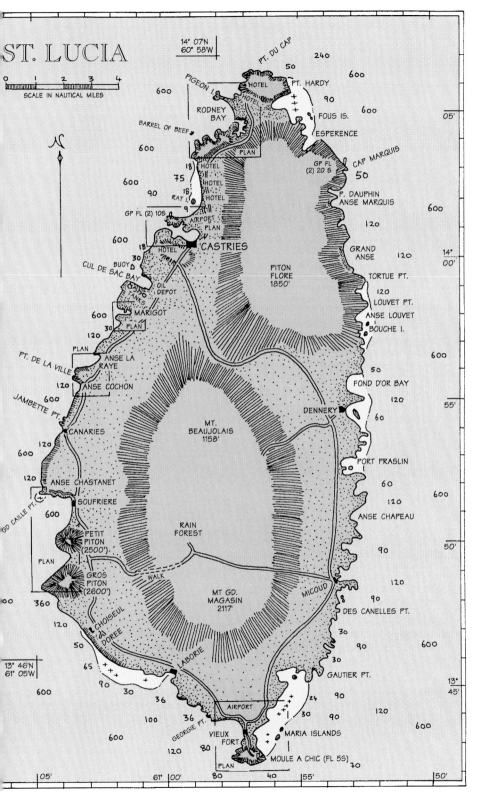

ST. LUCIA

SCALE IN NAUTICAL MILES

0 1 2 3 4

14° 07'N
60° 58'W

PT. DU CAP
50
240
600
600
PIGEON I.
600
PT. HARDY
HOTEL
HOTEL
90
05'
RODNEY
BAY
FOUS IS.
600
BARREL OF BEEF
ESPERENCE
600
PLAN
GP FL
(2) 20 S
CAP MARQUIS
50
18
HOTEL
75
18
HOTEL
90
RAT I.
HOTEL
P. DAUPHIN
ANSE MARQUIS
600
GP FL (2) 10S
9
AIRPORT
PLAN
120
600
18
HOTEL
CASTRIES
GRAND
ANSE
120
14°
00'
30
BUOY
CUL DE SAC BAY
PITON
FLORE
1850'
TORTUE PT.
OIL
DEPOT
120
LOUVET PT.
TANKS
ANSE LOUVET
600
MARIGOT
BOUCHE I.
120
30
PLAN
600
PLAN
ANSE LA
RAYE
FOND D'OR BAY
55'
PT. DE LA VILLE
120
ANSE COCHON
50
JAMBETTE PT.
600
DENNERY
120
MT.
BEAUJOLAIS
1158'
60
CANARIES
PORT PRASLIN
120
600
60
120
ANSE CHASTANET
120
ANSE CHAPEAU
GD CAILLE PT.
SOUFRIERE
600
RAIN
FOREST
90
PETIT
PITON
(2500')
120
PLAN
GROS
PITON
(2600')
WALK
MICOUD
90
360
MT GD.
MAGASIN
2117'
DES CANELLES PT.
120
CHOISEUL
DOREE
90
30
13° 46'N
61° 05'N
50
LABORIE
30
65
GAUTIER PT.
13°
45'
90
600
30
36
24
90
100
36
AIRPORT
30
90
120
GEORGIE PT.
600
VIEUX
FORT
MARIA ISLANDS
600
120
80
PLAN
MOULE A CHIC (FL 5S)
70
05'
61° 00'
80
40
55'
50'

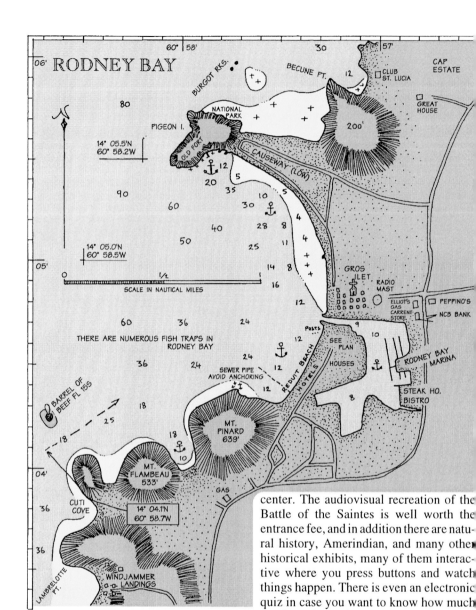

the British navy in this area. It was ideally situated, being in sight (on most days) of Martinique, the French main base. There used to be a fort, hospital buildings, barracks and storerooms. Now it is conserved by the St. Lucia National Trust as a delightful park. There are shady gardens and the fort has been partly restored. The climb to the top is well rewarded by the views. Strategically placed signboards tell you about the history. Near the causeway the old officers' barracks have been rebuilt to house the new interpretation center. The audiovisual recreation of the Battle of the Saintes is well worth the entrance fee, and in addition there are natural history, Amerindian, and many other historical exhibits, many of them interactive where you press buttons and watch things happen. There is even an electronic quiz in case you want to know how much you have learned.

There is a small entry charge to the park and interpretation center. This helps finance the National Trust, which works to preserve the environment as well as historical sites. The anchorage off Pigeon Island is good, but for those anchored in Rodney Bay lagoon, a ferry runs at 1015, 1215 and 1415. Le Pigeon restaurant [T:452-8166, VHF:16] is in the building that Snowball's Restaurant occupied way back before the causeway was built. Currently closed, it may reopen for snacks and

RODNEY BAY: THE LAGOON IS IN FRONT, PIGEON ISLAND IS TOP RIGHT

drinks.

Rodney Bay Lagoon is a large and completely protected inner lagoon which is entered via a man made channel between Reduit Beach and Gros Islet village. This is lit by port and starboard lights at the entrance and by range lights which make an excellent aid to good night sight. The lagoon is the home of Rodney Bay Marina.

Outside the lagoon, to the south of the channel entrance, is Reduit Beach, one of St. Lucia's finest beaches and the home of the St. Lucian Hotel and the St. Lucia Yacht Club.

Many yachts tie up at the marina. Otherwise the three main anchorages in the area are: inside the lagoon (dredged to 8-10 feet), to the southeast of Pigeon Island, and off Reduit Beach. Some people also anchor off Gros Islet village. The outside anchorages occasionally become untenable in northerly swells.

Regulations

Rodney Bay Marina is a port of entrance and a good place to clear in. If you plan to stay in the marina, you can go into a berth (see below) and walk down to the customs office. If you plan to anchor, clear in at the marina by using the customs slip which is opposite the customs office. It is about half way down the outer dock and marked by a yellow post. Customs are normally open daily from 0800 to 1800, but you pay overtime after 1600. Regular entry charges are $30-40 EC depending on the size of boat. Some customs officers have interpreted the law to charge yachts $25 EC for visiting some St. Lucian anchorages before they have cleared out. This was not the intent of the law. Full details of fees are given at the beginning of this chapter.

If you are too deep to enter the lagoon you can anchor outside and dinghy in.

Shipping in parts? Note that invoices and all shipping papers must be marked "for trans-shipment". Even though items are duty free there will be charges for documentation and transportation and customs often charge overtime.

Services

Rodney Bay Marina [Box 1538, Castries, St. Lucia, T:452-0324, F:452-

363, VHF:16] is large and pleasant, with lawns and coconut palms, as well as offices and shops. There is a convenient bus to town and a plethora of restaurants close by. Call for a dock space and, if you cannot get through, choose a spot and hope for the best. Eight foot draft is no problem. A swan 65 at 9' 3" can make it in comfortably on a good high tide. Boats of up to 10-foot draft have managed to enter on specially high tides. If in any doubt, sound out the channel before entering. "A", "D" and "E" docks are for visitors, "B" dock is a mixture of visitors and charter yachts, "C" dock is for local bareboat companies only. The outside of the outer dock has easier access and is the only space suitable for really large yachts, so there is a minimum fee rating here of 45 feet. There is ample water and electricity (220 volt, 50 cycle; transformers for 110 volts can be arranged). Pleasant features in the marina include hot showers, two banks, a first rate chandlery and an electronics shop. You can use Rodney Bay Marina as a postal drop and send faxes. There is a direct credit card telephone line to the States and several public card and coin phones. There is garbage disposal.

Rodney Bay Marina is the home of many charter companies, including Sunsail, Tradewind Yacht Charters, and Destination St. Lucia.

Rodney Bay Marina Boatyard [T&F:452 9725, VHF:68] is St. Lucia's largest haul-out facility with a 50-ton yacht hoist and room for about 90 yachts in long term storage and another dozen having work done on them. Labor is available or you can do the work yourself. The yard can handle any size job from a quick haul to a complete osmosis treatment and respray. The yard is ably managed by Hans Savimaki who oversees all the work. It has a paint store which stocks Proline anitfouling, a TBT co-polymer that beats the rest on price and works well. There is a machine shop (including SS welding), fiberglass repair shop, mechanical workshop, and a 10-boat work dock for lifting and working on engines. Their mechanic can tackle anything but is a specialist in

Cats and GMs. Here, too, is the fuel dock. The fuel dock is very service minded, opening at 0700 and going till the last person wants fuel. For big motor yachts taking on large quantities, Hans will even open in the middle of the night. Duty free fuel is available for anyone who has cleared out. Just show your papers. Day workers often offer their services to yachts in the lagoon; get a recommendation before hiring anyone.

Block ice may be bought from Sunsail and cube ice from the liquor store, the Bread Basket and the mini-market at the Mortar and Pestle. Sunsail [T:452-8848/8648, F:452-0839, VHF:16], the oldest charter company, has always helped visiting yachtspeople in any way they can. They offer a laundry service, fill all kinds of LPG cooking gas bottles and they do sail repairs, make biminis, covers and awnings. If you need a new sail Sunsail is the agent for Doyle Sails in Barbados. Sunsail is also agent for Furlex roller furling gear, and they can always help with rigging problems. They also run a yacht caretaking business.

Outfitters [T:452-8360, F:452-0722] is also in the Sunsail office. Outfitters is a well-run organization that specializes in yacht parts and fittings and getting them to you in good time. Their worldwide connections mean that they can find just about anything from anywhere, and they have a thousand-page catalogue of yacht hardware on hand. Because of their purchasing power, Outfitters can often equal or beat list prices. The best part is they can bring parts in fast. The faster you want it the more it costs, but charges are reasonable. They also handle all the customs clearance so it gets delivered duty free and hassle free to your yacht. Outfitters has stations in Antigua, Grenada and Venezuela, so you can order in one island and arrange collection in another. You can send faxes from Outfitters and use them as a mail drop [c/o Outfitters, P.O. Box 928, Castries, St Lucia, W.I.]

Sparkle Laundry [VHF:16] in Gros Islet will collect and deliver from the marina.

Quick Fix Refrigeration [T:484-9010 emergency:450-0587] is run by Wayne who will come by and get your system running again, or install a new one. He works with refrigeration and air-conditioning and even runs a 24-hour emergency service.

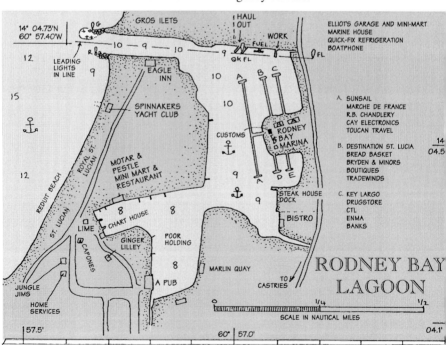

14° 04.73'N
60° 57.40'W

12
LEADING LIGHTS IN LINE

15

12

GROS ILETS
HAUL OUT
WORK
FUEL

ELLIOT'S GARAGE AND MINI-MART
MARINE HOUSE
QUICK-FIX REFRIGERATION
BOATPHONE

10 — 9 — 10
Qk FL
FL

EAGLE INN

10

A. SUNSAIL
MARCHE DE FRANCE
R.B. CHANDLERY
CAY ELECTRONICS
TOUCAN TRAVEL

SPINNAKERS YACHT CLUB

CUSTOMS

RODNEY BAY MARINA

B. DESTINATION ST. LUCIA
BREAD BASKET
BRYDEN & MINORS
BOUTIQUES
TRADEWINDS

14
04.5

MOTAR & PESTLE MINI MART & RESTAURANT

REDUIT BEACH

ROYAL ST. LUCIAN ST.

ST. LUCIAN

STEAK HOUSE DOCK

BISTRO

C. KEY LARGO
DRUGSTORE
CTL
ENMA
BANKS

CHART HOUSE

LIME

GINGER LILLEY

CAPONES

POOR HOLDING

8

8

MARLIN QUAY

TO CASTRIES

RODNEY BAY
LAGOON

JUNGLE JIMS

HOME SERVICES

A PUB

SCALE IN NAUTICAL MILES
1/4   1/2

57.5'

60° 57.0'

04.1'

If you have a problem with engine parts, it is worth trying the Marina and all the charter companies (see also Vigie). Destination St. Lucia can help with boat care and yacht management and they have a German language book swap.

The Bistro [T:452-9494, F:452-0453 VHF:16, cc:A,V] offers stern-to dockage with water and electricity (220 volt 50 cycle). They also have very reasonable houses for rent.

The Steak House marina [T:452-9800, F:452-9974, VHF:16/17] offers stern-to and alongside docking for about 20 boats with water and electricity (220 volt, 50 cycle).

Cay Electronics [T:452-9922, F:452-8524, cc:V], with stores in St. Lucia, Antigua, B.V.I and the U.S.A, is efficiently run by Mark Fruehauf. He offers sales and service for all your electronics, watermakers, generators, hydraulics, refrigeration and electrics, including alternators and generators. New stock includes electronics, gel filled batteries and a wide range of spares. He can quickly obtain anything that is not on hand.

Rodney Bay Marine Hardware [T:452-9973 F:452-9974, VHF:16 "RBSS"], part of Rodney Bay Ship Services is owned by Lucian Greg Glace and managed by well known St. Lucian yachtsman Ted Bull. It is one of the best stocked chandleries in the Windwards. Avon Tenders hang from the roof, and you can get a Johnson outboard backed by the full service facilities. Huge deep cycle batteries rub shoulders with watermakers, International paints, solar panels and windmills. You will find an-

chors, chain, rigging, fittings and ropes along with snorkeling gear and barbecues There is a small boutique and book swap Everything is duty free for all non St Lucian yachts. By agreement with the boatyard they do not sell antifouling.

Rodney Bay Ship Services also runs a full maintenance team with a fully qualified marine engineer. They work on all makes of outboard, all marine electrics most diesel engines and generators, including Detroit, Perkins, Cummins, Onan and Westerbeke, hydraulics, and watermakers. They carry out on-board repairs at the Steak House dock.

Blue Water Holdings [T:450-0688 F:450-9697, VHF:16] is run by four energetic young Englishmen who love sailing and racing. Hugh is the sailmaker (Blue Water Sails), David is the fiberglass specialist and Duncan, more newly arrived, is setting up a rigging shop.

MC [Marine Covers, T&F:452-0186] is just a short walk from the marina, but you don't have to walk, just call the owners Adriana and Tim Boyce, and they will

MARINE COVERS
WE MAKE AND REPAIR

biminis   cushions
awnings   windscoops
sailcovers   dinghy
dodgers   covers, etc.

*Call us for prompt service
and on time delivery*

come to see you. They make and repair cushions, dodgers, awnings, sail covers, biminis, and everything else except sails.

Other people who have workshops outside the area and pay house calls to Rodney Bay include: Andrew Tyson [T:452-5794], cabinet work; Richard Cox [T:453-2361], fiberglass repairs and spray painting; B&L Upholstery Clinic [T:452-7644], cushions and drapes; Remy and Parris Enterprises [T:450-1037], woodwork, recaulking, fiberglass repairs and fixing broken tape decks and radios; and Trevor Joseph [T:450-8864] for sail repairs. In addition, some businesses in the Castries area also pay marina visits. These include Chris Kessell for surveys, alternator and electrical repairs and International Marine Diesel for engine work.

Windward Island Gases [T:452-8514, 452-0339], just beyond Glace Motors, test scuba tanks and can fill most kinds of gas bottles, including CO_2, argon, helium and nitrogen.

There are two first rate travel agents in the area. Right in the marina nothing could be more convenient than to walk into Jane Tipson's Toucan Travel [T:452-0896/9963, F:452-9806, VHF:16, cc:A,V, Ds]. They often have special rates for trips to the U.K. and U.S.A. and they also arrange car rentals and island tours to help you get to know St. Lucia better. Ask for Kathy or Charlene.

World Travel [T:452-5574, F:451-7445, VHF:planned] is owned and run by Joycelyn. Her office is upstairs over American Drywall on the way to town, but you don't have to go near the office; just call Joycelyn on the phone and tell her what you want – tickets, car rentals or tours and she will arrange everything and deliver your tickets to you. Joycelyn is helpful and enthusiastic and works hard to get the best rates.

If you wish to rent a car, there are two local agencies willing to help. CTL [T:452-0732, F:452-0401] is right in the marina and National Car Rental [T:450-8500, F:450-8577], on the road to Gros Islet, has been offering discounts through an ad in this guide.

GRASSHOPPER TROPICAL ART & GIFTS GABLEWOODS MALL 451-7159

JUNGLE JIMS HOT TROPICAL GIFTS OPPOSITE CENTRE RODNEY BAY 452-8240

PIECES OF EIGHT RODNEY BAY

LOTS OF INVENTIVE GIFTS, POSTCARDS, STAMPS & MAIL BOX UK SUNDAY PAPERS 452-0896

TOUCAN TRAVEL RODNEY BAY MARINA TEL: 452-9963 FAX: 452-9906 VHF 16

IN MARIGOT USE OUR FREE TRAVEL HOTLINE AT DOOLITTLES RESORT

If you are looking for somewhere inexpensive to stay while you recommission your boat, the Blue Lagoon is close by. La Panache Guest House [T:450-0765] is a little farther away, a 10 minute walk down the Cas en Bas road, but it has a very pleasant garden atmosphere and overlooks the whole Rodney Bay area. Owner Henry Augustin turns out a first rate satisfying home meal at dinnertime for only $25 EC. Non residents can also eat at La Panache, but you have to let Henry know in the morning.

Ashore

Rodney Bay Marina itself is a small shopping center. The Marche De France [T:452-8484] is a conveniently placed supermarket offering a selection of meats, vegetables, and canned goods as well as wines and cheeses from Martinique.

The Bread Basket sells fresh bread, croissants and baked goods, and Bryden and Partners [T:452-8221] is a fully stocked liquor store with some basic stationery supplies as well. There are several other small supermarkets in the area. In the inner lagoon, the Mortar and Pestle has a well stocked mini-mart, including cube ice, good fresh vegetables, meat, wine, beer and soft drinks. They open weekdays 0800-1900, Saturdays 0700-1600, and Sundays and holidays 1000-1300. You can park your dinghy right outside.

Elliot's Mini Mart [T:452-8721, F:452-8577] is another convenient mini-market which is also the closest gas station. It is just a few minutes walk in the Gros Islet direction from the marina gates, and it is open every day. A larger supermarket and gas station can be found at Glace Motors [T:452-8814, F:452-9669], three miles from the marina toward Castries. They are open weekdays from 0630 to 2030. Apart from food, Glace Supermarket has good prices on beer and they sell quite a few hardware items such as sandpaper and brushes.

The new Gablewoods Shopping Center is about half way between Rodney Bay Marina and Castries. This complete shopping center has the large Julie'n Supermarket, a post office, pharmacy, Radio Shack,

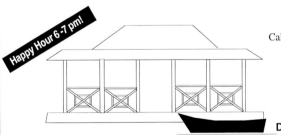

music center, Home Center Hardware, Sunshine Bookstore (the best bookshop in St. Lucia and they also sell telephone cards), an optician, a complete medical center and a variety of shops selling clothing, linen, handicrafts, jewelry, office supplies and more. One good reason to visit is Choice Meats and Delicatessen [T:451-7117], an excellent shop to buy meat, some fish and lambi. In addition, their black forest cake is rumored to be addictive. Also in Gablewoods Mall is Chateaux des Fleurs [T:451-7422], a shop selling flowers which also provides elegant fruit, cheese and wine hampers.

Should shopping time run over the lunch hour, there is a restaurant and complete arcade of fast foods. One of these, Miss Saigon, serves terrific oriental food.

J Q's is a large supermarket on the road to town, near the airport and a dollar bus ride away. They have the widest variety of food products and are best for a major provisioning.

You can sometimes find good seafood at the fishermen's co-op near Pointe Seraphine.

Caribbean Chateaux [T:451-7421, F:451-7413] are the wine people. Call them for a list of their latest offerings at good wholesale prices. They will deliver to your boat.

Shops around the marina include Pieces of Eight [T:452-0896, F:452-9806, cc:V], a delightful shop with everything from local books, videos and paintings to unusual gift items and objets d'art. It is owned by Jane Tipson who is planning an arty coffee shop to be called The Snooty Agouti [T:452-0321] in the inner lagoon. Erma's [cc:A,V] sells Kokonut t-shirts, Caribelle Batik and a mass of handicrafts. Colleta II [T:452-8054, cc:A,V] has casual and beach wear as well as evening wear and accessories. The Drug Store [cc:V] sells everything from sunglasses and sunlotion to aspirin and beach balls. It offers fast film processing.

You will find a hairdressing salon and several boutiques over by the A Pub. One of these, Dockside Trading, is run by yachtsman Don Baker. Here you will find

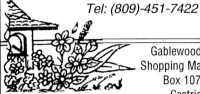

Trekker shorts that will follow you through countless seasons of hard work, excellent sailing hats, Topsider shoes and a good variety of flags. Don also keeps a good bookswap and you are welcome to go over and trade. Another is Creola, specializing in handpainted t-shirts, calabashes and other handicrafts. The St. Lucian Hotel has a good selection of gift shops.

Start the day in the marina anytime after 0730 at Nick's Bread Basket, [T:452-0647, $D] for coffee with a full cooked breakfast or plate of fresh croissants. Return at lunch for a really good ham and cheese sandwich or one of their special lunch plates, followed by ice cream or cake.

If pizza is your thing, you will love Key Largo [T:452-0282, $D]. Run by an enthusiastic young St. Lucian/Italian family, it is set under a loggia around a wood-fired brick pizza oven, presided over by Carlo from Rome. Key Largo is open for lunch and dinner and kids are welcome. The real Italian pizza is consistently excellent; also salads, sandwiches, ice creams and freshly ground Espresso coffee. Nightly happy hour is from 1730-1830.

The Marina Yacht Club [$C-D] bar and restaurant has a pleasant location overlooking the bay. Open 0800 to 2300 every day, it is an inexpensive yachtie hangout, selling both snacks and more elaborate dishes.

The Rodney Bay area offers a large variety of bars and restaurants. You can visit by dinghy or catch the ferry which tours the lagoon every half hour in the evenings. Dinghy tie up is available at A-Frame, The Lime, Mortar and Pestle, and After Deck.

There is much to see, so if your time is limited you could try a tour, coordinating happy hours as you go. Here is a run down of what you will find:

The A Pub [T:452-8725, F:452-9073, VHF:68, $B-D, cc:A,V] has a quaint and nautical atmosphere. Tie your dinghy right up outside. Owners Chris and Jenny create a cheerful informal atmosphere where you can drink, chat, play darts, and enjoy musical entertainment. The A-pub includes the Dockside Restaurant where you can sit in comfort and get anything from English style fish and chips and sandwiches to filet mignon au poivre and shrimp creole. For dessert they bake their own pies and pastries.

The A-Pub does a traditional English roast on Sunday nights, they have a band on Friday nights and Karaoke on Wednesdays and Saturdays, happy hour is 2030-2130. The A-Pub is the base for the St. Lucia Sailing Club and you are welcome to attend their races and meetings. An important event is the Pitons Regatta with four days of racing out of Rodney Bay at the end of the second week in February. Ask Chris about yacht club events and he is also the man to give you a local CYA rating. A second hand chandlery and end of line discount store is planned.

The Lime [T:452-0761, $B-D, cc:A,V] offers consistently good Caribbean cuisine, including seafood, meat and fowl in a pleasant atmosphere. It is very popular, so reservations are advisable, but you can often get in without one. Outside they also offer the best value snacks on the island. Try their rotis, fish, or chicken 'n chips,

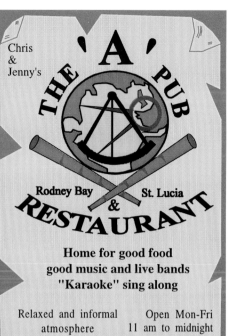

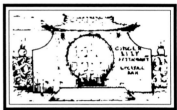
follow with one of their desserts and you
have a veritable feast. For late night entertainment they have a small night club/
disco.

Capone's [T:452-0284, $A-B, cc:A,V]
is an art deco restaurant in 1920's Miami
style. Smart and snazzy inside with efficient service, they serve good Italian food
in the appropriate American tradition and
have a pizza parlor [$D] for snacks and ice
creams. Try their Prohibition Punch. It is
served in a coffee mug by a waiter wearing
a shoulder holster and the mug is yours to
keep.

Right on the waterfront with its own
dock, Nick's Charthouse [T:452-8115,
F:450-8252, $B-C, cc:A,V] has a cheerful
decor with lots of jungly plants. Nick is
always on hand and greets guests personally; the service is excellent and the food
consistently good. Specialities are steak,
seafood and ribs, but on a lucky night you
can get freshwater crayfish. Happy hour is
1700-1800, when a few regulars gather to
sample Nick's collection of well over 100
rums. The Charthouse is often full so res-

ervations are advisable.

The Bistro [T:452-9494, $B, cc:A,V] is
small, cheerful French restaurant right c
the waterfront. Around 1700 Pat comes o
and starts writing up the menu on a larg
blackboard. Items such as lambi au grati
filet of sole layered with shrimp mouss
and wrapped in puff pastry, and her f
mous filet au poivre, are often feature
along with about 15 other entrees. This
the latest success for Pat and Nick wh
have previously owned three other tc
restaurants, including San Antoine. F
those with less gourmet tastes, simple pt
food specials are also available. There a
discounts for those eating between 170
1800. The Bistro gets full so reservatio
are advisable.

A new branch of Miss Saigon [$C-I
should have opened before this boc
comes out. Like the one in the Gablewoo
Mall it will be run by Myrna from t
Philippines. Myrna plans both a pleasa
dining room and takeout service. If it is li
her other branch, the food should be exce
lent and inexpensive.

The Steak House [T:452-9800, $B, VHF:16/17, cc: A,V] is open for both lunch and dinner and offers a variety of steak, lobster, fish and shrimp dishes, along with some chicken, lamb and pork.

Spinnaker's [T:452-8491, $B-D] has a perfect location right on the beach by the yacht club. Lunches are cheap and cheerful, featuring tasty rotis, chilis and hamburgers. Dinners are informal and less expensive than in many of the surrounding restaurants. The main feature is the carvery – a choice of meats, local vegetables and salads, buffet style. But they also offer local catch of the day, a seafood skillet and lobster. John Wright is your host and happy hour is 1800-1900 daily.

The Eagle's Inn [T:452-0650, $B-D, cc:A,V] has a great location looking out over the canal. You can enjoy good local food at a leisurely pace and many items are inexpensive. There is usually dancing after dinner. Happy hour is 1700-1930 and they feature a wine cellar. You can tie your dinghy right outside.

Those hankering after Chinese food should try the Ginger Lily [T:452-8303, $C-D, cc:A,V], a first rate Chinese restaurant with full take-away service and a happy hour on Fridays from 1800-1900.

You won't need a dinghy lock when visiting Julie Betts' Mortar and Pestle [T:452-0336/8756, $B, cc:A,V], where the tables are right on dockside. Whispering palms and traditional Caribbean style chairs and decor make this the most elegant restaurant on the bay. Julie offers exotic Caribbean specialities and national dishes from a host of islands. Expect a peaceful atmosphere and a pleasant mixture of both local and visiting customers. If you are in a party mood, turn up on Tuesday night in time for a rum punch party which is followed by a barbecue and steel band.

The St. Lucian Hotel [T:452-8351, cc:A,V] is right on the beach. They have two restaurants and nightly entertainment. Tuesday to Saturday there is a disco called Splash and for Sunday lunch they offer a buffet and steel band.

The Islander [T:452-8757, cc:V,A] is

Spinnakers!!
Beach Bar and Carvery
Phone: 452-8491

Right on St. Lucia's Rodney Bay
For breakfast, lunch and dinner
Good food at fair prices
Every day 9 am-11 pm
Happy hour 6-7pm

slightly off the main road, but it is worth finding for that big game on TV. Happy hour:1730-1900.

Going the other way, toward Gros Islet, Peppino's Pizza [T:450-9778, $D] offers inexpensive beers and pizzas with rich, satisfying toppings. Dude and Marie's Marine House offers excellent value in tasty local rotis, snacks, and full meals. It is ideally located for those on the slip.

The small town of Gros Islet is picturesque and very local. It is within walking distance of Rodney Bay and you can get a good meal at O'Reilly's [T:452-8830, $C]. This cute restaurant is tiny, so if a group is going, it is best to call O'Reilly and let him know you are coming. You sit out at a table on the street and watch life go by. Fresh creole seafood and all the local vegetables.

One night you wouldn't go to eat in a Gros Islet restaurant is Friday when the village is closed to traffic and everyone dances in the streets, or wanders from bar to bar. All along the street there are stalls selling such goodies as barbecued conch on a skewer and barbecued fish and chicken. If you like to eat sitting down, the lovely old Scottie's Bar right in the center of town puts chairs out on the street. In recent times Friday night at Gros Islet has attracted undesirable elements; to be safe, go in a group or by cab or bus and return the same way. Stay in well lit areas.

If all that eating out has left you with a heavy feeling, you can burn up some calories horse riding at Trims [T:452-8273]. Then for a thrilling sky high view of the anchorage (you can take your camera), try a parasailing ride with Jacobs. If you like St. Lucia so much that you want buy a house or piece of land, speak to fellow yachtsman Jonathan Everett at Home Services.

Water sports

The water in front of the St. Lucian Hotel is completely flat water and good for beginner windsurfing. Boards are available for rent at the hotel.

There is some reasonable snorkeling around Pigeon Island. Great scuba is a little farther away, but within reach by fast boat if you contact Dolphin Divers in the marina [T:452-9485, F:452-0802, cc:V]. Their boat goes out every day at 0830; you just have to turn up a little before to get fitted out with gear. They have a good shop with all kinds of diving and snorkeling gear for sale. They can also offer direct purchasing of scuba gear to your own home in Europe or the U.S. at discount prices. You can get tanks filled here and they will service equipment.

Windjammer Landings

Windjammer Landings [T:452-1311 $B, cc:A,V] is a brand new up-market villa development just south of Rodney Bay. The anchorage is tricky so those wanting to go in there by boat should contact the managers who will provide a guide. It is also just a short cab ride from Rodney Bay. They offer a particularly good Sunday jazz brunch and you can get your fill of fire eating and limbo on Thursday's Caribbean night. Windjammer Landings has boutiques, a full diving facility, and entertainment several nights a week.

BRIG UNICORN, VIGIE

CASTRIES AND VIGIE

When entering Castries Harbor, the only danger to avoid is the shoal that extends to the west of Tapion Rock. There are two main anchorages: Vigie Creek and close to Castries town itself. Neither location is particularly scenic and both are noisy, but they are conveniently located for shopping and services. Of the two, Vigie is more secluded but farther from town.

Castries Town

Castries has burned down twice and was most recently rebuilt in the early 1950's. Some post-disaster architecture lacks charm, but there are pretty spots. There are picturesque old buildings around Derek Walcott Square and along Brazil Street. The area between Peynier Street and Chausee Road along Brazil, Micoud, Chisel and Coral Streets has an interesting creole atmosphere, with balconies, gingerbread, old and new buildings.

Regulations

Castries is a port of entry, though it is currently easier to clear in Rodney Bay or Marigot. The officials insist that entering yachts come straight to the customs dock, or if there is no room, to the anchorage east of the customs buoy.

Services

Water is available at the dock and ice may be bought from one of the plants in town.

Valmonts [T:452-3817/8, ext 62] has a Yamaha dealership opposite the fire station. They sell duty free outboards to yachts in transit at good prices. They will also fix your broken Yamaha.

Ray's Refrigeration [T:452-4462] will fix your freezer.

There are two bus stations. Buses toward Marigot and Vieux Fort run from Micoud and Monigraud Streets. All the rest run from the north end of Chausee Road.

Ashore

Shopping hours are 0800 to 1230 and 1330 to 1600. Banks usually open mornings only to 1200, except on Friday when they also open from 1500 - 1700. (Barclays stays open till 1300, except on Wednesdays.)

The big market has wonderful fresh foods, straw goods and pottery coal pots. Now it spreads all along the streets, but by the time this guide comes out everyone should be in a new building.

The best supermarket in town is J.Q. Charles on the Boulevard and for the best meats try Maison Salaison [T:452-6599] or Chef's Choice [T:453-0086/4433]. Bryden's is a good liquor store and will deliver large orders to the marina. They also have a big new pharmacy and stationery store on Bridge Street.

You will find yachting gear, fishing equipment and tools at Johnson's Hardware [T:452-2392, cc:A,V] and for general hardware there is Ace, Homecenter and J.Q. Charles. If you need acrylic sheet then J. N. Baptiste [T:452-1139] is the specialist.

For in town boutique shopping don't miss Noah's Arkade [T:452-2523, cc:A,V,Dn] for handmade items, the Sea Island Cotton Shop [T:452-3674, cc:A,V] for batik and Windjammer [T:453-1586, cc:A,V] for silk screen. Art lovers should visit the Artsibit Gallery [T:452-7865]. Real boutique enthusiasts will want to go over to the Pointe Seraphine duty free shopping mall. (Take your boat papers with you for the duty free.) Here you will find over 17 tourist shops pleasantly laid out. A trip out to Bagshaw's clothing factory [T:452-2139, cc:A,V] is well worth the short taxi ride from town. Their large showroom is beautifully laid out in a

lovely setting overlooking the sea.

Paul Simmonds is a colorful Caribbean character whose somewhat restless nature has led him to start enterprises all over the world. He is a brilliant chef and a very talented artist. When his energies are directed into a new venture it is always exceptional. He and his Philippine wife Myrna run two restaurants in town. Paul's Place [T:453-1588, $C-D], the cheap and cheerful one, is upstairs on Bridge street opposite the post office. They offer an imaginative menu, including far eastern recipes and lots of specials. The food is excellent value. The new Chez Paul [$B-C, cc:A,V] is set in the lovely old Rain building on Derek Walcott Square. It is in the classiest location in town with great views from the balcony over Derek Walcott Square. It is open every day for breakfast, lunch and dinner. They serve Pacific rim and haute French cuisine, with plenty of inexpensive dishes for lunch.

There are plenty of local snack bars. The Subway (the sign outside says the "White House") is run by the Taylor family who also own the Bread Basket in Rodney Bay Marina. It has an agreeable upstairs dining room, serves good local lunches and snacks, but it can be crowded, so go early. The Pink Elephant [T:453-2847, $D

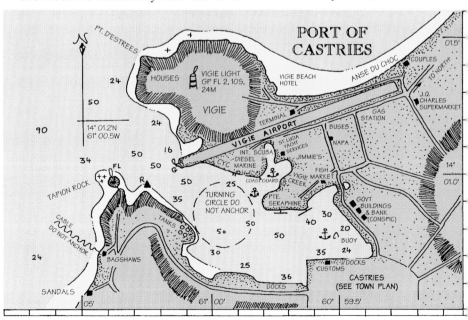

126

PORT OF CASTRIES

cc:A,V] on William Peter Boulevard is airy and pleasant with daily specials and snacks, including rotis. The Natural Cafe [T:452-6421, $D] on the Chausee Road is a vegetarian health food store and restaurant. It has a pleasant atmosphere, is clean and serves good food.

Other places to try include Flintstones on Jeremie Street or Kimlins on Derek Walcott Square.

There are two hillside restaurants up on the Morne with magnificent views over Castries. San Antoine [T:452-4660, $A, cc:A,V] is unmatched for elegant ambience. Originally built as a grand residence in the 1880's, it was converted to a hotel in the 1920's, then burned to the ground in 1970, leaving only massive stone walls with lovely arches. It has been beautifully recreated without regard to cost, and has a sumptuous atmosphere, with excellent service. Current owners Michael and Alison come from a catering family which has been in the business since the 1880's. The other famous restaurant on the Morne is Chef Harry's Green Parrot [T:452-3399, cc:A,V]. Harry is a superb MC who gets everyone dancing and having fun. The nights to go are Wednesday and Saturday when he has entertainment.

Vigie

There is a light on Vigie Hill (group flashing 2 every 10 seconds) which is helpful in identifying Castries Harbor at night.

You can anchor either inside or outside Vigie Creek, but leave room for the large brig Unicorn, which takes day charterers out from here. Anchoring here before clearing customs will incur the full and expensive fury of official wrath.

Services

Castries Yacht Center (CYC) [T:542-6234/5348, F:453-2653, VHF:16] is a relatively inexpensive, full service haul out facility using a 35-ton travel lift, with accommodation for both short term haul outs and long term storage. There is a perimeter fence and 24-hour security, showers, and a marine chandlery to cover haul-out needs, including paint, zincs, and safety gear. Do your own work, or they can do it for you. Fiberglass repairs are available and power tools may be rented. CYC sells water and the owner plans to supply high volume, duty free fuel bunkering. They offer a free water taxi to town and a book exchange. Inexpensive apartments

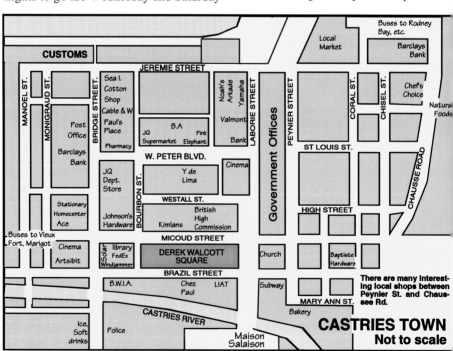

128

are available nearby.

In the same yard as CYC, International Diesel and Marine Services [T:453-1311, F:453-2523] is the Windward's first really comprehensive diesel shop. Run by Derek Morton, a fully qualified British diesel engineer, they have a small machine shop and equipment for fully servicing fuel injection pumps and injectors. They are agents for CAV and Perkins and can arrange spares for most brands of engine at short notice. They offer every kind of service, from routine maintenance and repair to a complete rebuild.

St. Lucia Yacht Services (SLYC) [T:452-5057, VHF:16, cc:V] is a ramshackle marina, home to a few local boats. Their fuel dock is fine and they offer water, fuel and a good car rental agency. You can talk to them about docking, but look at the docks first. Although apparently well protected, St. Lucia Yacht Services can suffer from a surge in a hurricane or other large weather system. There is a mechanic shop on the premises. Inside the fading exterior of their long building you will smell the fresh bread from CMC Exclusive Bakery.

You can buy freshly made white and whole wheat bread.

Christopher Kessell [T:452-4499 VHF:16 "Chrisalis"] is the local yacht surveyor. He also does excellent work on yacht electrics and can help with light machining. His prices are reasonable and you can arrange for him to come and visit you in Rodney Bay or Marigot.

A short walk on the road to town is Leroy James' big NAPA agency [T:542-5034 which stocks loads of filters, parts, sprays seals, polishes and tools. They are agents for Evinrude outboards and offer full sales and service. In addition they stock OMC inflatables, ropes and some marine hardware.

Ashore

A good reason for coming into Vigie is to visit one of the two excellent restaurants that grace its shores. Jimmie's Restaurant [T:452-5142, $B-C, cc:V] has a tropical garden setting by the waterfront with a view across the bay and is conveniently situated at St. Lucia Yacht Services. Jimmie's is one of St. Lucia's best seafood restaurants with some excellent recipes try the Harbor Catch). Jimmie is a St. Lucian who has spent years in the catering trade and really knows the business. He offers an interesting light lunch menu, and best of all he keeps the atmosphere very pleasant, without getting too formal. It is the kind of place where you can feel comfortable just going for soup and dessert.

The Coal Pot [T:452-6811, $B, cc:V] has a very romantic setting right on the waterfront in an old boat store-house, which gives it a nautical atmosphere. The restaurant is run by Sonia and Michelle whose cooking is excellent, with the emphasis on seafood. They are open for both lunch and dinner.

Up the hill between CYC and SLYS is Windjammer Clothing [T:452-1041, cc:A,V], with 100% cotton and easy styles.

Water sports

Buddy's Scuba [T:452-5288, VHF:16, cc:V] in St. Lucia Yacht Services is a small personal dive shop run by Phil. Phil rents gear to charter yachts, will provide transportation from Rodney Bay or arrange to rendezvous with you as you sail down the coast.

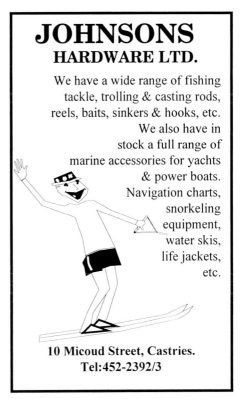
MARIGOT BAY

Marigot Bay is another of the Caribbean's spectacularly beautiful anchorages, completely sheltered and affording a perfect backdrop to that sunset rum punch. It lies about a mile south of Hess Oil's huge tanker depot at Cul De Sac Bay. By staying fairly close inshore and watching for a prominent house with a conspicuous red roof on the hill of the southern entrance, you should not miss Marigot. However, it is so well tucked away that a British admiral is reputed to have hidden his fleet here, disguising the masts by tying coconut fronds in the rigging. The pursuing French sailed right by.

Favor the southern side of the channel as you enter. This is not always easy as many yachts anchor on this side of the channel. Pass close to them or you will touch the shoal that extends a long way out from Doolittles. The Moorings plan to place a green flashing marker on the shoal, which you should leave to port as you enter.

Anchor anywhere in the inner harbor, where holding is fair in soft mud. Depths are 18 to 24 feet. Costly and delicate underwater electric cables and water pipes cross right at the entrance to the inner harbor. Anchoring is strictly forbidden here.

Regulations

Marigot Bay is an official port of entry, with customs and immigration. Linus

Leon, the man in charge, is friendly and helpful.

There are dinghy docks outside the customs house, close under Hurricane Hole Hotel and directly in front of Doolittles Restaurant. Dinghies must not be tied to the yacht docks.

The only place to dump garbage is in the facility behind the customs/police station.

There is a five-knot speed limit in the harbor.

Services

The Moorings Marina is secure, pleasant and offers long and short term dockage, electricity, water and ice. The Moorings [T:451-4357, F:451 4353] stand by on VHF 16 & 85 from 0800 to 1630. VHF channel 85 is the working channel and has a much greater range. Contact Hurricane Hole Hotel [T:451-4357, VHF:85] outside working hours. Diesel and gasoline (ask about duty free fuel) are available on The Moorings fuel dock next to the customs dock. There is a laundry, sail loft, mechanics, and a chandlery and they can sometimes help with spare parts.

The Moorings offers free showers and toilets upstairs above the Mariner Market. Anchored yachts are asked to use the shore toilet facilities. This is the base of The

Moorings charter company with a fleet of 40 yachts for bareboat or skippered charter.

A free 24-hour ferry service connects all parts of the bay.

Ashore

On the south shore is The Moorings Hurricane Hole Hotel [VHF:85, $A, cc:A,V] with a swimming pool and the elegant Rusty Anchor restaurant where you can peruse their gourmet menu. They offer entertainment in season when the occasion demands. Happy hour is nightly from 1700-1900, two for the price of one. While here visit The Moorings boutique with a full range of swim and casual wear, local books and holiday essentials. Visit the boutique during happy hour and you get a gift or a 10% reduction (you choose) on purchases over $50 EC.

The Mariner Market [cc:A,V] is a well stocked mini-market with a wide range of French and other wines. It is open in season from 0800-1800, except Sunday when it closes at 1630. In the summer time it closes a couple of hours earlier. The Mariner Market has daily happy hours (1700-1900) with a free bottle of champagne if you spend over $100 EC.

On the north shore is Doolittles [T451

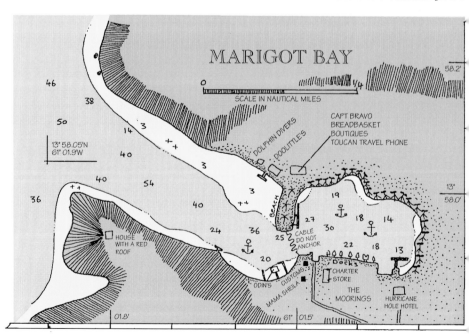

132

Marigot Bay Resort And Marina.

Refuel. Restock. Relax.

Retreat to a little time spent readying yourself and your yacht for more sailing adventure. Spend some time onshore at Marigot Bay Resort. Enjoy elegant dining and authentic West Indian cuisine at Hurricane Hole Restaurant, or eat casually at our new patio bar overlooking the marina.

Call ahead on VHF channel 16 or 85, for reservations. Then follow the navigational buoys to The Moorings Marina at Marigot Bay Resort.

- Reserve long- and short-term slips
- Ample fresh water, free steamy showers
- 110/220 volt power
- Supermarket with ice, beer, liquor, wine, duty-free diesel, gasoline
- Boutiques
- Laundry service available
- Accommodations available

The Moorings Marinas

P.O. Box 101, Castries, St. Lucia, West Indies • Tel: (809) 451-4357, Fax: (809) 451-4230

4761, VHF:16/68/85, $B-D]. This is a Canadian operation run for fun with hopes of maybe making a profit one day. Their ferry service will collect you from your yacht, or you can come into their dock with your dinghy. Seating is by the waterfront. Happy hour is 1730-1830 nightly. Inexpensive food includes fish creole, curry, pizza (delivered to your boat if you want), and hamburgers. If holding down the barstool makes you hungry, nachos and chicken wings are available.

Behind Dolittles are several shops and businesses. These include a Toucan Travel hotline [T:451 4978, VHF:16], a complete travel and tour agent, The Breadbasket, a great place to buy bread, sandwiches, croissants and other baked goodies, and Captain Bravo, a store selling fishing gear and chandlery. This is a good place to buy flags, cruising guides and a handline to keep you in fish while you cruise. There is also a branch of Bagshaws [cc:A,V] here selling silk-screened clothing, fabrics and linens designed and screened at their own studio. They artfully depict local scenes, flowers and birds. The largest boutique on the block is Doolittles [T: 451-4357 cc:A,V] run by The Moorings. It has a good selection of swimwear and clothing, with many smart t-shirts, along with handicrafts, perfume and costume jewelry.

If you walk about a mile to the main road you can catch a bus to town for $2 EC. Taxis are normally available at the resort or by the customs/police station.

There are also a couple of other restaurants nearby. Right near the customs is Mama Sheila's [D]. Mama Sheila is a great lady; you will enjoy talking with her and she does inexpensive and tasty Indian style cooking. Mama Sheila is a 7th Day so she does not serve alcohol. However, you are most welcome to bring your own with you,

MARIGOT BAY

or buy it in the Mariner Market. Mama Sheila also closes at sunset on Friday and opens again at sunset on Saturday.

JJ's [T:451-4076, VHF:16, $B-C, cc:V] is up the hill and local and rowdy in character. JJ serves conch, chicken and fish to the accompaniment of loud music. If you call and let him know you are coming, he will arrange free transport from the customs at about 1930.

Odin's Restaurant and Bar [T:451-4098, $B-C] hangs out over the water at the entrance to the inner harbor and you can tie your dinghy right alongside. They serve lobster, fish, chicken or conch.

Ready for a night ashore? Charo and Mike's Seahorse Inn [T:451-4436, cc:V] is simple, charming and inexpensive with a dock where you can tie your yacht right outside. In addition both Hurricane Hole Hotel and Doolittles offer overnight accommodation.

Water sports

Dolphin Divers [T452-9485/451-4357, F:452-0802, VHF:16] is in the Doolittles complex. It is a Padi five star operation and St. Lucian manager Rosemond Clery is one of the best-qualified divers in the Windwards. He also happens to be the Caribbean welterweight boxing champion. Rosemond is an enthusiastic diver and underwater photographer who teaches diving at all levels, including specialty courses. He is helped by three instructors and two dive masters. They are happy to rent gear and fill tanks.

Dolphin Divers take regular trips to Anse Cochon and Soufriere (for details of the dives, see the water sports sections for these areas). They are happy to take you diving from your yacht anywhere down the leeward coast. You can arrange a rendezvous over the radio. However, if you are in the Soufriere area you will probably have to telephone.

ANSE COCHON

Anse Cochon is a small bay with an attractive deserted beach. Many day charter boats make brief stops here on their day tours. It lies about three miles south of Marigot. First you pass Anse La Raye, then there is a rocky headland. Anse Cochon is tucked up in the corner just past this headland. It is the first beach after the headland. There are rocky patches to the south end of the beach, but there is no problem anchoring off the middle. If you get hooked into sand, rather than weed, you can find excellent holding in about 12 to 20 feet of water. There are currents in the bay, and your boat may swing around. If you have an anchor that can trip itself, keep a good eye on it or set a second anchor. Anse Cochon makes a good daytime anchorage and overnight stop in settled conditions.

Water sports

Snorkeling off the rocky headland at the north end of the bay is fair with brightly colored sponges, corals and parrotfish.

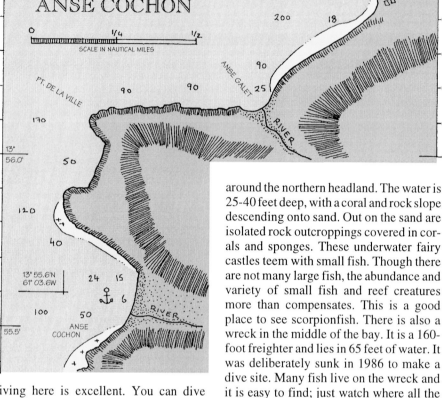

ANSE COCHON

SCALE IN NAUTICAL MILES

around the northern headland. The water is 25-40 feet deep, with a coral and rock slope descending onto sand. Out on the sand are isolated rock outcroppings covered in corals and sponges. These underwater fairy castles teem with small fish. Though there are not many large fish, the abundance and variety of small fish and reef creatures more than compensates. This is a good place to see scorpionfish. There is also a wreck in the middle of the bay. It is a 160-foot freighter and lies in 65 feet of water. It was deliberately sunk in 1986 to make a dive site. Many fish live on the wreck and it is easy to find; just watch where all the dive boats anchor.

Diving here is excellent. You can dive right off your yacht and work your way out

SOUFRIERE AND THE PITONS

Soufriere is a small, rustic, picturesque town set amid a scenic wonderland dominated by the towering twin Pitons. Its exceptional beauty will enthrall hikers and photographers.

When approaching Soufriere Bay from the north, beware of the shoal which extends out from the south side of Anse Chastanet.

It is deep nearly everywhere else, so anchoring is often in 60 to 80 feet of water and tying bow or stern to a palm tree or dock is obligatory. You will have plenty of local help willing and keen to do business, and a $7 EC tie up fee is average. Always negotiate in advance. Feel free to swim or dinghy with your own line if you don't

want help.

The whole bay is part of a marine national park. Spearfishing, anchoring on coral, removing coral or shells and dumping garbage are strictly forbidden.

Anse Chastanet

Anse Chastanet [T:459-7000, $A-C, cc:A,V] is a delightful cottage hotel built on a hill which slopes to the sea. The whole bay is a marine park, and anchoring is not permitted, but three or four yacht moorings are planned. Best to call and book one in advance. The Anse Chastanet beach bar is a congenial lunch spot and one can browse in the two boutiques. For dinner, they have a delightful a la carte restaurant up the hill

Where the Mountains Meet the Sea

$\mathcal{I}$n a tranquil bay where the landmark Les Piton
mountains of St. Lucia slope down to meet the sea,
discover Jalousie Cove Marina.

Jalousie Cove Marina is an ideal deep draft marina, fully equipped
to meet every need of pleasure and charter vessels including clean,
filtered diesel fuel. At this official southern point of entry to
St. Lucia you'll also find a staffed customs facility.

While your vessel is docked at the marina,
you may enjoy all the amenities of the luxurious
Jalousie Plantation Resort & Spa, including
restaurants, boutiques, a deluxe spa program, and full range of
recreational activities and water sports. Some facilities
are subject to fees and surcharges.

Castries is only 50 minutes away by use of Jalousie's fast
sea transports. A helicopter service from the resort can take you
to St. Lucia's two airports or other islands such as Martinique or Barbados.
For more information on Jalousie Cove Marina, contact:

Jalousie Plantation
R E S O R T & S P A

ST. LUCIA, WEST INDIES
809.459.7666 Fax **809.459.7667**
Operated by Resort Services Management Company

where the emphasis is on creole and international seafood. Anse Chastanet is also accessible by dinghy or the road from Soufriere, or you can hire a local pirogue to bring you over.

Water sports

Scuba St. Lucia at Anse Chastanet [T:459-7000, F:459-7700, VHF:16, cc:A,V] is the largest dive operation in the Windwards, with two resort courses and four dives daily. It has a range of facilities, from an equipment shop to photo and video labs. They do not fill tanks.

The Anse Chastanet reef is unquestionably one of the best dives in the Windwards. This flawless reef extends out from the beach seaward. The shallower parts are good for snorkeling and the diving is excellent along the length of the reef which slopes from about 30 to 80 feet. Sheet coral, fungus corals, solitary corals and brain corals are abundant, as are a delightful variety of sponges from the azure vase sponge to large barrel sponges. The water is clear and reef fish abound with clouds of brown and blue chromis, along with sergeant majors, brilliantly colored parrotfish and goatfish. Groupers are particularly tame and easy to see here. One sees all kinds of jacks and snappers cruising just off the reef. Because of the pristine quality of the reef and the possibility of currents which can sweep you out to sea, Scuba St Lucia prefers you dive on this site with them. If you want to dive on your own, we mention several other dives in the sections below.

Hummingbird anchorage

Anchorage off the Hummingbird restaurant is scenic and generally calm. Fishermen sometimes cast nets along the beach so anchor as far to the northwest, up under the cliff, as safely possible.

Ashore

The Hummingbird Restaurant [T:459-7232, F:459-7033, VHF:16, $B-C, cc:V is one of the best waterside restaurants in the Windwards, artistically designed with a wall made of pottery coal pots, and wonderful hand carvings. There is an exquisite

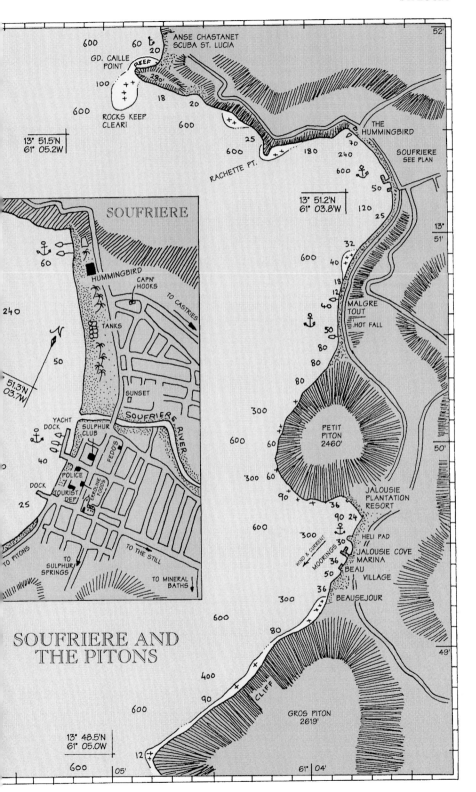

SOUFRIERE AND
THE PITONS

view across the pool to the Pitons beyond. The food is a blend of French and creole cuisine, with seafoods a specialty. Owner Joyce gets much of her business from yachts and welcomes them warmly. So much so that a skipper bringing in a party of four or more gets his or her fish or chicken dinner (any style) free.

Hot and cold showers are available, and Joyce will arrange taxis for her customers at a fair local rate. The staff will help customers with telephone calls or faxes during normal office hours; they can also recharge video batteries for a small fee. They will help you get rid of well-wrapped garbage. Rooms are available.

Boat boys insisting on watching your dinghy can be a nuisance here if you let them. The police are currently trying to deal with the problem and would appreciate your help in not encouraging them. Further, if you have any problem, the police will try to sort it out. If you are eating at the Hummingbird, call on the VHF just before you go ashore and have Harry, Thomas, Victor or Joseph, the uniformed security guards, meet you on the beach. They will help you pull your dinghy to the hotel entrance and they will watch it.

A short distance behind the Hummingbird lies Captain Hook's Hideaway [T:459-7365, $C-D] a small cheap and cheerful restaurant good for local plates and snacks.

The Hummingbird anchorage is just a short walk or dinghy ride from town.

Water sports

There are two good dives close to this anchorage, easily accessible by dinghy. The first is right off the cliff on the northwest side of the anchorage. You can start close to the beach and work outwards around the cliff. There are interesting rock formations and overhangs, plenty of corals, decorative blue sponges and lots of reef fish. You can go as deep as you dare. Notice the bubbles of sulfur rising from the seabed over the sand close to the beach. In some areas the bottom is warm to the

welcome to the

VHF Channel 16
Telephone:459-7232
Fax:459-7033

HUMMINGBIRD RESORT

Gourmet Restuarant
With a perfect Pitons view
Open breakfast, lunch and dinner
(breakfast 7-10 am)

Hot and cold showers
Overnight Accommodation

The Yachtsman's Favorite Bar
Our guards will watch your
dinghy and your yacht.

Batik Studio
exclusive designs
at reasonable prices

JOYCE (YOUR HOSTESS)

touch. The other dive is right under the former garbage dump just around the corner. There are four underwater pitons which rise dramatically from the drop off. You can see the top of at least one of them just below the surface from the dinghy. The current can be very strong here.

Soufriere town

The town of Soufriere was the set of the movie "Water," starring Michael Caine and it has many charming old buildings. Much has been done recently to upgrade the town and waterfront.

You can anchor stern to the specially constructed yacht dock right outside the police station. There is a charge for this, and no control is exerted over the local boat boys. Keep your yacht a good distance from the dock as swells can come in suddenly. There is a dinghy dock at the end, and there is a landing charge of $5EC per person for using it.

Regulations

Soufriere will soon be a full port of entry. Meanwhile, if you arrive here from abroad, you can get a temporary permit to moor from the police station which costs $25EC.

Ashore

The area has many points of interest and you may want to go to the new tourism center close by the waterfront for details.

In town you will find a great little supermarket, sparkling clean with an ample array of foods to provision your boat. We were pleased to see they had local frozen fish on sale. It is called Eroline's Foods [T:459-7125, cc:A,V] and is open Monday to Saturday. Normal hours are 0800-1800, but on Saturday it stays open till 1900. There is also a first rate pharmacy and drug store called Clarke's. For a local restaurant try Fedo's New Venture [T:459-5220, $C-D]. It is very small and you would not go for the ambience, but Fedo is an excellent chef and can produce a first class meal. There is also the Sunset Bar [T:459-7100, $D], an upstairs restaurant that does good pizzas and local meals. The Still [T:459-7224, $C, cc:V], just out of town, is a large restaurant offering good local food and they have a handicraft boutique. A beach bar is planned next to the Hummingbird.

If you visit just one place in this area, it should be the Dasheene Restaurant at Ladera Resort [T:459-7850/7323, $A-B cc:A,V,Ds]. The view here, straight down the valley between the Pitons, is exquisite probably the most spectacular in the Caribbean. There is a swimming pool and bar with a friendly atmosphere. They serve both lunch and dinner. I would recommend lunch so you can see the view though dinner on a full moon night can be terrific. The energetic can walk up to Dasheene from between the Pitons. You can also take a taxi or the Vieux Fort bus from Soufriere. It is a long but pleasant walk back down.

The Sulphur Springs, between Ladera Resort and Soufriere, look like a scene straight from hell, with barren, brightly colored earth, bubbling pools and huge spurts of steam. More scenic and pleasant are the naturally hot Diamond Baths built by Louis the 16th (a fair walk or short ride out the back of town). Take a few dollars and your towel, and you can luxuriate in these baths set amid a well-tended tropical garden. Start at the top where the indoor baths are the hottest and most therapeutic then graduate to the outside pools. You can also visit the Soufriere Estate, Museum and mini-zoo. The rainforest area near Morne Fond St. Jacques offers exquisite views for walking or hiking. The road is sometimes bad so you may have to ask around to find a taxi driver willing to take you up there. You are required to have a guide when hiking in the rainforest reserve, but walking on the road leading to it, amid the lush vegetation with hidden glimpses of the Pitons below, is also beautiful.

Malgre Tout

There is a good, and very attractive anchorage stern to Malgre Tout beach close to Petit Piton. Odd coral heads can chafe lines here, so snorkel on your anchor. This anchorage may be difficult in heavy northerly swells, so treat it with caution during

the winter months. Local youths will be willing to help you with your lines.

There is an interesting small hot waterfall on Jah I's land, with a nominal entrance fee. Walk back from the beach to the road and turn toward Petit Piton and you will see a sign to the waterfall. Get permission from Jah I in his small wooden house. This is the best hot shower available, and an unbeatable value.

Diving and snorkeling is good around Petit Piton.

Between the Pitons

The beach between the Pitons is now part of Jalousie Plantation Resort [T:459-7666, $A, cc:A,V,Ds,Dn]. This is one of the Windward's glitziest resorts, with all-inclusive room rates that run around $900 a night. Jalousie Cove Marina [T&F:459-7666, VHF:68, cc:A,V,Ds] is neither in a cove nor is it a marina but it does have strong docks capable of taking just about any size of yacht stern-to. Water, telephone and electricity (220 volt, 50 cycle and 415 volt 3-phase) are on the dock and

there is a fuel dock with both diesel and gasoline. Dinghies may be left inside the main dock. This area is generally calm but it can roll and blow hard here, especially when the wind and swell is from the north. Jalousie Cove has also put down some moorings. They will send their boatman to help tie you up to a mooring if you call them on VHF:68. There is a charge of $40EC a night for using these moorings, which can be credited against a meal ashore at the hotel.

Ashore

There is always one hotel restaurant available to yachtsmen, usually The Pier restaurant beside the marina. Half or full day passes to the hotel are also available. They include meals in any of the restaurants and most activities. Current entertainment includes a Tuesday buffet and Sunday afternoon jazz brunch. You can leave your yacht here and go on one of the many tours the hotel offers, including a helicopter tour which starts right beside the marina. Frog Haven and Femme de L'ile are two elegant boutiques selling everything from bathing and casual to evening wear. Coconuts is a small essentials store with liquor, beer, ice, household essentials and a few marine items. They can also do a full provisioning to order including fine meats and cheeses through the hotel. If you fax a couple of days in advance they can probably get everything you need for a major provisioning.

Those who do not wish to pay for a mooring can, with difficulty, anchor stern to the rocky shore among the moorings off Beausejour Estate. Once anchored you will be broadside to wind and current, though facing into the swells.

Right next door to Jalousie is Beau Village, a collection of four artistically chosen local houses and a dinghy wharf. Ashore there is a rum shop, boutique, and a restaurant called Bang Between the Pitons [T:459-7864, $C-D]. The village is designed to be low key and entertaining, where locals and visitors can mix. A playground for children is planned. Eating is outside under moveable shelters. Food is barbecued jerk meat and fish with local vegetables. The toilets have showers which you are welcome to use. Beau Village was designed and is owned and run by Colin Tenant (Lord Glenconner) who started the Mustique development.

Water sports

The dive around the base of Petit Piton is one of St. Lucia's great dive sites. You can start from close to the beach and explore at whatever depth you feel comfortable. There are wonderful sponges, good coral formations and an extraordinary variety of fish. Sometimes huge schools of fish make magical patterns in the sunlight. Apart from reef fish such as angelfish, blue chromis, parrotfish, scorpionfish and damselfish, there are lots of hunters out there; jacks and snappers swim in fair sized schools and occasionally one sees a monster. The snorkeling here is also quite good. Another good site for both snorkeling and scuba is under Gros Piton just below the prominent cliff. A sloping drop off with plenty of fish and coral goes down to great depths. There are sometimes currents in this area.

There is a dive shop at Jalousie Plantation. You can arrange a dive with them and they will fill tanks when they are not too busy.

ANSE CHASTANET BEACH

NAVIGATION SOUTH COAST, PITONS TO VIEUX FORT

The trip from the Pitons to Vieux Fort is a tough one against both wind and current. There are reefs extending about half a mile offshore between Choiseul and Laborie, so this coast is best given a good clearance. There are no good anchorages until you reach Vieux Fort.

VIEUX FORT

As the beaten track becomes trampled these days with the arrival of more and more boats, Vieux Fort gains charm by virtue of being away from it all. The town, with its old wooden buildings and large fishing fleet, has a quaint attraction. The anchorage is well protected, and a long walk (or short ride) away is one of the Caribbean's most magnificent windward beaches, a beach so long you can guarantee a mile or so to yourself. I would recommend this stop to those who want to get away from the obvious charms of the tourist spots and savor something really local. It is an obvious pickup or drop-off point for those arriving or leaving from Hewanorra, St. Lucia's international airport.

Navigation

The sail to Vieux Fort from the Pitons is a beat to windward, often against the current. It takes about two hours in a weatherly boat. Keep well clear of the reef that stretches about half a mile offshore between Choiseul and Laborie.

You can anchor either in the first bay southwest of the main ship harbor marked on our chart, or off the town to the northwest of the port. To approach the town anchorage, leave the green beacon to port, head slowly for the Kimatri Hotel on the hill and choose your spot.

Getting ashore and leaving the dinghy is a problem. The port authority suggests leaving them on the south side of the main dock near the shore. The dock is very high and there is one ladder you can use to ascend which is steep and long enough to demand some agility. You will then have to move your dinghy along the dock to

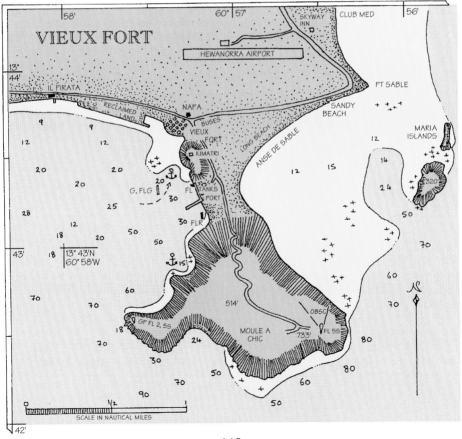

leave the ladder clear for others. You can also beach your dinghy among the fishing boats. However, a few people have complained that local youths demand large sums to guard your dinghy.

Regulations

Vieux Fort is an official port of entry and customs may be found at the head of the large ship dock. You will probably have to travel two miles to the airport to clear immigration, though there are plans to have an immigration station at the dock.

Services

Telephone calls may be made from any of the hotels. The Club Med keeps their diving fleet here and the staff is usually helpful.

Cooking gas is available at the gas depot just outside the port. You can dinghy over to town to get outboard gasoline where all the fishing boats are beached.

Ashore

You can find basic food supplies and a good selection of fruits and vegetables in town which are less expensive than in Castries. There are two restaurants ashore that make Vieux Fort a pleasant destination.

The Kimatrai [T:454-6328, $C-D] stands on the hill over the yacht anchorage. You can walk up from the ship dock. Head toward town, keep bearing left and look for a sign. The Kimatrai is an old fashioned kind of hotel, cool and breezy, with a marvelous view of the harbor. It is open all day and is a great place to hang out, relax, write postcards or catch up on your diary. It has the perfect location for sunset. The meals are very inexpensive and excellent value.

Il Pirata Restaurant [T:454-6610, $B-C, closed Monday] is a superb Italian restaurant run by an Italian family. Their pasta is all homemade and cooked perfectly. Their Zuppa cake is out of this world. If you don't feel like a full meal you can eat inexpensive pastas and pizzas. The service is friendly and the waiters wear cheerful pirate uniforms. You are welcome to use the showers. Il Pirata lies a mile west of the town of Vieux Fort. It has its own dock but the dock is a little high to climb up, and the beach can be surfy. Improvements are planned but meanwhile you can easily get there by land. Walk or taxi the mile from town, or take a bus heading toward Choiseul or Laborie. There is a Club Med farther afield, east of the airport.

East of Vieux Fort are the Maria Islands, a nature reserve and home to a species of lizard and a snake unknown anywhere else in the world. You can call the National Trust [T:452-5005] to arrange a guided trip. The energetic should hike up to the Moule a Chique lighthouse for the view.

There is a great art and craft center [T:459-3226, cc:A,V] at Choiseul, accessible by bus or taxi, which has baskets, carvings, seed jewelry, pottery, and household items made from natural local materials.

Northbound

The northbound passage between St. Vincent and St. Lucia can be hard on the wind and hard on the body. The north end of St. Vincent is unbelievably gusty on occasion and more than a little bumpy. It is not unusual to have gusts of 30 to 40 knots. These will steady down about six miles offshore. It pays to be prepared. I often do this trip single handed and am not over fond of it, but find the easiest way to do it is as follows: Motor sail close up the coast under reefed main and engine and wait until the full force of the wind hits before deciding what to do. If you are comfortable under main and engine, keep going that way until the wind steadies down. Otherwise, if you have roller furling, just unroll a little of the jib until it gets calmer. The main thing is not to arrive at the north end with too much canvas, where reducing sail can degenerate into hanging onto flailing dacron as the boat bucks about and tries to throw you over. Once you get about five miles north of St. Vincent, wind and seas generally become much more constant and you can adjust sail accordingly. The current will set you to the west, so head up if possible. It is going to be a long day, so plan to leave early from Cumberland Bay or Wallilabou, as that will make it seem shorter.

Southbound

The southbound trip is usually a lovely broad reach. If you cannot see St. Vincent from St. Lucia, a course of 205° magnetic should start you in the right direction. Most people know how far they like to go in one day. I personally favor starting at the Pitons

and stopping in St. Vincent. Nature lovers will favor Cumberland or Wallilabou and those who like waterfront bars can clear customs in Wallilabou or Barrouallie and continue onto Young Island Cut. If you plan to go all the way to Bequia, make sure you allow plenty of time.

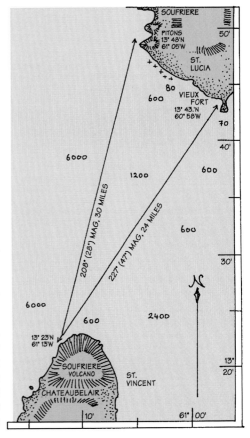

VINCENT & THE GRENADINES

CRUISING COMPANIONS

Whether your next cruise is to the Virgin Islands, the Leeward Islands,
Windward Islands, Trinidad & Tobago, Venezuela, Bonaire or Cuba,
Cruising Guide Publications are the ideal companion.

Cruising Guide Publications' books are a must for Caribbean cruising. Providing colorful photography, award winning design and the most up-to-date information on marinas, haul-out facilities, anchorages, resorts, restaurants, shops and watersports activities.

The guides are illustrated with sketch charts for safe, comfortable passages and anchorages, as well as being packed with information, tips and pointers that will help you make the most of your voyages.

Ideally suited for the chartering yachtsman, or the yacht owner travelling the Caribbean, the guides are updated regularly to ensure the most accurate and current information.

Also available is an extensive selection of Caribbean Art and Admiralty Collection prints. They include reproductions of historical charts and scenes dating back into the 1700's.

Call or write for a catalog of our many other titles and color brochures featuring Caribbean Art prints and Admiralty Collection charts.

CRUISING GUIDE PUBLICATIONS

P.O. Box 1017, Dunedin, FL 34697-1017
Phone: (813) 733-5322 • 800-330-9542 (Orders Only) • Fax: (813) 734-8179

Regulations

St. Vincent together with the Grenadine, make up one country. The main customs stations are Wallilabou, Kingstown, Bequia and Union Island. In a pinch you can find customs in Mustique and Canouan.

There is an entry charge of $10 EC per person. Yachts on charter are charged $2US per foot per month. You may stay as long as you like. Those clearing outside normal office hours (weekdays 0800-1200, 1300-1600) will pay a moderate overtime fee.

No jet skis, aquascooters, or similar craft are allowed anywhere in St. Vincent and the Grenadines.

Fishing in the waters of St. Vincent and the Grenadines is strictly regulated. You may only fish for your own consumption. You can do this by trolling when sailing, or hand-lining at anchor or from the shore, but not in protected areas where all fishing is forbidden. Protected areas include: The northeast coast and Devil's Table in Bequia, Isle de Quatre, all Mustique, the eastern coast of Canouan, all of Mayreau and the Tobago Cays, the whole of Palm, PSV and the surrounding reefs. Spearfishing is strictly forbidden to all visitors. Buying lobster out of season (the lobstering season is the 1st October to 31st April) is also illegal, as is buying a female lobster with eggs (easily seen as red "caviar" under the tail) or any lobster less than 9" in length. Corals must not be damaged. Fines run at around $5000 EC.

Holidays

Jan 1st - New Years Day
Jan 2nd - Recovery Day
Jan 22nd - Discovery Day
Easter Friday through Monday
First Monday in May - Labor Day
Whit Monday (7 weeks after Easter)

Carnival - 2nd Monday and Tuesday in July
1st Monday in August - August bank holiday
October 27th - Independence Day
Dec 25th - Christmas
Dec 26th - Boxing Day

Shopping hours

Are normally 0800-1200, and 1300-1600. Saturday is half day and most places are closed by noon. Banks normally open weekdays till 1300, and on Fridays 1500-1700 as well.

Telephones

Card and coin phones may be found all over the island. You can buy cards for the phone in post offices and selected shops. For overseas calls dial 0+country code+number. Soon you will be able to dial 115 from a public call box to get an operator for credit card and collect calls. When dialing from overseas the area code is 809, followed by a 7 digit number.

Transport

There are inexpensive ($1.50-6 EC) buses running to most villages. If you are going a long way check on the time of the last returning bus. Taxis are plentiful. Sample taxi rates are:

	EC
Kingstown - Airport	20
Kingstown - Young Island	25
Airport - Young Island	20
Kingstown - CSY/Bimini	30
Short ride	10
By the hour	40

Rental cars or motorbikes are available (see our directory). You will need to buy a local license which costs $30 EC. Drive on the left.

St. Vincent is an island of towering mountains, craggy peaks and dramatic precipices. Everything is dressed in a tangle of dense green forest. St. Vincent's steep and wild terrain was among the last to be settled by Europeans. At the time Columbus sailed through the islands, St. Vincent was inhabited by amber colored Caribs who had migrated from South America and had a more poetic name for the island: Hairoun, which means "home of the blessed." They were a fierce tribe who had wrested the land from the previous and more peace loving residents, the Arawaks. While the other islands were being exploited by the newly arrived Europeans, a slave ship was wrecked off Bequia and the Caribs took the slaves as their own. However, these slaves were a fierce and warlike tribe and gave the Caribs lots of problems. To control this, the Caribs decided to kill all the young male black children. This caused a revolt among the slaves who killed those Caribs they could, stole their women and ran into the hills. They kept the names the Caribs had given them, followed some Carib customs and became known as the Black Caribs. Over the years they took control of the land from the original Caribs and put up fierce resistance to British settlement. Finally, in the late 18th century, they were defeated by a superior British force and shipped en masse to Honduras.

The northern end of the island is dominated by Soufriere, a 3000-foot volcano. I had a friend who was anchored under the volcano in April 1979 with an amateur geologist on board. Together they scaled the volcano and peered into the depths. The geologist declared it was safely dormant. That night, which happened to be both Friday the 13th and Good Friday there was a rumbling from the very bowels of the earth and it erupted with a massive cloud that landed dust hundreds of miles away. It created a murk in the area so thick they couldn't see to the bow of the boat and had to leave completely blind, steering by compass to get away. The eruption, which lasted for some days, was Soufriere's second since 1902. The other was in 1973. As you sail by you can see some rivers of dark lava that flowed down from the summit. Despite the absence of any warning, everyone left the area in time and there were no casualties. The enthusiastic can hike up Soufriere and it is unquestionably one of the Windwards' best and most exciting hikes. Starting on the Windward side there is a clear trail that starts in farmland and goes through rain forest, montane forest, and then into an area where only tiny plants can survive. The top is often in cloud, and you need a little luck to see down into the crater or get the views over the island. The wind often blows a gale at the top and it is cool and damp, so take a rain jacket. You have to be careful not to get blown down into the crater which is a sheer thousand foot drop with no guard rail. Take lunch with you and eat it near the top, as the longer you spend there, the more likely you are to get windows in the clouds and see into the crater. The crater is an impressive cone with a huge smoking volcanic dome in the middle. Call any taxi driver for details. The crater rim is at 3000 feet; the mountains to the north attain 3800 feet.

In St. Vincent it seems that neither God nor man was completely sure they wanted tourism, for it lacks tourist type resorts, the acres of white sand beach and the convenient, easy anchorages of the Grenadines. In compensation, this very beautiful island remains unspoiled and you can drive

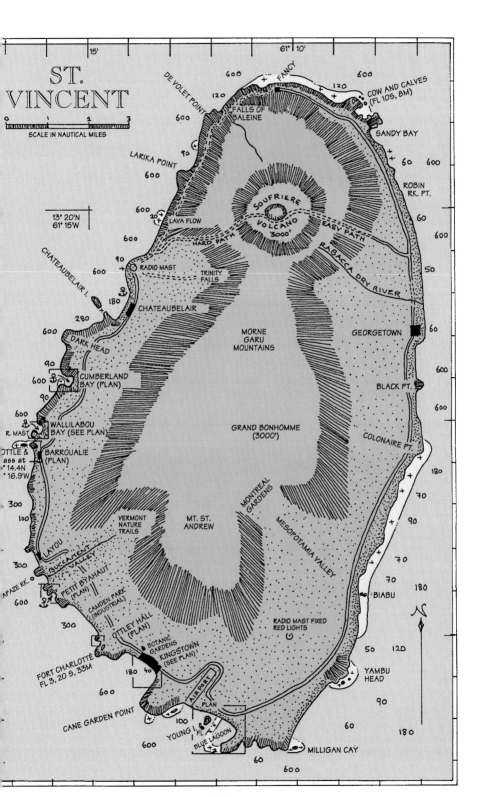

ST.
VINCENT

SCALE IN NAUTICAL MILES

15'   61° 10'

DE VOLET POINT
FANCY   600
608   120   COW AND CALVES
600   (FL 10S, 8M)
FALLS OF
BALEINE   SANDY BAY
LARIKA POINT   60   600
90
600   ROBIN
RK. PT.
13° 20'N
61° 15'W   600   SOUFRIERE   60
20   LAVA FLOW   VOLCANO
600   3000'   EASY PATH   600
HARD PATH   RABACCA DRY RIVER
90   50
CHATEAUBELAIR I.   RADIO MAST   TRINITY
600   FALLS
180
280   CHATEAUBELAIR
600   DARK HEAD   MORNE   GEORGETOWN   60
GARU
90   MOUNTAINS   600
600   CUMBERLAND
BAY (PLAN)   BLACK PT.
90
600   WALLILABOU   600
R. MAST   BAY (SEE PLAN)
OTTLE &   BARROUALIE   GRAND BONHOMME   COLONAIRE PT.
ass at   (PLAN)   (3000')
14.4N   180
16.9'W   MONTREAL   70
GARDENS
300   VERMONT   90
100   NATURE
TRAILS   MT. ST.   MESOPOTAMIA VALLEY
LAYOU   ANDREW   70
300   BUCCAMENT
VALLEY   70
APAZE RK.   PETIT BYAHAUT   BIABU   180
(PLAN)
600   CAMDEN PARK
(INDUSTRIAL)   RADIO MAST FIXED
300   OTTLEY HALL   RED LIGHTS
(PLAN)   50   120
BOTANIC
GARDENS
FORT CHARLOTTE   KINGSTOWN   YAMBU
FL 3, 20 S, 33M   (SEE PLAN)   HEAD
180   40   90
600   AIR PORT
PLAN
CANE GARDEN POINT   PLAN   60   180
100
600   YOUNG I.   FL
BLUE LAGOON   MILLIGAN CAY
60
600

153

CUMBERLAND BAY

or hike amid exotic, almost theatrical, scenery. Its fierce, uncompromising form is the perfect scenic complement to the appealing and gentle Grenadines farther south. Those doing a round trip from St. Lucia who only wish to stop one way are better off visiting St. Vincent on the way north, as this makes the hard windward north bound trip shorter.

Try to see some of St. Vincent's interior, much of which has stayed out of the hands of man and is totally wild. Roads run up both of St. Vincent's coasts, but none goes all the way round or crosses the middle. Climbing the volcano or a boat trip to the Falls of Baleine are recommended. I also like Montreal Gardens in the Mesopotamia Valley. Perched upon the very threshold of the mountains, they are at the end of the road. They are not well maintained, but that perhaps is part of the charm. There are little paths, dense vegetation, a river, and broad views. The gardens are a perfect place to spend an hour away from it all, communing with nature. (Reorganization of Montreal Gardens may come soon.) Those who like to be more organized can take a tour of the Botanical Gardens and Fort Charlotte. The Botanical Gardens are the oldest in the western hemisphere, and it was here tha Captain Bligh brought the breadfruit tre after the mutiny on the Bounty fiasco. direct "sucker" descendant from his origin; tree is on display. You will find man youths to guide you through the garden; one or two are good and entertaining, b negotiate fees in advance. There is also pre-Columbian museum on the grounds c the Botanical Gardens open only o Wednesdays (0945-1145) and Saturday (1600-1800).

Navigation, West Coast North to Soutl

Navigation along this section of the coa; is straightforward as the land is steep-tc except for the clearly visible Bottle an Glass rocks near Barrouallie. A quarter c a mile offshore clears all other danger Some yachts manage to anchor i Chateaubelair, stern to the shore, right u in the northern end of the bay. This can b a passable anchorage in the summer month in settled conditions, but it is uncomfortabl in any kind of swell and dangerous in a ba northerly swell.

CUMBERLAND BAY

This deep and enchanting bay is part of an estate in the heart of St. Vincent's wildest and richest land. A forest of coconut trees and bananas flows down the valley to the beach. At dusk a flock of cattle egrets roosts in nearby trees, and at night the tree frogs set up a rich throaty chorus. Sometimes the bay becomes a boiling mass of jumpin tuna and fishermen can often be seen wit their seine nets waiting patiently. For th cruising sailor there is a river to do a fres water clothes wash. Enter toward the nort of the bay to avoid the large rocky shoa which extends from the southwestern pai of the bay. Cumberland is very deep and you will need to anchor bow or stern to a palm tree. There will be many eager to help.

Regulations

There is no customs at Cumberland Bay, but you can clear in or out at Wallilabou or Barrouallie, which are close by.

Ashore

Although many of the locals look like bad guys in a spaghetti western, for the most part they couldn't be nicer and more helpful.

You can buy vegetables from Maxwell, fish from Joseph and crayfish from his brother Uncle Sam. Maxwell is always willing to come down and cook you a fish dinner.

These men are good about not overwhelming yachtspeople when they arrive, and they generally keep an eye on the bay but very occasionally, in the wee hours after they have gone home, dinghies have been known to go missing and once or twice the lines tied to the palm trees have been stolen. It is therefore advisable to keep the outboard on deck, the dinghy locked to the boat, and to use an older piece of line across the beach.

The only restaurant is Stephens and Stevens Hideaway [T:458-2325, VHF:68, $C], right on the beach. Mr. and Mrs. Stephens are well known characters in the area. You can check out their prices when Mr. Stephens comes by the boat or you can call them on the VHF. Mrs. Stephens cooks

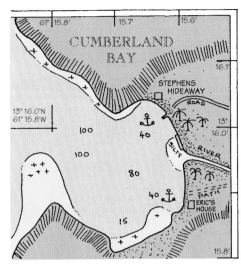

a great crayfish and callaloo soup as well as local mutton, chicken and goat.

The house at the other end of the bay belongs to Eric, a well traveled Vincentian who is retiring to go fishing. He may one day open a bar and meanwhile will always give good advice to passing yachts.

You should definitely take a walk here. An easy one is up the hill to the north which gives you a great view of the anchorage. Walk back to the road, turn left and keep going. (Unless you land at the north side of the bay, you must ford a small river, but that is part of the fun.)

Over the last year there has been large works plant ashore which is part of a road project. This should soon be removed.

WALLILABOU

Wallilabou is a picturesque bay about a mile south of Cumberland with a pleasant waterfront restaurant. Enter in the middle of the bay and pick up the bow and stern moorings put down by the Wallilabou Anchorage Restaurant, or anchor off the north end of the beach and tie bow or stern to the trees. The only disadvantage to this bay is the excessive number of boat boys, some of whom are rude. These boys are a problem created by yachts and can easily be solved by them. We suggest you deal only with the first set of boys who come up

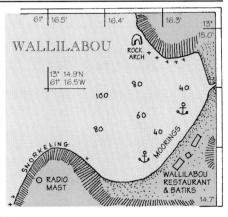

and tell all the others you are only dealing with the first set. The going rate for someone to help you with your lines is $7EC. Many people complain about the quality of fruits and vegetables they have bought here from the vendors. Steve and Jan, from the Wallilabou Restaurant hope to organize the boat boys by the time this guide comes out.

Regulations

Customs clearance is available daily between 1600-1800. Those clearing on weekends and after 1600 will be charged overtime. At other times, customs are available in Barrouallie.

Services

Steve and Jane Russell, who run the Wallilabou Anchorage Restaurant, are keen to attract yachting customers. They offer free moorings, showers and water via a long hose from the dock. A phone is available as is ice and overnight accommodation.

Ashore

The Wallilabou Anchorage Restaurant and boutique [T:458-7270, VHF:68, $C D] has a delightful location where you can eat looking out over your yacht. Steve, who is from St. Vincent and his wife Jane from England are very pleasant and usually in the bar in the evenings. The restaurant serves generous portions of local style food particularly fish and shrimp. Behind the restaurant is a mini zoo with agoutis

ortoises and parrots. Brightly colored locally made batiks are on sale.

There is a small but photogenic waterfall, good for a hearty shower, about a mile up the road. The walk through the lush countryside is quite delightful and the falls are easy to find. (Just get to the road and turn left; look for the falls on your right.)

Water sports

Snorkeling is interesting around the southern headland of Wallilabou.

Diving along this part of the St. Vincent's coast is great, but there is no dive shop so you have to do it on your own. For those who have high speed tenders, one easy dive to find is on the south side of Chateaubelair

Island. Here a steep wall has been sculpted by the sea into a rich pattern of ravines, hollows, and tiny caves which are home to eels, soapfish and other creatures. It is decorated by a variety of black corals including wire coral. Giant gray angelfish often gather over the sand at about 90 feet. There is also a reef 40 feet deep where huge structures, covered with a colorful mixture of corals, rise from the sand like fairy castles. Pufferfish swim by with what look like broad smiles on their faces. Huge schools of tiny silver fish catch the sun in a brilliant display. You will see a good variety of brightly colored reef fish and creatures such as Christmas tree worms, snake eels and maybe an octopus.

BARROUALLIE

Barrouallie is easily identified by the conspicuous Bottle and Glass rocks. It is a picturesque local town with a few quaint buildings. The main reason to stop here is to clear customs (see below). However, the anchorage is pleasant and good enough for an overnight stop. Those who prefer can move on to Cumberland, Wallilabou, Petit Byahaut or Young Island Cut. Some people anchor in one of the bays to the north and visit by dinghy.

Navigation

If you are coming from the north give a reasonable clearance to the last visible rock in Bottle and Glass as there is an underwater rock that extends seawards a few hundred feet. The best anchorage is close to shore between the town dock and Pint Rock. There is an adequate anchoring shelf for a quick stop in about 25 feet of water. For overnighting it would be advisable to get one anchor hooked in the shallow water, drop back and set another in the deeper water, holding the boat bow to the beach. You can tie your dinghy to the town dock. I can't think what you would need any boat boys for here, but if you do, try Winston, who is pleasant.

Regulations

You can clear in or out at the police station opposite the playing field. The police seem very efficient and friendly here and are not currently charging overtime even on weekends. Clearance is also possible in Wallilabou between about 1300-1800. (Those clearing in after 1600 will pay an overtime fee.) It is not possible to clear in Barrouallie during the hours the customs officer is in Wallilabou.

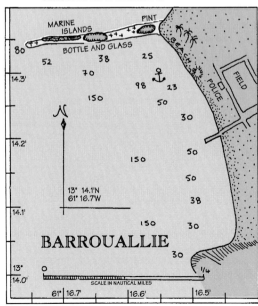

This small and delightful bay usually makes a good overnight anchorage, though it can be uncomfortable in some sea swells. A stern anchor may cut the roll. Ashore there is a small beach backed by hills with several conspicuous peaky outcroppings of rock. If you are coming from the north you pass the village of Layou, then Buccament Bay (just after the island called Lapaze Rock), then the next headland is Byahaut Point, a distinctive rounded headland with a diving flag sometimes flying from the top. Pass the headland, head into the bay and pick up a mooring or anchor in about 24 feet of water off the beach on a sand bottom. If you are coming from Kingstown, Byahaut Point is the headland you see after you leave Kingstown Bay. Ashore Petit Byahaut looks private; you mainly see some small green roofs poking out of the vegetation. If you are coming from abroad, Chuck and Sharon at Petit Byahaut will run you to the police station in Barrouallie to clear in for $25US.

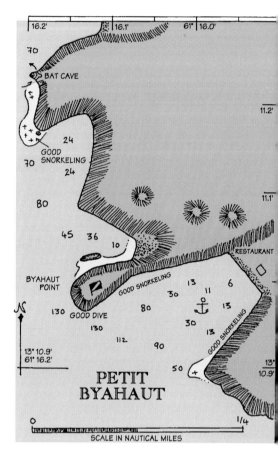

Ashore

Petit Byahaut [T:457-7008, VHF:68, $B, cc:V], approachable only by sea, is a delightful small resort where guest accommodations are in luxurious tents under roofs. It is owned by Chuck and Sharon, originally from Canada and California. They have four moorings available for yachts which is a pleasant number to share the bay with. If you use their moorings, there is a $10 US a night fee, deducted from your bill if you are eating dinner ashore. The restaurant is excellent in a beautiful setting of flower gardens with the sea beyond. There are lovely walks over the headlands. Their new chef speaks French, German and English Special overnight rates are available when there is room. The best place to beach your dinghy is to the south of the dock remains

Chuck and Sharon organize great hikes and it is a safe place to leave your boat Their most popular energetic all day hike is the volcano. You travel by taxi up the lee side of the island, taking in the sights such as the Mesopotamia valley. You hike with a guide up the eastern side of the volcano and then down the western side where Petit Byahaut picks you up by boat and brings you back. For the less vigorous there are lovely nature trails at Vermont which you can visit with knowledgeable guide Elroy They also arrange hikes to Trinity waterfalls (2.5 hours each way).

Petit Byahaut

"the natural place to be"

(809) 457-7008
MESSAGE OR FAX
VHF 68

major photos Carol Lee

Water sports

Snorkeling and diving between Petit Byahaut and Buccament Bay is superb and easily accessible by dinghy, though the current is strong. Petit Byahaut has a dive shop, fills tanks, and rents gear.

Dinosaur Head is the face of Byahaut Pt. that faces the anchorage. There is a 120-foot wall covered in coral, sponges and seafans. You swim through large schools of tangs and see queen angelfish, eels, snappers and spotted drums.

The Bat Cave is a short dinghy ride away and can be done as a dive or a snorkel as long as the swells are slight. There is about three feet of water at the cave entrance. You can find somewhere to anchor your dinghy outside and there is also good snorkeling in this area. Inside the cave it is quite dark, but you can see the bats which cling by the hundreds to the cave walls and roof. Crabs climb up among the bats. You catch a glimpse of the tunnel which leads off to the left because you can see a hint of light at the end of it. This tunnel is about 30 feet long and about four feet wide. You rise and fall on the swells and if the swells are bad it could be dangerous. The tunnel leads out into a fissure about 30 feet high and 40 feet deep. Below the water is a brilliant blue. You swim out through the fissure and divers go down to two huge rocks at 80 and 130 feet which are covered in sponges and corals and teeming with all kinds of fish. The ascent is up a wall textured with nooks and crannies. If you do the bat cave dive, it is most important not to disturb the bats. Two species live here, fishing bats (*Noctilio leporinus*), which eat fish and insects, and the St. Vincent fruit eating bat (*Brachyphylia cavernarum*) which was thought to be extirpated and are endangered. So swim quietly through the cave, without talking or splashing, and under no circumstances take flashlights or flash photographs.

Ottley Hall lies just to the west of Kingstown on the far side of Fort Charlotte. Here you will find a new yachting facility under the management of the Caribbean Charter Yacht Yard (CCYY) company [T:457 2178, VHF:68].

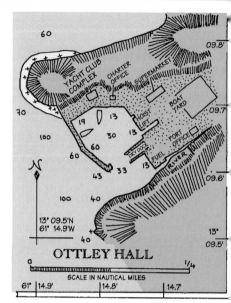

Services

This is a new combination 40 berth marina and yacht yard. There is a 65-ton marine hoist, a 700-ton synchro-lift and shunting system and a dry dock capable of handling anything up to 65 meters long, 15 meters wide and six meters deep. Special covered sheds on rails can be rolled over yachts on the hard or in the dry-dock so that respraying and repainting can be done in controlled conditions. The yard will be able to handle the construction and repair of all sizes of yacht, using local staff who have been trained in Italy. There is a fuel dock and long term storage for smaller yachts is planned.

Regulations

It is planned that Ottley Hall will be a port of entry.

Ashore

The marina is a short taxi ride from Kingstown and will include a restaurant, hotel and a modern supermarket. Passing yachts will be welcome to stop.

CCYY will also be running a fleet of three charter maxi yachts. This is a new project and at the time of writing construction had been completed on all major structures and the marina should be in operation before this guide reaches the bookshops.

KINGSTOWN

Kingstown, St. Vincent's capital, has some charming corners with old stone buildings, cobblestone sidewalks and handsome arches. The market is colorful and the shopping for both tourist items and provisioning is good. Yachts anchor up in the eastern corner of the bay to the east of the ferry dock. It is not particularly scenic, but it is right in town. A new cruise ship dock is planned in this area, which might restrict the anchoring. It is unwise to leave a yacht or dinghy unattended. There are lots of youths ashore who can be a little overwhelming, but if you need help to provision, they can help you accomplish a lot in a short time. Many prefer to visit Kingstown by road. Taxis and buses are readily available from both Young Island

Cut and Blue Lagoon.

Regulations

You can clear customs in Kingstown, but it is more cumbersome than elsewhere: you have to deal with customs, port authority and then go down to immigration at the other end of town. Yacht clearances are a sideline in these offices and there are sometimes lines of people doing other business. It is much easier to use the yacht facility in Wallilabou.

Services

Carlton King [T:457-9311] runs a first rate machine shop 150 yards from the Botanical Gardens toward the Prime Minister's residence. Whatever you break he can probably fix, including stainless, cast iron and aluminum.

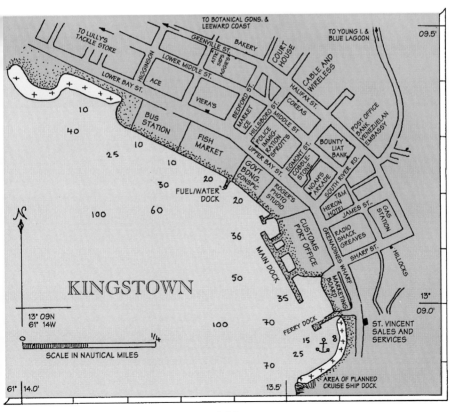

There is an excellent small dock where you can take on fuel and water right opposite the fish market, provided there is no swell. It is run by the Fisherman's Cooperative [T:456-2015]. You can also make contact by calling St. Vincent Signal Station [VHF:16] for a phone relay. Pull along the west side of the dock where it is 15-30 feet deep. Water here is inexpensive and available from 0600-1900. The diesel and gasoline pumps open about 0800. Ice is available in the fish market. A big perimeter fence and security guards separate this area from the general fish market. There is also an ice factory by the general market that sells inexpensive bags of chipped ice.

See also "Services" under Young Island Cut and Blue Lagoon.

Ashore

There are many supermarkets to choose from, but the biggest and most convenient is Greaves [T:457-1074], which stays open till 1900 on Fridays. Its subsidiary by the airport opens till 2000 nightly, except Sundays when it opens from 0700-1000. Greaves in town offers a charter yacht discount and delivery to Young Island Cu is negotiable. The Marketing Board ofte has good deals, especially on produce. Th local market is lively and colorful wit many local ladies eager to offer yo excellent buys in local produce. Mario Mills' T & M [T:456-1616, cc:A,V] is a excellent wine shop, selling not only wines but also a variety of gourmet items including coffee, chocolate, creams cheeses, asparagus, smoked fish and cavia

Upstairs in the same building as T & M i Shades of Faces [T:457-2069], a beaut therapy clinic that offers anything fror facial treatments to back and body massage

The best place to look for yacht items i St. Vincent Sales and Service [T:457-182C F:456-2620], owned by Paddy Punnet himself a keen boating man, and someon who can give you good advice whateve your problem. His modern shop is in brand new building conveniently place opposite the ferry dock. St. Vincent Sale and Service sells both auto spares an general marine hardware. It is a sales an

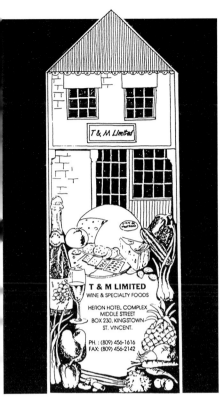

T & M LIMITED
WINE & SPECIALTY FOODS

HERON HOTEL COMPLEX
MIDDLE STREET
BOX 230, KINGSTOWN
ST. VINCENT.

PH. : (809) 456-1616
FAX: (809) 456-2142

service agent for Yamaha and outboards in St. Vincent are duty free. St. Vincent Sales and Service is a NAPA jobber and has excellent buys on filters. They keep a selection of resins and marine paints, including antifouling. Rope, chain, anchors, stainless fittings and boat batteries are available. They can make hydraulic hoses.

Lully's has a fishing tackle store on Lower Middle Street which also stocks snorkeling gear and ropes.

Radio Shack on Bay Street [T:457-2504] has the same range of electronic equipment and service you would expect to find in the U.S. Stock includes VHF radios and computers. Anything in the catalog that they don't have can be brought down fast. For more general hardware, try Ace [T:457-1639] just beyond the bus station. Ace often has good buys on silicone seal, 5200, sandpaper and tools. Sprotts has an excellent selection of tools and household hardware. Trottman's has a good range of electrical supplies and there are also several lumberyards and plumbing and hardware stores around town.

If you are shopping for fun, take a walk along Bay Street. Pop into 96 Degrees [T:457-2408, cc:V,A] for casual wear. Next look in at Noah's Arkade [T:457-1513, cc:A,V], a delightful shop with a wide range of Caribbean handicrafts and literature. The crafts side includes brightly colored batiks, ornaments, gifts, sculptures, household items, t-shirts, and clothing. The book selection ranges from children's books and fiction to nature, cooking and cruising guides, all with a local flavor, and many are unavailable outside the region.

At the Cobblestone Inn there is an arcade with more shops, such as Stechers [T:457-1142, cc:A,V], which sells duty-free porcelain, china, crystal, jewelry, and perfumes, and Giggles [T:457-1174, cc:A,V], a clothing boutique. Combination [T:457-1063] is a hairdressing salon and clothing store. Upstairs in the new Sprotts department store, Sprotties Silk Screen Shop [T:456-1647, cc:V] offers delightful clothing and household items, all made from their own silk screened fabrics. Jitterbugs [T:457-2637] is a new sports store with casual wear, snorkeling gear and other sports accessories.

Other shops to look at are Hibiscus or the local Handicraft Center for local crafts, and Made in De Shade [T:457-2364, cc:V] for casual clothing.

Rogers Photo Studio on Bay Street sells film and does one-day processing when the machines are working.

You can choose a lunch spot to suit your mood: we mention just a few of many. Clean and inexpensive, The Bounty [T:456-1776, $D] is perfect for light snacks (rotis and small lunch plates). When you go in, head straight up to the cash desk, select and pay. They give you a slip which you hand over to the food counter. Then you sit down and the food arrives. You must know this because if you sit first, nothing happens. The Bounty may move sometime during the life of this guide. For a little more atmosphere Sid's Pub [T:456-2315, $C-D], on Grenville Street, offers good local food in an English style pub. For really good local food in a friendly atmosphere, visit Aggies Bar and Restaurant [T:456-2110, $C-D, cc:V, Ds, closed Sunday lunch]. If you want something cooler, more spacious and social, then go to Basil's in the Cobblestone Inn [T:457-2713, $C-D], where you can get a first rate lunch buffet, or climb up the stairs to the Rooftop Restaurant [T:456-1937, cc:A,V, breakfast and lunch only] for a breezy open atmosphere with a view.

The Heron Hotel serves a wonderful breakfast at a reasonable price and is a big favorite with the "ferry from Bequia" crowd.

St. Vincent Nightlife

Those who like to go out on the town should try The Attic [T:457-2558], an attractive jazz club in Kingstown which sometimes has excellent groups on weekends. Other times it is a quiet bar with good background music. See also the Aquatic Club in Young Island Cut.

THE SOUTH COAST OF ST. VINCENT

Navigation

The current along this coast is predominantly westwards, up to two knots. It reverses weakly for a few hours which can create choppy seas.

When leaving Kingstown heading for Young Island, give the headland a good clearance as there is a submerged rock about 200 feet south of its eastern end.

There are two good anchorages close together: Young Island Cut and Blue Lagoon. They are both well serviced by bus

YOUNG ISLAND CUT

and taxi to town. The nearest larg supermarket is near the airport. If you vi the Calliaqua fish market around 1600, yc have a chance of meeting the fishermen they return with the day's catch. For cookin gas, go to the filling station just before t airport (a short bus or taxi ride). Bo anchorages are within dinghy reach of eac other, so read about services and sho facilities for both anchorages.

Young Island Cu

Young Island is open and easily enter from the west. The channel to the east Young Island is narrow, curves, and is be given a miss, even with the new beacon Young Island Cut is a favorite wit yachtsmen. It is scenic and both Your Island and the mainland have small pleasa beaches. There are several restaurants ar bars.

You have to anchor with care. The curre sweeps through both ways and the center the cut goes as deep as 65 feet. There good holding in the north or western par of the anchorage, but it occasionally roll Anchoring bow and stern is essential your boat will swing with the change current and bang into someone else. Th sea bed close to Young Island offers po holding. Young Island's electrical cab carries 11,000 volts, enough to make yo whole boat glow, so anchor well clear.

Service

To make life easy there are a couple businesses here that operate moorings for fee of $10 per night. Their boats will me you as you arrive. After you have tied u test the mooring by putting your boat har in reverse.

Sam Taxi Service [T:456-4338/447 F:456-4233, VHF:68] is one of those wh rents out moorings. Sam also offers a fu taxi service that includes not only tow trips and tours but fetching gas, doin laundry, shopping or anything else yo need. Sam will also clear yachts in. Th service costs $50 US so is more likely to b used by the larger charter yachts. Sam Ta also offers a complete communication service, including sending faxes, telephon calls, and flight reconfirmations.

RESTAURANT

Opposite Young Island

*S*t. Vincent's most popular bar & restaurant specializing in fresh locally caught seafood.
For romantic candlelight dinners
where the service, food, wines, and
ambience are first class.
Live lobster in season from our pool,
choice meats, as well as
pub snacks and gourmet pizzas.

INTERNATIONALLY AND
LOCALLY ACCLAIMED TO BE
ST. VINCENT'S LEADING RESTAURANT

The island's only Espresso Coffee Bar

YACHT PROVISIONS WITH FROZEN SPECIALTIES

Pub: 10 am - last order
Happy hour 9-10 pm daily
The greatest selection of cocktails,
draught beer served in chilled mugs
Restaurant: Throughout the day
'til last order
reservations recommended

Phone 458-4227   VHF 68

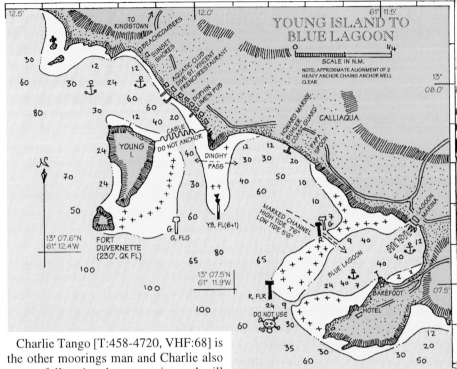

Charlie Tango [T:458-4720, VHF:68] is the other moorings man and Charlie also runs a full taxi and tour service and will help in any way he can.

Some yachtspeople visit town by bus to clear customs.

The Aquatic Club [T:458-4205, VHF:68, cc:V] sells water and cube ice from their new dock. You can pull alongside, but keep an eye on the current. The Lime'n Pub offers showers.

Verrol at Nichols Marine [T:456-4118] has an efficient mechanized workshop where he repairs and reconditions alternators and starter motors in a few hours. They come back looking and working like new. Verrol also does aluminum and stainless welding. Call him on the telephone and he will come and sort out your problem wherever you are in St. Vincent. (In Bequia you can leave things for him with GYE or Sam Taxi Tours.) Verrol's workshop is in Belaire, just behind the airport, which is closer to the south coast than town. A few houses down from Verrol is Oscar's Machine Center, a good new machine shop. They can do all manner of jobs here on all kinds of metals and can resurface engine blocks. Contact Oscar through Verrol if

their new telephone has not yet been installed.

Buhler in Calliaqua builds boats and does fiberglass work and spray painting.

Howard's Marine [T:457-4328, F:457-4268, VHF:68] is a sales and service agent for OMC and Yamaha. They keep plenty of motors and spares in stock and will repair any kind of outboard and will even help with inboards.

Ashore

Young Island Cut is lined with restaurants and is a good place to visit some bars and eat out. The premier place for gourmet food is The French Restaurant (known as "The French") [T:458-4972, VHF:68, $A-B, cc:V]. Prices are on a par with other good restaurants and owners Jacques and Martine make you feel like important guests. Their cuisine is excellent – as good as you will find anywhere in the Windwards – and this is a perfect place to eat lobster (in season). Choose your own right out of their pool. They offer background piano music

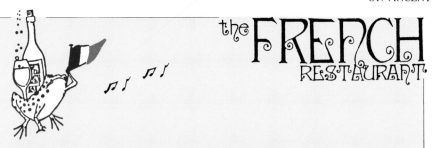

the FRENCH RESTAURANT

Famous throughout the islands for its gourmet cooking

at Villa (Young Island Cut), St. Vincent

The French Restaurant is unanimously acclaimed to be the best restaurant in the Grenadines. We have the original live lobster pool in St. Vincent. You choose your own lobster. The only restaurant in St Vincent to earn ☆☆☆☆ in The Best Hotels, Restaurants and Shops in the Caribbean '94 -'95.

Open every day for breakfast, lunch and dinner.
Piano music Thursdays and Saturdays
Reservations advisable in season

Tel: (809) 458-4972, Fax: (809) 457-4930, VHF channel 68

on Thursdays and Saturdays. They also offer delightful and very inexpensive lunches. Reservations for dinner are advisable.

The Lime'n Pub [T:458-4227, $B-D] is more informal. You can relax, play darts, meet people, and prop up the bar with draft beer in an iced mug. Owner Dave Dunn aims for a huge variety of food so he has something for everyone. For the cheap and cheerful crowd there is English pub food, rotis, burgers, "gourmet" pizzas, ice cream and espresso coffee. The bon vivant will find a vast menu with the emphasis on seafood, including lobster straight from their holding tank. For something different try their Caribbean salmon lightly smoked with fine herbs and served with a spinach sauce.

The Lime 'n Pub is managed by Desiree and Andrew. There is a dinghy dock and ice cream parlor. Happy hour is 2100-2200 daily.

Beachcombers [T:458-4283, VHF:68, $B-D] is an intimate restaurant where the view of the anchorage and sea beyond is framed by almond trees. Seafood and local specialties are served, as well as pizzas and snacks.

Dolphins [T:457-4337, F:457-7241, $B-C, cc:A,V,Dc] is run by Austin Patterson who hails from Scotland. It is set in a fine traditional Caribbean building. Happy hour is 1700-1900 daily with half-priced beer and a special on banana daquiris. Austin is an artist and he has lined the walls of the building with paintings and sculptures both by himself and other local artists.

Stilly's Aquatic Club is where the action gets heavy on Friday, Saturday and holiday nights into the early hours.

Browne's [T:457-4000, cc:A,V] (ex-Mariners Inn) has recently been taken over by Vidal Browne of Young Island and is still being renovated. You can expect a top quality operation.

Paradise Inn [T:457-4795, $C-D, cc:V], run by Shirley Layne, offers local food and occasional Friday night barbecues with live music.

Young Island Resort [T:458-4826, VHF:68, $A, cc:A,V] is a delight of tropical flowers and trees and is well worth a visit for a sundowner. Their Thursday night cocktail party on Fort Duvernette is good (the cost is around $15 US), and they have a jump up to a steel band on Saturdays. If you wish you can dine at Young Island Resort (reservations advisable).

For an adventure in inexpensive local food, wander down the road to Papa Spoon's Rasta Ranch [$D] on the Calliaqua playing field. He serves good all natural food in calabash bowls and sells beer and fresh juices.

Boutiques include the Young Island Dock Shop [T:458-4826, cc:V,A] and The Lime'n Pub boutique [T:458-4272, cc:V,A]. You can ask at the Lime'n Pub about food for charter yachts, including frozen meals and Villamar's smoked fish.

Right on the dock, The Aquatic General Store [T:458 4205] keeps a selection of beers, soft drinks and basics. Next door, the Aquatic Flower and Food Center [T:457 4749 cc:A] has freshly cut flowers and some local fruit.

Fort Duvernette stands behind Young Island, a monument to the ingenuity of the soldiers of a bygone age who managed to get cannons up to the top. There is a place to tie the dinghy, and 250 steps take you to the cannons. The panoramic view is your reward. Fort Duvernette was used in the late 18th century when the settlers were fighting off the Black Caribs from inland. You will notice that cannons face in both directions.

Watersports

Diving in St. Vincent is really wonderful. The rugged shoreline is equally dramatic below the surface. Walls and reefs that drop far deeper than any sane person can dive are common, fish are everywhere - feeding in schools, tucked under rocks and hiding in sponges.

Dive St. Vincent [T:457-4714, VHF:68, cc:A,V] is run by Padi/Naui instructor Bill Tewes. Bill has been here about a decade and is on nodding terms with most of the fish and sea creatures. He has the honor of appearing on a St. Vincent and Grenadines postage stamp in full diving regalia, part of an underwater series that features his

BLUE LAGOON SHOWING POSITION OF MARKED CHANNEL

photographs. He has stations in Young Island Cut, Canouan and Union Island and is associated with Dive Bequia. Dive packages good in all these places, or learn-as-you-go full certification programs, are available. Bill also offers trips to the Falls of Baleine. Charter skippers should know that Bill can pick up a group from a yacht heading north, take them to the falls of Baleine as the yacht powers up the coast and deliver them back at the north end of the island.

Those diving on their own will find the base of Fort Duvernette easily accessible, though you do have to be careful of the current which tries to sweep you out to sea. Anchor your dinghy to the west of the Fort Duvernette dinghy dock. Follow the base of Fort Duvernette down. Almost as soon as you begin you will be surrounded by large schools of brown chromis. At 40 feet you find yourself in a pleasant area of house-sized boulders with nooks and crannies where eels, shrimps and angelfish hide out. Large schools of sergeant majors hug the rocks while offshore jacks, mackerels and schools of margates patrol.

Other even better dives are best done with a local dive shop as the anchorages are dangerous for yachts and local knowledge about the currents is essential. Bottle Reef under Fort Charlotte starts at 25 feet. You descend along the foot of an underwater rock headland. On your right is a gentle slope of coral decorated by sponges and many smaller soft corals. On the left the headland turns into a sheer wall adorned by deep water sea fans. There are small bushes of black coral in several colors. At the bottom we found several cherub fish. These little critters, the smallest of the angelfish, are only a couple of inches long. You round the bottom of the headland at 100 feet and ascend through huge schools of grunts and even larger schools of brown chromis that seem to explode into a variety of patterns all around. There is always a chance of finding ancient bottles. A curious current pattern here makes it possible to have the current with you the whole way.

Kingstown South is on the south side of Kingstown Harbor. You can see by looking at the sheer cliffs above and the schooling chromis below that this will be an interesting dive. The descent is down a steep slope and this is the place to look for the unusual red banded lobster. This colorful little crustacean is clearly marked in bands and spots of red, white and gold. Unlike other Caribbean lobsters, it has claws, though they are tiny. We saw one when we finished our descent and three more later, as well as a slipper lobster and the more normal spiny lobster. We circled slowly anti-clockwise up the slope looking at sponges, corals and big rocks. You often see large pelagic fish swimming out toward the sea. Among the many reef fish you will meet are spotted drums and filefish.

New Guinea Reef is on the east side of Petit Byahaut. This spectacular dive takes you down a wall to 90 feet where large black corals occur in bushes of white, pink, dark green, light green, brown and red. All three black coral species are here. Fish include black jacks, parrotfish, French angelfish and occasional sightings of the rather rare frilled goby, frogfish and sea horses. An overhang near the bottom makes this dive visually spectacular.

Blue Lagoon

Blue Lagoon is a pleasant anchorage with a beach and plenty of palm trees. You can lie comfortably, protected by land and reef. The main shoals between Blue Lagoon and Young Island are marked by large beacons (see sketch chart). These are in fairly shallow water, so do not cut them too fine.

The opening of the west entrance is marked by two large beacons. After that, if you are lucky you will see one or two stakes. If not, head straight across the reef into the deep water. Depths vary with tide from about five foot nine inches to about seven and a half feet. Call Lagoon Marina or Barefoot Yacht Charters on VHF:68 to ask about the state of the tide. Do not attempt to use the deeper south entrance as it is dangerous and has gotten many a yacht in trouble. The anchorage is quite deep, so be prepared to use plenty of scope. You will need a stern anchor to keep your stern into the small swells. If you anchor in the region of the two old mooring chains (see our sketch chart), use a trip line in case your anchor gets hooked on one. You can also come stern-to at either of the yacht facilities.

Services

The Lagoon Marina and Hotel [T:458-4308, F:457-4716, VFH:68, cc:V] is small and personal and a sub-base for Tradewind Yacht Charters. Electricity (220 volt, 50 cycles) can be arranged at the dock. Beverly, the dock master, sells water, fuel and ice. There is a marine chandlery, showers, laundry and a telephone service. When available, rooms are offered at special rates. They will help if you have a mechanical or electrical problem, and look after your yacht if you want to leave it here. Those wishing to pick up or drop off charterers here should discuss it first with the management. A large, seaworthy, light dinghy suitable for charter work is built on the premises.

Mary Barnard's Barefoot Yacht Charters [T:456-9526, F:456-9238, VHF:68, cc:V] is a charter company which welcomes visiting yachts. They offer communications, a full travel agency, an air charter service, diesel, water, ice and a provisioning shop with prime U.S. steaks. They usually have room for visiting yachts to tie up overnight at their dock.

Ashore

The Lagoon Marina and Hotel's bar has a perfect view over the harbor and their restaurant [T:458-4308, VHF:68, $B-C, cc:V] offers well prepared creole and international food.

Bimini's Restaurant [T:456-9526, VHF:68, cc:V, $B-C], set in the open amid the rocks overlooking the sea, is quaint and intimate. Good food with a local flavor.

Both The Lagoon and Bimini have interesting small boutiques.

Blue Lagoon is a good place to leave your boat while you explore ashore. If you decide to do this by taxi, Robert of Robert Taxi [T:456-4873, VHF:68] is a real gentleman and very reliable.

Water sports

St. Vincent Dive Experience [T:458-4283, F:457-2768, VHF:68] at The Lagoon Marina is run by Vincentian Perry Hughes. Perry is young and keen. He will collect divers from their yachts, he rents dive gear and runs trips to the Falls of Baleine. He generally sets off in the morning on a two-dive package which will get you back in time for a relaxed lunch. Special trips can be scheduled on request. The dive sites include those described under Young Island Cut.

The snorkeling on the reef that protects the harbor is fair.

NORTHERN GRENADINES PASSAGES

Bequia and Mustique, in the northern Grenadines, are both frequently visited by yachtsmen. Although only about eight miles apart geographically at their closest points, they are very different from each other.

Navigation

There is a strong westerly current throughout the Grenadines. Its effect is particularly noticeable in the Bequia and Canouan channels so it is advisable to point eastwards of your destination and check your bearings periodically to see how much you are being set. There is least set when the tidal stream runs counter to the regular current, but this is a mixed blessing since the seas become rougher and sometimes positively uncomfortable. The roughest seas are to be found just north of Canouan and off the Bequia side of the Bequia Channel, especially up by Bequia Head. It is not unusual for the current to be going in two different directions on opposite sides of the channel.

St. Vincent to Bequia

The passage from St. Vincent to Bequia is usually pleasant off-the-wind sailing. Although Admiralty Bay is hidden till you get quite close, you can usually see the headland that you have to round because it stands out against the more distant land behind. Look behind you to see which way you are being set by the current, and make

SCALE IN NAUTICAL MILES

ST. VINCENT TO
BEQUIA AND MUSTIQUE

adjustments so you stay on course. Big seas can lead to a little exciting surfing and one often covers the eight or nine miles in about an hour and a half. Be prepared for the Bequia Blast after the lee of Devil's Table. Many drop their sails here, but if you fancy an exhilarating short beat, keep going. When sailing in you might notice what appears to be a madman zooming around your yacht standing up in a tiny inflatable, being badly bounced by the waves. Fear not, it is just Tim Wright who makes his living taking marine photographs. If he takes your yacht he will probably bring a proof for you to see. There is no obligation to buy. And yes, he has flipped over and lost his camera gear at least once. If you want to be sure Tim comes by your boat, you can always call him [T:457-3212, VHF:77] and let him know when you will be sailing by.

Sailing the other way is a different matter. To make Young Island or Blue Lagoon from Admiralty Bay you usually have to tack to windward against a foul current. It usually takes two hours and can take three

or more. It is generally quicker to tack or motor sail up the Bequia coast and then shoot across from Anse Chemin, the bay just southwest of Bequia Head. This is fine in calm weather, but on rough days one can sail straight into a range of liquid mountains near Bequia Head. If the seas are rough, head straight over to St. Vincent and then work back up the coast.

St. Vincent to Mustique

The trip between St. Vincent and Mustique is about 15 miles, and in good going it takes two and a half to three hours. The seas around the north end of Bequia can be very rough, but one often gets an exhilarating reach. Whether you are sailing north or south, keep well off Bequia Head and The Bullet as the current pulls you down that way. Otherwise just strap everything down, hang on tight and ride 'em!

Bequia to Mustique

Most people approach Mustique from Admiralty Bay. The easiest way is to round

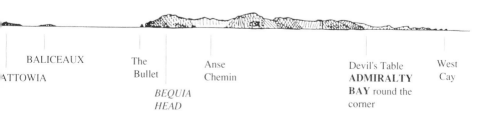

BALICEAUX		The	Anse		Devil's Table	West
ATTOWIA		Bullet	Chemin		**ADMIRALTY**	Cay
	BEQUIA				**BAY** round the	
	HEAD				corner	

Approaching Bequia from St. Vincent

175

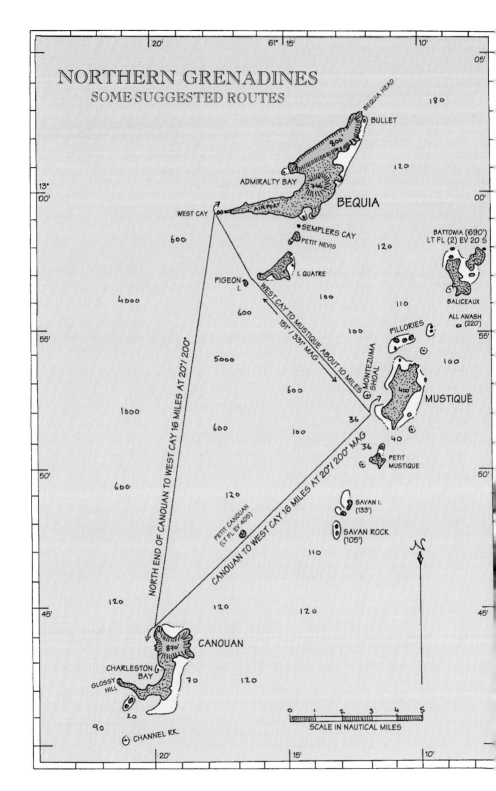

NORTHERN GRENADINES
SOME SUGGESTED ROUTES

BEQUIA HEAD

BULLET

180

800

120

ADMIRALTY BAY   746

BEQUIA

WEST CAY   AIRPORT

SEMPLERS CAY

PETIT NEVIS

120

BATTOWIA (690')
LT FL (2) EV 20 S

600

I. QUATRE

PIGEON I.

4000

600

160

110

BALICEAUX

ALL AWASH
(220')

55'

5000

100

PILLORIES

100

MONTEZUMA SHOAL

55'

WEST CAY TO MUSTIQUE ABOUT 10 MILES

151° / 331° MAG

600

600

400

MUSTIQUÉ

1600

600

36

40

NORTH END OF CANOUAN TO WEST CAY 16 MILES AT 20'/ 200°

5000

160

36

PETIT MUSTIQUE

50'

600

120

CANOUAN TO WEST CAY 16 MILES AT 20'/ 200° MAG

SAVAN I. (133')

50'

PETIT CANOUAN
(LT FL EV 40S)

SAVAN ROCK
(105')

110

120

120

120

120

45'

45'

CANOUAN

870'

CHARLESTON BAY

GLOSSY HILL

70

120

20

90   CHANNEL RK.

0 1 2 3 4 5
SCALE IN NAUTICAL MILES

West Cay and sail out between Pigeon Island and Isle de Quatre. As you approach Mustique, Montezuma Shoal is a real danger. It is marked by a beacon placed right on the middle of the reef. Pass either side but keep at least a quarter of a mile clear of the beacon. The beacon is red and black, but if you get close enough to see the colors you will probably run aground.

There are passages between Semples Cay and Petit Nevis, and between Petit Nevis and Isle de Quatre, but they can be very rough and the current extremely rapid. Furthermore, there is a reef extending well south of Petit Nevis, so serious thought should be given to prevailing conditions before choosing either of these routes. It is

an easy seven-mile reach from Friendship Bay to Mustique or back.

Bequia to Canouan

As you round West Cay (Bequia) and head south, it will be possible to see Petit Canouan; if the visibility is good Canouan itself will be in sight. Glossy (Glass) Hill, the southwestern point of Canouan, is joined to the rest of the land by a low isthmus which stays below the horizon till you get quite close, so Glossy Hill appears initially as a separate island.

Mustique to Canouan

This trip can be a rolly run with the wind right behind. I often tack downwind to make it a reach.

177

gingerbread
BEQUIA

Tel: 809-458-3800
Fax: 809-458-3907
VHF:68

Restaurant & Bar. Upstairs, for breakfast, lunch and dinner in comfort, with elegance. Evening specialties - seafood and curries.
Live music (non amplified) most nights.

Cafe & Lunch Barbecue under the trees by the sea, for fresh coffee and baked goodies.
And from 12 noon to 3.00 p.m. daily
- barbecued fish, chicken, kebabs.

Apartments self contained, fans, hot water, daily and weekly rates

Telephone and Fax Service
7 a.m. to 7 p.m., upstairs

BEQUIA BOATS

Regulations

Port Elizabeth is a port of entry for St. Vincent and the Grenadines. The procedure is simple, though the lines are sometimes long. Customs open at 0900 and close at 1500. Fees are given under St. Vincent.

Jet skis and the like are strictly forbidden, as is spearfishing, throughout the Grenadines (see St. Vincent).

Holidays

See St. Vincent.

Shopping Hours

Office and bank hours are as for St. Vincent. Most stores open from 0800-1200 and from 1400-1700.

Telephones

Card and coin phones may be found near the tourist office. You can buy phone cards in the post office and Solana's. By the time you get this guide you should be able to dial 115 for credit card and reverse charge calls. See also St. Vincent.

Transport

There are inexpensive buses which run to many parts of the island (ask in the little tourist office on the quay). Taxis are plentiful and reasonable. Sample taxi rates are:

	$EC
Most rides	15
Longer rides	20

Rental jeeps and motor bikes are available (see our directory). You need to buy a local license which costs $30 EC. Drive on the left.

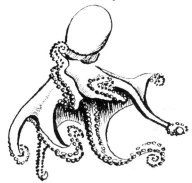

179

BEQUIA

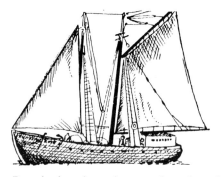

Bequia has long been a favorite of yachtspeople. Isolated enough to remain relatively unspoiled, yet lively enough to be stimulating and entertaining, it provides a blend of the old and new that many find perfect. It is well connected with St. Vincent and the other Grenadines both by the new airport and by the cheaper and more traditional ferries. The Admiral makes two trips on weekdays, leaving Bequia at 0630 and 1400 and returning at 1030 and 1630. They often offer a supplementary service with a boat leaving Bequia at 0730 and 1700, returning at 0900 and 1900. The traditional sailing schooner Friendship Rose which served as the Bequia ferry for many years, has now been refitted as a charter boat. Some yachtspeople leave their boats anchored in Bequia and take a ferry over to visit St. Vincent. Check in the tourist office behind the main dock for weekend schedules.

Bequia is an island of sailors and boats. Linked to the outside world mainly by the sea, the old traditions still go on. Boats are built on the beach in the shade of palm trees. Everything from little "two bow" fishing boats to grand schooners are built by eye, using only simple hand tools. A big launching is always a festive occasion with rum flowing freely, music playing and hundreds of brightly dressed people helping to roll the boat down the beach into the sea. Bequians travel all over the world on cargo vessels and quite a few have ended up owning their own. Some are intrepid fishermen who venture all over the Grenadines in little open boats.

The island used to be an active whaling station, and though the tradition is now dying out, Bequians still make an occasional foray during the whaling season between February and April. At this time of year humpback and sperm whales leave their northern feeding grounds and head south to mate and bear young. Few people are left in Bequia with the skills necessary to hunt them - a daring feat in an open sailing boat, using hand thrown harpoons. On the rare occasions that they make a kill the hunters tow the whale to Petit Nevis for butchering.

Bequians are a proud people, descendants of settlers who came from North America on whaling boats, from farms in Scotland, from French freebooters and from Africa.

Bequia's main harbor is Admiralty Bay and there is also a harbor on the south coast called Friendship Bay, and a daytime anchorage at Petit Nevis.

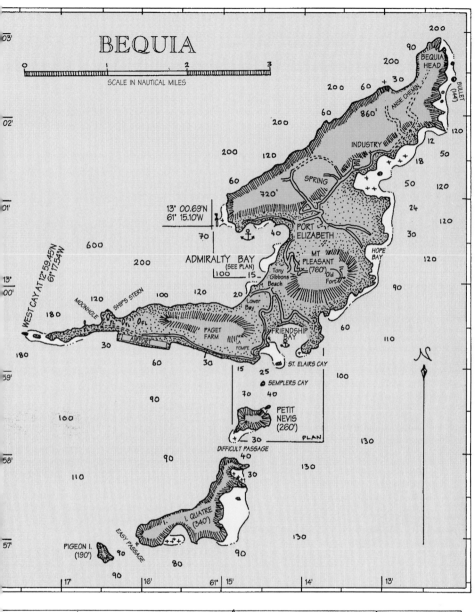

BEQUIA

SCALE IN NAUTICAL MILES
0   1   2   3

200
90
BEQUIA HEAD
200
BULLET (144')
200   60   + 30
ANGE CHEMIN
120
200   60
860'
12
INDUSTRY
200
120
18   50
SPRING
+ + +
50
720'
24
120
60
+ +
30
120
13° 00.69'N
61° 15.10'W
70
40
PORT ELIZABETH
HOPE BAY
600
200
ADMIRALTY BAY
(SEE PLAN)
MT PLEASANT (760')
120
WEST CAY AT 12°59.45N 61°17.54W
100   15
Tony Gibbons Beach
Old Fort
90
120
SHIPS STERN
100
120
20
MOONHOLE
Lower Bay
60
180
PAGET FARM
FRIENDSHIP BAY
110
O FL
LA POMPE
30
AIRPORT
60
30
15
St. ELAIRS CAY
180
25
90
SEMPLERS CAY
100
70   40
100
PETIT NEVIS (260')
+ 30
130
DIFFICULT PASSAGE
40
110
90
30
130
110
I. QUATRE (340')
130
PIGEON I. (190')
90
EASY PASSAGE
+ + +
90
80
90

Admiralty Bay is a huge, well-protected bay with Bequia's town, Port Elizabeth, at its head. Small hotels, bars, restaurants and shops spread from town along the southeastern shore, strung together by a tiny path that threads its way along the seashore. In most conditions it is possible to walk from town to the Sunny Caribbee without getting your feet wet. However, during northerly swells (most prevalent between Christmas and February) one has to run the gauntlet below the wall, past The Old Fig Tree, dodging the swells. Occasionally a giant wave rolls in, smashing on the wall in a massive flurry of spray catching even the nimblest traveler. My friend Too Tall Tom watching this from his yacht So Long, aptly calls these waves "Tourist Busters."

Navigation

The entrance to Admiralty Bay is straightforward. As you approach from the north and the bay begins to open up you can see two fine beaches, Lower Bay and Tony Gibbons (aka Princess Margaret) Beach. Each is separated by a distinct headland. East of Tony Gibbons Beach it becomes more built up, starting with the Sunny Caribbee Plantation House and continuing to town.

Approaching the bay you must allow plenty of room for Devil's Table, a reef which extends a good way from shore: it is marked by a yellow and black beacon. The beacon is on the outer part of the shoal; allow plenty of room when you go round. Once in the harbor, take care not to hit the shoals that lie offshore between the eastern end of Tony Gibbons Beach and the Green Boley. Yachts anchor inside some of these shoals, so they look like tempting empty space.

Anchor well clear of the local ferry channel to the main dock. The ferries are large and need plenty of turning room. It is advisable to keep out of their way at all times. Yachts may not tie up to the ferry dock or the dinghy dock.

As you arrive boat boys may approach you in small open boats offering to pilot you in. Best not to accept this service as they are not qualified either as pilots or skippers. These lads can be of help, however, in putting out a second anchor for you.

The main anchorage is up in town off the Frangipani Hotel. The water is deep and it takes lots of anchor line and sometimes a couple of tries to get hooked in the muddy sand.

The area by the Bequia Marina is calm and has good holding. Some yachts like to anchor off the Old Fig Tree and Sunny Caribbee. Enter inside the shoals by following a line between the ruined fort and the Sunny Caribbee Plantation House. The anchorage is eight to ten feet deep, shoaling toward the shore. The holding can be tricky in hard sand. Sometimes this is a beautiful spot, calm as a lake, the water decorated with floating pink blossoms from the white cedar trees that line the shore. Yet in times of northerly swells it can be untenable.

ADMIRALTY BAY

Tony Gibbon's Beach and Lower Bay are picturesque anchorages with good holding in sand, but they become very rolly in northerly swells, when landing a dinghy can be hazardous.

Regulations

Port Elizabeth is a port of entry. Customs and immigration are both in one building, along with the Post Office, right behind the ferry dock. Lines are occasionally long. Customs are open 0900-1500. There is a five-knot speed limit in the harbor. This applies to dinghies, tenders and water taxis as well as yachts and ships. If you need to speed into town, do so only in the main shipping channel in the center of the harbor. Currently fast small boats are the most

serious danger to life and limb in this harbor. We have already had one death and several maiming accidents. Is five minutes worth it?

Services

Bequia Marina [T:458-3272, VFH:68, cc:V], is now under new management. The docks have been repaired and expansion is planned. You can pull alongside to take on water, diesel and cube ice, or to get your laundry done. Showers are available and there is room for a couple of boats stern-to with shore power. There are also a few moorings available for rent.

An easy way to get fuel and water is to call Daffodil Marine Services [VHF:68] which will deliver it alongside in a mobile service station. The water they sell comes from their own large desalinization plant.

You can also get diesel and gasoline at the Shell station in town.

There is an over-worked garbage collection point near the head of the dinghy dock. Never accept offers from local youths to "take your garbage."

There are two places for sorting out your

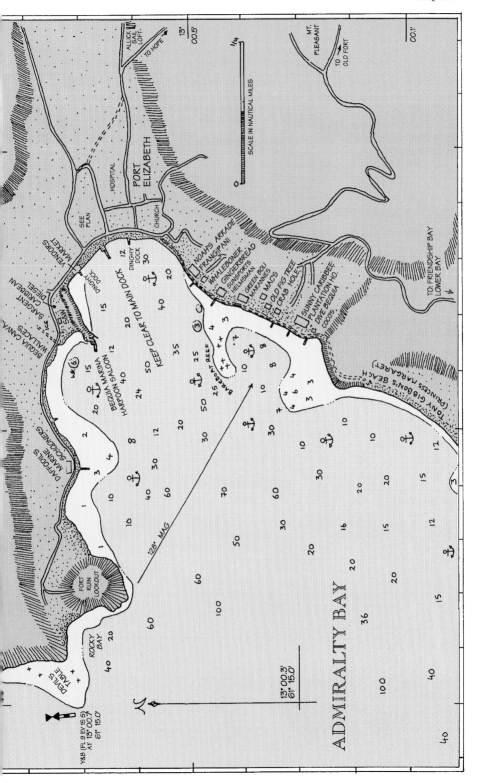

ADMIRALTY BAY

186

mechanical problems. Tyrone Caesar at Caribbean Diesel [T:458-3191, 457-3201, F:457-3203, VHF:68] is a first rate diesel mechanic. He spent nine years as an engineer on large cargo carriers, then several more working in Miami for many large organizations including Cummins. His experience covers all sizes of engine from giants to lightweights, and he knows Detroit Diesels, GM's, Perkins and Yanmar particularly well. He can bring in most parts in three days. Tyrone is good at basic electrical trouble shooting, and knows

when to pass the job on. He can also arrange for refrigeration repairs.

Grenadine Yacht Equipment (GYE), along with Peter from Fredag, now offer a full repair facility for any boat problems, from a clogged head to a broken engine. Peter (who can also be reached on VHF: 16 "Fredag") sailed here from Norway with his wife Maryanne on Fredag, a large boat they built themselves. After years of adventure and misadventure, including a sinking and dismasting, Peter seems to have found his metier fixing other people's problems

rather than sailing into his own. He has a first rate small work shop with a lathe at GYE and can do light machine work. He deals with all kinds of mechanical and electrical problems and he can bring in parts for Perkins and Bourgwarner within a few days. Peter handles breakdowns for many charter companies, including The Moorings and Stardust.

Nowhere in the Caribbean is better than Bequia for getting laundry done. One call on the radio [VHF:68] brings a rapid collection service to your yacht and same-day delivery at fair prices. There are two companies offering this service: Daffodil Marine and The Lighthouse. Both have water taxis and also deliver ice, beers, soft drinks or whatever else you need. In addition, The Lighthouse [T:458-3084, VHF:68] has a land taxi, offers showers by their office and has an apartment to rent. Daffodil Marine Services [T:458-3942, F:458-3369, VHF:68] offers water and fuel delivered to your yacht. They also have a carpentry and mechanical shop, send faxes, and sell duty free Carib dinghies. A new deli style mini-mart is planned where you can cart all your shopping directly to the dinghy dock. They will carry a full range of groceries, wines, beers and soft drinks.

Block ice is also available from Grenadines Yacht Equipment (GYE), The Old Fig Tree and the Gooding's house behind Bequia Marina. Cube ice may be found in the Shoreline Mini-market, Kingfisher Cafe, and the Frangipani.

There is a travel agency at the Gingerbread called Grenadine Travel [T:458-3795, F:458-3775, VHF:16,68, cc:V,A].

David de Lloyd's Bosun's Locker [T:458-3246/3634, F:458-3925, cc:V] is a fine chandlery where you can buy most items duty free. It is the sole agent for Simpson Lawrence and has a good line of their manual and electric windlasses. David also sells Avon inflatables, wind generators, toilets, stoves, Seagull outboards and spares. He has a good stock of Blake and other paints, along with rope, anchors, chain, bilge pumps, spares, resins, rigging, stainless hardware, and all the usual yacht necessities, including Admi-

188

ralty Charts. He also carries nautical gifts. GYE [T:458-3347, F:458-3696, VHF:16,68] is the sales and service agent for Evinrude outboards, along with all the accessories. (They can also repair other outboards.) GYE can fill your gas bottles (including French ones) and have an excellent stock of brass pipe fittings, stainless steel hardware, rigging wire, rope, epoxy, marine ply and Danforth anchors. You can send a fax here or make a photocopy. Owners Daniel and Missy Foulon speak French, Dutch and English.

The new Bequia Marine Supply [T:457-3157] is in Bequia Marina. It is a full sales and service agent for Mariner Outboards and carries a range of regular chandlery gear, including guides, charts, flags, resins, paints, cleaners and some hardware.

There are several places for sail and canvas work. Allick [T:458-3992, VHF:68] is up the hill behind town. He is local, low key, personable, thorough and reasonably priced. He nearly always has the materials on hand for repair jobs, and you can ask him about new sails, awnings, cushions and covers. Jobs can be dropped off at Daffodil Marine Services.

Bequia Canvas [T:458-3369, VHF:68] does just about everything but sails – interior and exterior cushions, awnings, covers, even tote bags. It is an efficient operation run by Carol Farrington from the U.S. They keep a wide range of materials, including closed-cell foam. You can go to their shop in Wallace's fishing tackle store behind Bequia Marina, or if you call them on the radio, Carol will come to your yacht to discuss the job.

There is a new North Sails agent in Bequia [T:457-3213, VHF:68] run by Richard from France. They are hooked right into the big North organization and you can order your new North Sails here and get quick computerized quotes. They also handle repairs and do canvas work. Richard also offers a complete spar and rigging shop. He can solve all your problems and doesn't mind working up at the top of your mast. Should you have the bad luck to be dismasted, he can arrange a whole new rig in as little as 10 days if everything goes smoothly. Richard is agent for Profurl and Harken and installs many of these systems.

Bequia also has many shipwrights and carpenters.

Frangipani Yacht Services [Box 1, Bequia, St. Vincent, W.I., T:458-3244, F:458-3824, VHF:68] are open weekdays from 0830 to 1300 and 1400 to 1700. They offer a mail drop, telephone, fax, telex, send cables and will help in any way they can. You can have mail sent here.

Sam Taxi Tours [T:458-3686, F:458-3427, VHF:68] opens occasionally in Bequia to offer a full communications service, photocopy machine, and will make airline reconfirmations.

What better way to see the island than by pedal or motor bike? Andrew Mitchell's Handy Andy [T:458-3370] rents these as well as running a laundry. Andrew is also a professional yacht refinisher and you can arrange anything from a full awl-grip spray job to fixing up your teak decks.

Taxis in Bequia are inexpensive and sight seeing in Bequia is highly recommended.

Gideon has three taxis, runs a good operation and is always listening to VHF:68, as are Lighthouse Taxi, Noel, Ricky, Pikie, and Donovan.

Ashore

Nowadays Bequia has become quite a good place to stock up on provisions. Small supermarkets include S&W [T:458-3447], Knights [T:458-3379], and Shoreline [T:458-3458, VHF:68]. Between them they should serve most of your needs. A big improvement in Bequia is having several small delicatessen type shops. Doris Fresh Food [T:458-3625, VHF:68,16] and Dieter's Deli [T:457-3213, VHF:68] were once one, and have now split into two, side by side. Between them you will find excellent meat, cheese, wine, local chutney, gourmet items, including Villamar's smoked fish, and some fresh produce. In addition Deiter's does hearty Russian bread, popular with those setting out to sea and Doris does French bread.

Joan, right opposite Doris, is my favorite supplier of fruits and vegetables. She is

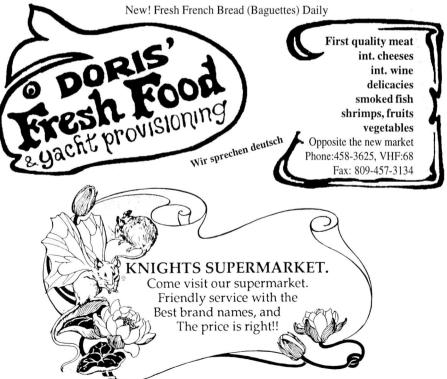

always there with a good selection and a friendly welcome and the prices are always fair. You can also buy fruit and vegetables in the new market block. Stalls have also opened along the waterfront toward Barclays Bank which are handy if you are at that end of town.

Few people realize that Daphne bakes her own bread, as does Mac's Pizzeria, Kingfisher Cafe and The Harpoon Saloon. You can also get good bread in the supermarkets. The Whaleboner sells yogurt and fresh milk from their own cows, as well as bread and cookies. The Gingerbread Coffee shop has baked goods, coffee, wine, caviar and gourmet items. Maranne's has yogurt and gourmet ice cream.

The waterfront in Port Elizabeth is colorful, with vendors selling t-shirts, model boats and handicrafts. Here you may see Baillar, a French Canadian artist, who now lives in Bequia and often sits in the square doing instant portraits or seascapes.

Bequia has a large range of small, pleasant boutiques. The new market has its own dinghy dock and long term plans include a small marina. Many shops here sell t-shirts and gifts and there is an ice cream shop and a bar.

The building of model boats is a Bequia specialty and you can find them at Mauvin's [T:458-3669] near the market (look also for Laura's handpainted shirts or Sergeant's [T:458-3344], toward Bequia Marina. They will build to order but my favorites are the model whaling boats. You will find attractive local handmade clothing in Daphne's Restaurant where she does her own hand screening.

In the new Shoreline Plaza there is a bakery, bank, stationery store, Baby Things, video rental shop, drug store (non prescription), The Wine Rack [T:458-3777, cc:V], for wine and liquors, and the Potpourri shop which sells the New York Times. The boutique 96 Degrees in the Shade [T:458-3118, cc:A,V,Ds] sells elegant hand painted and batik wear.

On Back Street next to Petit Jardin is the Vinsure building which houses Sam Taxi Service.

Solana's [T:458-3554, cc:V,A] has a

Yacht
Communications
Service

Phone: 809-458-3244
Fax: 809-458-3824
VHF:68

Hotel, Restaurant, Bar,
P.O. Box 1, Bequia,
St. Vincent Grenadines, West Indies.
Phone:809-458-3255. Fax:809-458-3824
**Don't miss our famous barbecue & Jump
up Thursday nights**

Dieter's Delicatessen
Deútscher Käse - & Saftladen
Fleisch, Wein & Volkorn Brot
Vhf:68
Phone(809) 457-3213

large collection of hand painted t-shirts, shorts and batik work, also handicrafts, film, jewelry, books, videos, flags, phone cards and maps. Solana's is also the Federal Express agent. Creative Universe [cc:A,V] has jewelry, t-shirts and film. The Almond Tree Boutique [T:458-3889, cc:V] sells clothing and souvenir items.

Do not miss the Bequia Bookshop [T:458-3905, cc:V] which has an excellent range of nautical books and charts, local books, videos and novels. They also sell film, postcards, local art and locally handcrafted scrimshaw. There are some seats outside the store in a shaded patio. From time to time the Bequia Bookshop brings in English newspapers. These are not for sale, but for customers to sit and enjoy.

A few steps back from the church you will find Island Things [T:458-3903, cc:V], with a wide range of clothing and souvenirs, all locally made. Behind the church are the Lighthouse Laundry, The Patriot hair dressing shop for men and Lulley's Tackle Shop [T:458-3088, F:458-3797]. This is a new town branch of the oldest fishing shop in Bequia, with a really wide range, not only of fishing gear, but also ropes, snorkeling gear and knives.

In its spacious upstairs location, Local Color [T:458-3202, cc:V,A] is full of products from all over the Caribbean. There are many handicrafts and an even bigger range of clothing.

Melinda [T:458-3895, cc:A,V] is an artist and was the first in Bequia to hand paint t-shirts. She used to row around the harbor,

Bequia's most complete boutique. Beachware, casual clothing, t-shirts and gifts. Located next to Barclays Bank (upstairs). Major credit cards accepted.
Phone: 809-458-3202
Fax: 809-457-3071
Port Elizabeth, Bequia

accompanied by her pet Labrador, selling them to the yachts. Now Melinda is in her new boutique, where you will find Bequia's most elegantly hand painted t-shirts, with shorts, caps and visors to match. In addition there are silk pants and tops, semi-precious stone necklaces, hand painted masks and exotic odds and ends. Next door Sprotties [cc:A,V] specializes in silk screen clothing. The Garden [T:458-3892] has some pareos, batiks and long dresses.

As you wander toward the Frangipani on the waterfront track, you pass Noah's Arkade [T:458-3424, cc:V,A] which has a wide range of Caribbean crafts, spices, handicrafts and local books, as well as some casual wear.

Along the waterfront, the Whaleboner Boutique [T:458-3233, cc:V,A] offers hand made clothing from screened and batik fabrics and they also sell shorts and local model boats. Down at the Gingerbread you will find the Helmsman [cc:V] selling elegant swimwear and casual wear, including a range of brightly screened t-

shirts from Trinidad.

By the time you've seen all these shops and walked to the Green Boley you will probably need a break. Stop at Maranne's and try some of her famous gourmet ice cream, frozen yogurt or sorbet. Everything is home made from fresh ingredients with local fruit flavors, unobtainable elsewhere in the world. Right next door the Green Boley Boutique [T:458-3247, cc:A] has applique, locally made clothes and souvenirs.

No shopping trip would be complete without a visit to the Crab Hole [T:458-3290, cc:V,A] where they operate their own silk screen factory. You are welcome to visit the factory and see the process at work. In the shop you can choose from their fabrics and elegant casual wear with accessories to match.

You've been hanging a line over the stern for miles, but never have any luck? Get Wallace's [T:458-3360], near Bequia Marina, to recommend a lure, or sell you a made up rig. Steadman Wallace has always given good fishing advice, and has turned

many no-luckers into happy anglers. Jergen, a long time Bequia visitor, may soon take over this shop. He knows the business well, and Steadman will not be far away. You will also find some rope and if you need to freshen up your reading matter, the Wallaces keep a book swap here. The price of using this is to make a small contribution to the Sunshine School for disabled kids.

Bequia has lovely walks. You can follow the path from the Sunny Caribbee over to Tony Gibbons Beach and on down to Lower Bay. If you laze on the beach and swim, keep an eye on your handbags and cameras. Don't set them down and wander away, as they too have been known to walk.

Watch a sunset from Mount Pleasant, walk to Friendship Bay, Spring or Industry for lunch or dinner and enjoy the great variety of views along the way. Spring makes an especially good destination on a Sunday when they have their famous curry lunch. One can hike to Hope, a lovely remote beach where the shallow water sets up long lines of breakers often suitable for

body surfing (watch the undertow). Those on limited time or who don't like hiking should take a taxi tour. The taxi drivers are proud of their island, and will take you to all the best and most scenic spots in a leisurely 3-hour tour. Each place you visit seems so different, sometimes Bequia feels like several islands in one. Highlights include an old fort looking over the harbor; Bequia's summit, Mount Pleasant, with a stop at The Old Fort bar and restaurant; the beautiful windward beach of Spring and a visit to the home of Athneal Olliviere, the island's head whale harpooner, who has a small whaling museum.

If you just want to visit Spring, Friendship or Lower Bay, hop on a taxi – the island is small so the fares are reasonable.

Tennis courts are available at Spring, Friendship Bay, the Plantation House and Sunsports. If you come at Easter you can get involved in the Bequia Regatta, a four-day extravaganza of local boat races, yacht races and lots of partying. Christmas is also a popular time in Bequia, but "9 Mornings" which starts some two weeks before Christ-

mas, can make the town anchorage throb with disco music through the night.

The waterfront offers a wonderful mixture of bars and restaurants. The Frangipani Hotel [T:458-3255, $B, cc:A,V, closed September] is owned by Son Mitchell, the prime minister of St. Vincent and the Grenadines, and has been in his family since the turn of the century. The upper floor of the main building used to be the family home and downstairs was the storehouse for the Glorea Colita, which, at 131 feet long, was the largest schooner ever to be built in Bequia. In 1940 she disappeared and was found drifting empty in the Bermuda triangle. Today the Frangipani is ably managed by Marie. By day it is a good place to meet people and enjoy a great fresh tuna sandwich for lunch. By night they offer romantic candlelight dinners of Caribbean specialties. Everyone comes by on a Thursday night when they have a barbecue and jump up to a steel band. They also have a string band on Mondays in season.

The most sociable and entertaining evening rendezvous is at Pat Mitchell's

Gingerbread [T:458-3800, VFH:68, $B-C cc:V,A,]. The impressive Caribbean style building features highly intricate gingerbread trim and an immensely high wooden roof supported by mast-like poles. The spacious upstairs dining room has a grand harbor view and comfortable seats. The atmosphere is enlivened by a string band on Wednesdays, Fridays and Sundays. The food is delicious, with curries a speciality. Reservations are advisable in season. You can also stop in for an after dinner drink and enjoy a tune from De Real Ting string band. The Gingerbread is also open for breakfast. At lunchtime you can get soups, salads and sandwiches upstairs or barbecue items outside under the trees downstairs. The coffee shop offers coffee and baked goodies.

Another place for those who enjoy entertainment is the Harpoon Saloon (T:458 3272, VHF:68, $B-C, cc:V), now under the new management of Noel Frazer, a Vincentian with years of hotel experience in the U.S. and St. Vincent. He has a steel band on Tuesdays and Saturdays, and a daily happy hour from 1700-1800. The wide-ranging menu has a good selection of items from land and sea.

Mac's Pizzeria [T:458-3474, VHF:68, $C-D] is a favorite haunt for yachtsmen. They offer pizzas, quiches, salads and delicious goodies from their bakeshop, along with occasional specials. The atmosphere is congenial, the food first class and inexpensive enough that you can gravitate here any time you do not feel like cooking. In season it is advisable to make a reservation to avoid a long wait.

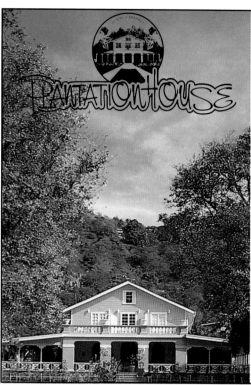

There are plenty of first rate places to get inexpensive local food. The Old Fig Tree [T:458-3201, VHF:68, $C-D] is right on the water overlooking the harbor. In times of northerly swells this part of the harbor seems to attract the biggest waves. During a hurricane the building nearly went into the sea, but was saved by the huge "Old Fig Tree" that gives it its name. Bryn Willer has now taken over this establishment. Bryn has been in the Caribbean for some 20 years, including a stint as part of The Moorings management team. Bryn's lunch menu includes rotis and local dishes, and in the evening she offers a wide range of food with many daily specials. These include a variety of dishes from places like China, Italy and Mexico, as well as local seafood. Bryn plans to run a small mini-mart which will offer frozen entrees to ease the cook's life at sea.

Noeline Taylor's Porthole [T:458-3458, VHF:68, $C-D] is a popular meeting place for a lunch roti. She also cooks dinner. Walk in for her famous fish and chips.

If you have time to plan a little ahead, call Daphne's [T:458-3271, VHF:68, $C] and discuss a special local meal with Daphne Grant, one of Bequia's really good local cooks whose meals have an individual flair. Daphne's is more like a private house than a restaurant and a great place to go in a small group.

The Hinkson's Whaleboner [T:458-3233, $C-D, cc:V,A] is conveniently situated next to the Frangipani and has its own dinghy dock. Much of the food comes from their farm so you know it is fresh. True to its name, the bar, stools and entrance have all been built of whalebone from the old whaling days. Angela will cook good snacks, pizzas, chicken and fish. They also do full evening meals at a reasonable price, including curried and roast pork. In both cases the meat comes from their own hand raised animals. Chicken and fish are always available, as is lobster in season.

Other local restaurants include the Lyston Williams' Green Boley [T:458-3247, $D], good for rotis and snacks and Isola McIntosh's Julie's Guest House [T:458-3304, VHF:68, $C] where advance

GOURMET FRENCH CUISINE
Daily Menu or A la Carte

Seafood is our specialty. We also offer first quality meat and poultry.

Relax on the terrace among the local fruits and flowers and watch your cares drift away!

Open: 11:30 am - 2 pm, 6:30 pm - 9:30 pm
For reservations: VHF:68, Tel:(809) 458-3318,
Fax: 457-3134. Back Street, Port Elizabeth, Bequia

booking is necessary. Yachties on a budget will appreciate the low prices for fried chicken and fish at the S & W snack bar [$D], upstairs over their supermarket. The Kingfisher Cafe near the town dinghy dock offers pastry, snacks and local fruit juices.

For upscale gourmet cooking visit Le Petit Jardin [T:458-3318, VHF:16,68, $B, cc:V], owned by Owen Belmar from Bequia. Owen has returned to his native Bequia after years as a chef on huge corporate charter yachts. He studied at the Culinary Institute in the U.S., but his ability to produce wonderful melt-in-the-mouth delicacies to rival any French chef is unquestionably a gift. The food is served in an appropriately quiet, simple and slightly formal setting in a house of natural stone and varnished wood, which has a garden of herbs and fruit trees. Le Petit Jardin is open for both lunch and dinner. Reservations are advisable.

The Sunny Caribbee Plantation House [T:458-3425, F:458-3612, VHF:68, $A-B, cc:V,A] is a gracious hotel in traditional Caribbean style surrounded by lawns and palm trees. A wide veranda forms the dining room, and you can relax in comfortable chairs. It is open for breakfast, lunch and elegant evening meals. They have a top-rated Italian chef, and they sometimes offer theme nights based on a different country or place. Although the restaurant is fancy, the manager Marcel likes yachting customers and will accept those who come in shorts, and they try to keep at least one dish at a reasonable price. When space is available, the hotel offers very substantial discounts to yachtsmen who want a night ashore. Their beach bar, Coco's, is another great place for a sundowner. Happy hour is nightly from 1800-1900, and musical entertainment is sometimes available. Coco's is also a good place for lunch when they get a big barbecue going.

Schooners [T:458-3658, VHF:68, $C] is the local hangout for those anchored on the north side of the harbor. It has a big balcony offering a commanding view of the harbor. Locals and yachting folk gather for happy hour from 1730-1830. There are several dishes on the menu every night, and snacks

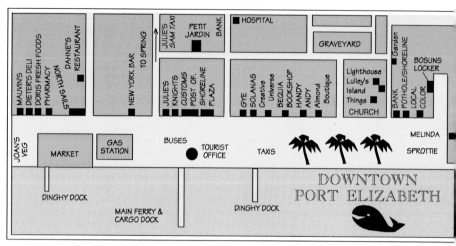

DOWNTOWN PORT ELIZABETH

are available if you ask. Schooners is also open for lunch, and they offer take-out frozen meals for yachts.

These are just the restaurants in town. There are also good restaurants in other places, and taxi fares are reasonable ($12-20 EC).

Spring on Bequia [T:458-3414, VHF:68, $B, cc:A,V], is both a hotel and a working estate and they grow most of their own produce. They are open from about November till June and are famous as a peaceful hideaway resort. Candy, the owner, works on the menus and they have a reputation for delicious food but you must call them up and book in advance. (If you cannot get them on VHF:68, ask a Bequia taxi to relay for you.) It is a pleasant walk, about a mile, in the cool of the evening to work up your appetite for dinner. Spring on Bequia is also famous for Sunday curry lunches, and during the season they run a beach bar on Spring Beach.

The Old Fort [T:458-3440, VHF:68,73 $A, cc:V,] is built on the ruins of an ancient fortified estate house up in the cool hills of Mt. Pleasant. Run by Germans Sonja and Otmar Schaedle, its wonderful views make it a good destination for hikers by day. At night atmosphere is their strong point with a fire in the dining room hearth where they serve a five-course set dinner. Call on the VHF before midday to make reservations.

Lower Bay has one of Bequia's best beaches, set in a low key rural atmosphere of fishing boats and strung out nets. Great for swimming by day and romantic on a full moon night, it is a popular place to hang out, especially on Sunday. Recently people have begun to gravitate there of an evening for inexpensive seafood dinners. Lower Bay makes an acceptable anchorage in settled conditions and is within dinghy reach of Admiralty Bay. However, there is usually enough swell to make landing on the beach a damp affair, so it is better to

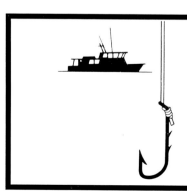

take a cab over ($12-15EC). By day it is interesting to follow the track from the Sunny Caribbee over the bluff to Tony Gibbon's Beach, then over the next bluff to Lower Bay. Once you arrive there are four local restaurants to choose from. Keegan's [T:458-3530, VHF:68, $C-D], opposite the beach, offers inexpensive three course dinners, featuring chicken, shrimp, fish or conch. By day they do fish or chicken'n chips and snacks. De Reef [T:457-3104, VHF:68, $C-D], right on the beach, is popular for lunch, and a gathering place for locals on Sundays. You can get chicken, fish or sandwiches any day of the week. By night they offer three course dinners by reservation and every other Friday in season they put on a seafood buffet dinner with a band.

Theresa's [T:458-3802, VHF:68, $C, reservations essential], just back from the beach, is a cutely converted little rum shop and a favorite watering hole for expatriates and holiday returnees. Monday nights Englishman John Bennett serves food from far away places such as Italy, Mexico,

China, or India. During the rest of the week his partner, Theresa, creates a splendid West Indian buffet. They also open at lunchtime for sandwiches and first rate hamburgers. Dawn's Creole [T:458-3154 VHF:68, $C] has a special kind of enchantment. It is up a steep driveway at the end of nowhere where one sits amid flowers and trees overlooking the sea in a perfect secret hideaway. Wander up for lunch or a snack

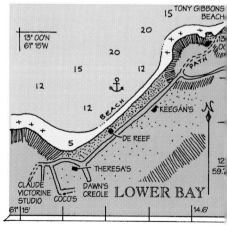

202

or try one of their full creole meals in the evening, including meat, fish and conch. They also make a wonderful thick "goat water" stew with all the local vegetables. There are only five tables so dinner reservations are essential. Dawn's Creole has a few hideaway rooms and the view from some are unbeatable.

Coco's Place [T:458-3463, VHF:68] right next to Dawn's will be in operation by the time this guide comes out. They plan inexpensive Bequia food and a pub style, friendly atmosphere. There will be a cable TV for those big games you just cannot miss.

While you are in Lower Bay, visit the home of French artist Claude Victorine [T:458-3150, VHF:16 "Pigeon"], whose work is displayed along with that of her daughter, Louloune. Both are exceptionally talented. Louloune does both realistic paintings and intricate weavings of imagination and dreams. Claude's main medium is painting on silk and she creates superb cushion covers, wall hangings and fabrics which are guaranteed to add a touch of class to any boat or home. Claude accepts visitors in the afternoons, and the sight of her pretty little house perched up in the hills is well worth the walk. She sometimes closes on Fridays.

Water sports

Sailboarding enthusiasts should check with Paradise Windsurfing at the Plantation House or at Friendship Bay. Basil, an accredited instructor, will teach you how to windsurf, or if you already know, you can rent a board for the afternoon, or take one along with you for your cruise.

Diving in Bequia is superb and not to be missed by scuba fans. For the uninitiated it is an ideal place for a resort course. There are two shops to choose from.

At the Sunny Caribbee Bob Sachs is one of scuba's greatest enthusiasts and Bequia's most experienced diver. He and his team of assistants have a flair for running groups that are always friendly and sociable. Call Dive Bequia [T:458-3504, F:458-3886, VHF:68,16, cc:V] and Bob or his manager Kristina will arrange to collect you from your yacht. Return to the bar later to socialize with them and other divers. Their seaworthy new dive boats allow for occasional diving and exploring trips up to the Falls of Baleine in St. Vincent or down to the Grenadines.

Dive Bequia also works with Dive St. Vincent and Grenadine Divers, so you can set up dive packages valid in all their locations or start a full certification course in one place and continue it through the others.

Sunsports [T:458-3577, F:458-3907, VHF:68, cc:V] is run by Bob Monnens from Minnesota. Bob is friendly, keen and experienced and likes to work with small groups – never more than eight divers on a trip. He enjoys night diving and will go to the more distant dive sites even for one person. The Sunsports retail shop has a good selection of fins, masks, dive books and accessories. Call Bob to arrange to be collected from your yacht.

For those diving on their own, the most accessible good dives are around Devil's Table. There is a pretty reef extending from the black and yellow beacon to the shore.

There are moorings so you can tie up your dinghy. From the shallow inshore end you can dive out along one side of the rocky shoal, and back on the other. The depth at the outer end of the reef is about 65 feet. There are plenty of different corals and reef fish. Sergeant majors may often be seen guarding their eggs. An even prettier dive is along the stretch of coast from inside this reef northwards to Northwest Point. There is a sloping reef all along this shore. The maximum depth is about 60 feet at Northwest Point. Coral formations include lots of pillar coral, and there are usually large schools of blue chromis. Over the sand garden eels undulate. On both dives you must mind the current.

The more exciting dives are a long way from the anchorage. There is usually a lot of current, so they are best done as drift dives and are most easily accessible by dive boat. The Boulders is a superb drift dive about two-thirds of the way between Admiralty Bay and Moonhole. A gentle descent 60 feet down a coral slope takes you into an area where hundreds of fish, including huge schools of blue chromis and sennets, make ever-changing patterns as you drift with the current. Barracudas patrol up and down; moray eels, lobsters, crabs and shrimps can be found. The reef gets deeper till you come to the boulders, which are tall rock formations, each about 20 feet high, starting from a bottom depth of 93 feet. There are tunnels to pass through and holes and caverns which provide hiding places for nurse sharks, groupers, angelfish and jacks. As you return to the dive boat, you may see a frogfish or seahorse.

Pigeon Island is an outstanding dive area. The island slopes off steeply to around 100 feet. There are walls, overhangs, rifts and hollows decorated by deepwater lace coral. The visibility is generally excellent and you will see huge schools of blue and brown chromis, big groupers, passing pelagic fish and sometimes rays and turtles.

Flat Rock Drift Dive is on Bequia's northwest coast, starting at the western end of Anse Chemin. This is a gentle easy dive where you hardly have to use your fins and

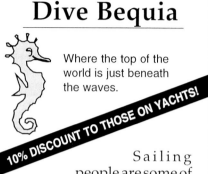
there is time to examine all the little creatures on the way. You swim along a captivating reef which slopes gently into sand at 60 feet. It offers an excellent selection of soft and hard corals, lots of fish, arrow crabs, lobsters, tube worms and anemones. A couple of spotted snake eels hang out here and one often sees a ray.

The Wall (West Cay, northern side) is an adventure dive to 114 feet, with dramatic vistas and the odd large pelagic. Moonhole (outside the Moonhole complex) offers temporary anchorage, though I would leave a crew member on board. The easiest dive is to start right in the bay and follow the reef round the point to the east, watching for currents. This is a gentle dive to 60 feet with hard and soft corals and a variety of smaller fish.

The snorkeling is good around Devil's Table and along the coast to Northwest Point. Both dive shops also offer snorkeling trips.

MOONHOLE TO FRIENDSHIP BAY

If you are sailing from Admiralty Bay to West Cay, you will undoubtedly catch sight of Moonhole. This rather isolated community, where American architect Tom Johnson is king, is not easily accessible by either land or sea, there being no road or good anchorage. Moonhole houses are certainly different; the original was built under a natural arch known as "Moonhole" – it was abandoned when a huge boulder fell from the ceiling and threatened to crush the bed. The other houses grow out of the rocks without straight lines or right angles. They have huge arches, fantastic views and lovely patios. There is seldom glass in the windows and the breeze is constant; there is no electricity. Moonhole is a special kind of vacation home for the right people. The architecture is worth marveling at as you sail by. Although Moonhole (T:458-3277,

VHF:06) is a very private place, Jim and Sheena Johnson do now offer tours (about $40 EC) on Tuesday afternoons. They can also arrange tours on other days for groups of six or so (all tours are by prior arrangement only). A tour lasts an hour or two and takes you through several houses. (They select ones which are empty at the time.) You also get to visit the original Moonhole and finish at their bar overlooking the sea, where you have time for a drink before going back. It is probably easiest to get to Moonhole by taxi, but the intrepid can dinghy down if there are no northerly swells. Landing takes some agility.

Bequia's new airport is built along the south coast. There is a dock about a third of a mile to its east off Paget Farm where you can get ashore from a tenable, if rolly, anchorage.

FRIENDSHIP BAY AND PETIT NEVIS

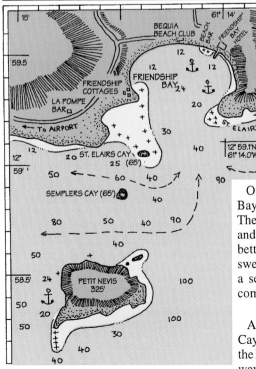

On the south side of Bequia, Friendship Bay is gorgeous, with a lovely white beach. The anchorage is secure with good holding and in times of northerly swells it offers better protection than Admiralty Bay. A swell often creeps in from the southeast so a second anchor from the stern to keep comfortable is advised.

Navigation

A reef extends from the shore to St. Elairs Cay and beyond. On the opposite side of the harbor there is a reef extending out a fair way from St. Elairs Point (locally called

FRIENDSHIP BAY WITH SEMPLERS AND ST. ELAIRS CAYS IN FOREGR(

"Hillary"). Keep in the center of the channel. Once inside, pick up a hotel mooring or anchor to the east of the bay or off the Friendship Bay Beach Bar. Note that a reef extends from the west side of the Friendship Bay Hotel dock to a small breakwater near the beach bar.

Ashore

The Friendship Bay Resort [T:458-3222, F:458-3840, VHF:68, $A-B, cc:A,V] has the air of a rather grand hotel, with lovely gardens and a cute "swing seat" beach bar called Herby 'n' Spicy. Cocktails, lunch and informal dinners are served here and as an alternative there is a panoramic glass-lined dining room. The view of Petit Nevis and Isle de Quatre is spectacular. It is run by Swedes Lars and Margit Abrahamson and Ulf Nohlas. They have a dock where you can come stern-to to take water when it is available. They offer telephone and fax communications and they sell cube ice and bread. They have several moorings for complimentary use by customers. The food is excellent; a blend of Swedish, French and local flavors with plenty of seafood and lobster in season. On Saturday night musical entertainment is often provided. Sandwiches and light lunches are available in the bar and are excellent value. Their lobster salad is great.

You can work off the calories on their tennis court or underwater with their dive shop. A boutique is planned next to the beach bar. Special rates for yachtspeople are available when there are vacancies.

Just down the beach, the Bequia Beach Club [T:458-3248, VHF:16, $B-C, cc:V,A] offers beach-side dining with local and continental food. They have a barbecue on Mondays with entertainment. Lunch time snacks are available and there is a scuba shop.

Over near Friendship Cottages, La Pompe International Bar has a good selection of basic groceries, a pool table, Sunday evening videos and the world's hottest domino tournament. This is the place to meet the local fishermen and whalers.

Water sports

The snorkeling is worth a go in Friendship Bay, both along the shore between the Friendship Bay Resort dock and Herby 'n Spicy beach bar, also between St. Elairs Cay and the shore. Both Friendship Bay Hotel and Bequia Beach Club have dive shops.

Petit Nevis

Petit Nevis makes an interesting daytime anchorage. The snorkeling along the shore is good (out of the lee the current gets strong) and the whale rendering facilities make interesting exploring. If passing southwards, note the long southerly reef.

MUSTIQUE

Regulations

Yachts do not often clear in or out of Mustique, but it can be done. Customs and immigration will be found at the airport.

Jet skis and the like are strictly forbidden, as is spearfishing and anchoring on coral.

Vessels carrying more than 25 passengers are not allowed in Mustique.

Shopping Hours

General store: weekdays 0800-1300, 1500-1800. Boutiques 0900-1200 and 1400-1800. Treasure boutique opens Sunday mornings.

Holidays

See St. Vincent.

Telephones

Calls can be made from the Mustique Co. office. See also St. Vincent.

Transport

Rental jeeps and motor bikes are available (see text). You need a local license which costs $30 EC. Drive on the left.

Mustique is unique among the Grenadines. It is a privately owned island that has been developed as an area of holiday homes for the ultra-rich. Mansions with tennis courts and swimming pools sit on rolling grassy hills and long lawns stretch to sandy beaches. Each house lies in spacious grounds; there are only about 80 on the whole island, plus one hotel, one beach bar, three boutiques, a small local village and a fishing camp. A roll call of property owners reveals some glamorous names, including Princess Margaret, Mick Jagger, David Bowie, and Raquel Welch. Parts of the island are wild; other areas are well tended. About half the houses are available for rent as holiday homes when the owners are not in residence. Many older homes were designed by Oliver Messel and are delightful to look at, with a showy but dignified appeal.

Montezuma Shoal is about half to three quarters of a mile west of Britannia Bay (called Grand Bay on some charts). It presents a real hazard and has ground pieces off the hulls of a cruise ship, a large charter yacht and many a bareboat. It is currently marked by a red and black striped beacon placed on the reef. Stay at least a quarter of a mile away. (If you can see the colors you are probably too close.) If you come from the south, do not follow the coast too closely as there is also quite a reef extending seaward from the southern point of Britannia Bay.

The only acceptable anchorage is in Britannia Bay. The Mustique Company has put down 18 moorings for medium sized yachts which you should use if possible (there is no charge for them at this time). You have to attach your own line to the top of the buoy. Leave as much scope as possible so you do not over-strain the mooring. Snorkel to check the condition of the chain.

If they are all taken, you can try to find a spot between them, or anchor to their west. Do not anchor to the south of the moorings as you are in danger of anchoring on the reef which is protected by law. There are large fines for damaging it. Leave a clear channel to the main dock for the Mustique cargo vessel.

The water is sparkling clear and this is a lovely area to snorkel over. The anchorage is generally rather rolly.

Services

It is possible to make phone calls from the Mustique Company office by the airport. You can buy ice at Johanna's Banana. Call Basil's Bar on VHF:68 about the possibility of a taxi. There is a garbage disposal. Wrap it well.

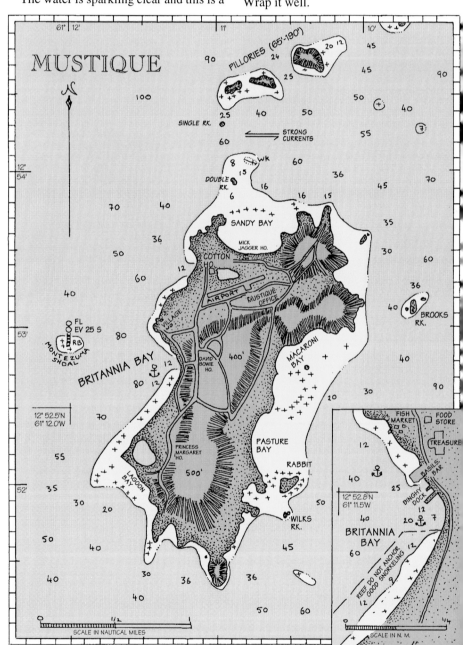

VIEW SOUTH FROM MUSTIQUE

Ashore

You will find a small supermarket ashore and in the fishing village on the waterfront there is a fish market where you can buy fresh fish and lobster in season. Basil plans to sell delicatessen items.

A good reason to step ashore is to visit Johanna Morris's little group of shops: Treasure, Johanna's Banana and Treasure Fashion. Treasure [T:456-3521, cc:V,A] has a delightful collection of clothes and toys, including casual wear and swim suits, featuring makes like Gottex and Jams. Plenty of hats, shoes, snorkeling gear, sunblocks and cosmetics are here, as are local books, film, maps, games and gifts of every description. There is also a wonderful collection of toys, from kites and teddy bears to endearing windup farm animals.

Treasure Fashion [T:458-4621 ext:522, cc:A,V] specializes in elegant and exotic clothing for both men and women. It has everything from bathing suits to long evening dresses. Men's clothing includes smart casual wear by Tommy Hilfiger, and for the women the wide range includes La Pearla Italian linen clothing.

Johanna's Banana is a coffee shop where you sit outside under big sunshades and watch the boats come and go. Between boats you can catch up on the news with the current U.K. newspapers Johanna keeps on hand for customers. They serve fresh Italian espresso coffee, fresh fruit juices, ice cream, frozen yogurt and delicious home-baked treats, including coconut tarts, pain au chocolat and croissants. Lunch time sandwiches are planned.

Basil's also has two shops. Basil's Boutique is over in Basil's Bar, and Across Forever, on the other side of the road, is an antique and collectibles shop. Basil travels to far eastern ports and brings back his favorite items for the shops.

Opening hours for the general store are weekdays 0800 to 1300, and 1500 to 1800. For the boutiques generally about 0900 to noon and 1500 to 1800. Most open Sunday mornings.

Mustique is well worth a tour on foot, by taxi, motor bike or horse. The latter two are probably the most enjoyable ways to see the island. Horse riding is done in the cool of the day either at 0800, 0900 or 1500 and 1600. Frances keeps her horses well trained and you can book through the Mustique Company [T:458-4621 ext:378, VHF:16, 68]. Mustique Mechanical Service (MMS) [T:458-4621, VHF:68] rents small motor bikes and jeeps, but these are often scarce at the height of the season. You will find the office over the hill to the north of Britannia Bay, near the gas station. You will have to buy a local license.

Martinique.

Mustique has wonderful walks and hikes with miles of unspoiled beaches and countryside. One easy walk is southwards from the anchorage to the beaches at Lagoon Bay.

Water sports

You can arrange to go sailboarding or diving with Lesley Dunning from New Zealand at Mustique Watersports [T:458-4621 ext 486, VHF:68,16, cc:A,V]. Lesley runs an excellent operation and is very personable. She will pick divers up from their yachts. The water is generally very clear and diving is pleasant.

Walk in Reef is just off the dive shop dock and ideal for beginners and those who haven't dived since last year. Afterwards try some of the more exciting dives:

South Britannia Drift Dive. Let the current carry you through this delightful garden of soft corals as you watch large schools of Bermuda chubs and creole wrasses. The occasional sight of an eagle ray makes it perfect.

The Wreck of the Jonas. The Jonas is a 90-foot dredge and it lies 40 feet deep on the east side of Montezuma Shoal. There are beautiful coral formations close to the wreck and barracudas and nurse sharks, as well as the usual reef fish.

South East Pillory Drift Dive. The current sweeps you along a steep slope which drops from 20 feet to 90 feet. The scenery is always changing as you go along, with lots of reef fish and large soft corals.

Dry Rock (south side of Petit Mustique). This is the place for the big fish; schools of barracudas, nurse sharks, turtles and rays.

Basil's Bar [T:458-4621, VHF:68, $A-B cc:A,V] is a thatch and bamboo structure perched on stilts over the water's edge. Wednesday night is a popular barbecue buffet night followed by a jump up.

For an elegant meal out, don your best evening pants or a dress and call The Cotton House [T:456-4777, F:456-5887, VHF:68, $A, cc:A,V]. It is about a 15 minute walk away, but if you make dinner reservations they are willing to come and get you (reservations are essential). The new manager, Warren Francis, is keen to attract yachtspeople. On Mondays, Wednesdays and Fridays between 1730 and 1930 they have sunset hour on the balcony at the main bar with two-for-one drinks. On Saturdays they have a beach barbecue with a band and on Tuesdays in season they sometimes have a creole buffet. During the day, their upstairs pool area, artistically surrounded by fake ruins, is a good watering hole.

The Cotton House also has its own Mill Boutique, run by Warren's wife Gilly. They stock elegant casual and beachwear, and a few gifts and gourmet items from

CANOUAN

(For customs, holidays and general information see St. Vincent.)

Canouan is an island of dumpy yellow and brown hills which turn green in the rainy season. The hiker will be rewarded by impressive views and lovely hidden beaches. There are a few hundred inhabitants, a handful of cars, including one or two taxis, and two major hotels. A large development has started in the northern part of Canouan and it may come to life soon.

Corbay and Rameau Bay are pleasant spots far from the rest of the island, though the new development may change this. You may have to try a couple of times to get the anchor well dug in, and the wind shifts around, so two anchors are advisable.

Charlestown Bay is the main anchorage

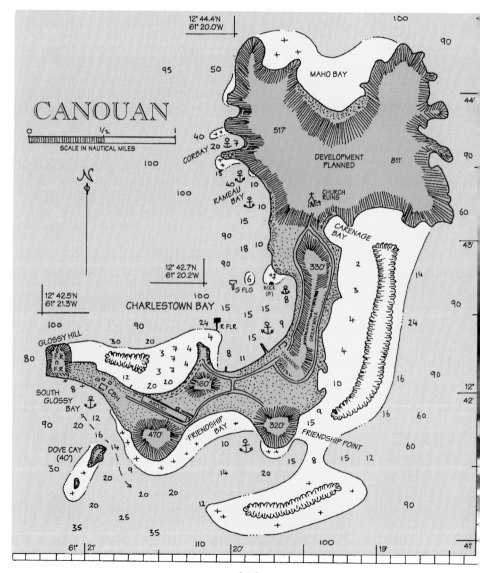

CANOUAN WITH YACHTS IN CHARLESTOWN BAY

and the entrance is marked by red and green beacons on either side. Pass between them. You can anchor anywhere in the bay. Some like to tuck up in the northern corner, others anchor off the Tamarind Bay Resort. This is a pleasant anchorage but northeasterly winds with northerly swells can make it uncomfortable. The wind tends to get held up in the hills and then shoots down from the north in intense gusts. There is a new large ferry dock off the beach and a small wooden dock in the southern part of the bay.

Ashore

You will find a few tiny shops selling corned beef, cooking margarine, rum, etc. If you run out of gasoline, go to the small wooden dock and raise the red flag outside the fuel shed. This should bring Mr. De Roche down the hill to sell you some.

The Tamarind Bay Resort is new and the first managers are a pleasant French couple. The restaurant will be open to passing yachts and a long dinghy dock is planned.

Villa La Bijou [T:458-8025, VHF:68] is a cute guest house and restaurant perched on top of the hill. It is sometimes open. Call before you hike up.

Just behind Tamarind Bay Resort is Yvonne and George's Anchor Guest House and Restaurant [T:458-8568, VHF:16, $C]. They will cook you a local meal if you give them a couple of hours' notice. Some rum shops in town serve fried chicken.

Other anchorages

There is a really rolly anchorage by the Canouan Beach Hotel in South Glossy Bay. The water here is gorgeous and so is the beach. I would recommend it for a lunch stop. There is a dinghy dock, which is perilous in swells, and currents make swimming ashore inadvisable.

Ashore

Canouan Beach Hotel (CBH) [T&F:458-8888, VHF:16, $A-B] is a classy French resort. They serve a great buffet lunch. This is also a good place for dinner, but you may want to anchor in Charlestown Bay and visit by cab. Yachtspeople are welcome but you must make a reservation and dress reasonably smartly. CBH can also occasionally

help with ice and they sometimes sell delicious bread.

Keen snorkelers might be interested in a daytime stop inside Friendship Point on Canouan's south coast. Approach past Glossy Bay, pass between Dove Cay and Canouan, and follow the coast, keeping a good look out for coral heads. In settled conditions you can dinghy up the windward side of Canouan inside the reefs where the snorkeling is excellent.

Water sports

There are a couple of good dives in Canouan and one often sees sharks, turtles and rays. Tony Alongi who runs Dive Canouan [T:458-8648, F:458-8875, VHF:68] is pleasant and puts himself out for yachting customers. He is based at the Canouan Beach Hotel. If you are anchored in Charlestown Bay, call him about coming to collect you for a dive.

For those diving on their own the easiest spot to anchor for a dive is in Corbay. Dive to seaward of the rocky headland on the northern side of the bay. You can also dinghy north up the coast and look for your own spot. Another good dive if you are anchored in South Glossy Bay is right around Glossy Hill. Watch out for currents. Snorkeling is good around the rocks in both Corbay and Rameau Bay.

FEEL REST ASSURED.

Experience the peace and tranquility of some of the beautiful ports and lagoons in the Caribbean and Tahiti, and feel rest assured that one of the largest yacht charter companies in the world is backing you up.

Tortola • St. Martin • Guadeloupe • Martinique • Union *(Grenadines)* • Tahiti

Bareboats and Crewed Yachts

2280 University Drive, Suite 102 • Newport Beach, California 92660 U.S.A.
(714) 650-0889 • FAX: (714) 642-1318

Call 1-800-634-8822 *US & Canada*

or contact your Yacht Charter Broker

formerly

SOUTHERN GRENADINES PASSAGES

From Canouan to Carriacou the Grenadines huddle together, each just a short hop from the next. The islands are generally small and very quiet.

Any island with a few inhabitants will also have a rum shop where you can meet people and learn to drink Jack Iron – a powerful, rough white rum, sometimes distilled far from government inspectors. A small shot is poured into a glass and the idea is to down it all in one gulp, preferably without tasting. Then you reach for a large glass of water to put out the fire.

Navigation

The current sets to the west most of the time, so head east of your destination until you have got the feel of its strength. The southern Grenadines are strewn with keel-hungry reefs. This is the area where people make the most mistakes and several yachts have been lost. Usually this is because people misidentify islands. If you approach this area with just a shade of apprehension and self-questioning, you should be okay.

A new series of navigational beacons is now in place. Most of them are on the edge of shoals so keep well clear.

Sailing south

When you round Glossy (Glass) Hill at Canouan, you must be sure you know which island is which. Mayreau lies in front of Union, and some people see the two as one island and then mistake the Tobago Cays for Mayreau. If you are heading for the lee of Mayreau your compass heading should be around 225-230° magnetic. If you find yourself sailing between south and 200° you are probably heading for the Tobago Cays....and trouble.

Tobago Cays. If you approach the Tobago Cays from the north, the easiest and best route is as follows: after you round Glossy Hill head for the middle of Mayreau (about 218° magnetic). As you approach Mayreau you can see Baline Rocks. Leave these to port, giving them reasonable clearance, and sail on until you are about half way between them and Mayreau before heading up into the Tobago Cays. Line up the day markers in the Cays if you can see them. (Note: Petit Rameau and Petit Bateau look like one island for much of the approach.)

An alternative and much trickier approach is to head a bit to the east of Mayreau from Glossy Hill, then sail a hundred yards to the east of Baline rocks, between the rocks and the northwest end of Horseshoe Reef. This entrance channel is about a quarter of a mile wide, and Horseshoe Reef is often not visible, so caution is advised. The current can be strong, so make sure you are not being set down on the rocks. Once past the rocks, hold course until the day markers line up (see Tobago Cays sketch chart), then head up into the islands.

Mayreau. When approaching Mayreau, pass well to the east of the black and yellow beacon marking Dry Shingle. When sailing round the lee of Mayreau, watch out for the reef off Grand Col Point (see Mayreau and

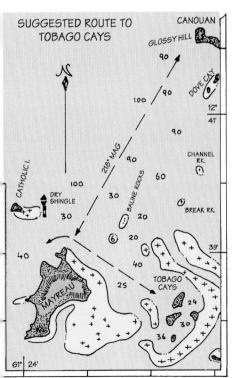

SUGGESTED ROUTE TO TOBAGO CAYS

Tobago Cays sketch chart). It is marked by a yellow and black beacon. Pass well outside this beacon as it is in quite shallow water. When heading over to Palm or Union, you need to head well up, at least to the middle of Palm Island, until you figure out how much you are being set down, as the current can be very strong. Watching the Union airport against Carriacou gives an idea of current set. Union's deadly windward reef (Newlands Reef) extends out half way to Palm Island, so you have to sail almost over to Palm before heading west into Clifton Harbor. Note that there are two red beacons on Newlands Reef. You leave these to starboard as you head into Clifton. You must swing in a curve well outside them. Don't run from one to the other or you will be hard aground.

Grand de Coi, between Union and Palm, is a dangerous reef, almost never seen till it is too late. Numerous yachts have gone aground here and one or two destroyed. Now there is a yellow and black beacon on its western side. You must always pass to the west (Union Island side) of this beacon, keeping well clear. The following pointers may also be helpful in gauging your position.

All Directions: When there is gap between PSV and Petite Martinique, you are too far south to hit Grand de Coi. When this gap is closed, keep clear of Grand de Coi by watching the western side of Mayreau against the new Union Island airport. If you keep Mayreau well behind the airport you will be west of Grand de Coi. A gap between the two stands you in danger.

For all directions south: sail right down to the entrance of Clifton Harbor then pass west of the Grand de Coi beacon.

To Carriacou: Head toward the northwest coast. When you approach Hillsborough it is safest to pass to the west of Jack a Dan before rounding up into town.

To PSV: When you have passed Grand de Coi, steer for the east side of Carriacou till PSV bears due east, then head on in, passing well to the south of Mopion, Pinese and all their surrounding reefs. Keep an eye on current set and compensate if necessary.

A much trickier and more dangerous way is to pass between the two little sand cays Mopion and Pinese. The course from the lee side of Grand de Coi is around 165-170° magnetic, though with current you may have to head considerably more to the east. A bearing of 160° magnetic on the highest peak of Petit Martinique takes you close enough to eyeball your way in. Mopion usually has a small thatch shelter on it. Always sail through the center of the passage, and do not round up too soon as the reef extends about a quarter of a mile southwest of Mopion (see our PSV and Petit Martinique chart). Treat this passage with caution.

Sailing north

From Carriacou to Clifton and Palm: The safest route is to pass to the west of Jack a Dan, then follow the coast up to Rapid Point. From Rapid Point aim for the east side of Union, checking on the current set

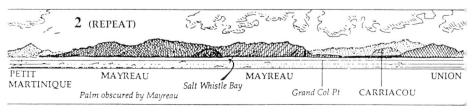

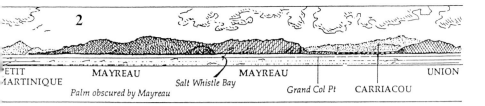

by watching Frigate Island against Union. As you near Union you should be able to see the reefs between Frigate and Clifton. Do not get too close to these as the current and

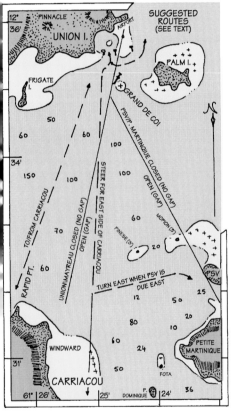

wind are setting you down on them. On the other hand keep a good eye out for the Grand de Coi reef to the east. Stay to the

west of the beacon that marks the reef (see also Grand de Coi notes above).

From PSV to Union: Sail due west till you are on a line between the east coasts of Carriacou and Union before changing course to Clifton. Before the gap closes between PSV and Petite Martinique, edge westward till the finger of land on the western side of Mayreau disappears behind the new Union Island airport. Pass to the west of the Grand de Coi beacon. Experienced sailors could head out between Mopion and Pinese and then head for the Pinnacle until the finger of land on the western side of Mayreau disappears behind the new Union Island airport, or until the Grand de Coi beacon is identified. Always pass well to the west of the Grand de Coi beacon.

From Palm northwards: Always sail round the lee of Mayreau. Pass to the west of Grand Col Point staying well clear of the beacon. Then, as you get to the north of Mayreau, stay well east of Dry Shingle (marked by a black and yellow beacon) which extends eastwards from Catholic Island.

Approaching the Tobago Cays from the south: Sail round the lee of Mayreau, then head straight up toward the middle of the Cays. If you are tacking under sail, favor the Mayreau side of the channel when passing Baline Rocks to avoid the shoal to their south. There is a southern entrance to the Cays, but it is tricky and should not be attempted without local knowledge. Many charter yachts have run aground here. How-

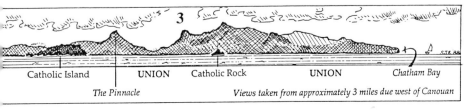

ever, if you are in the Cays on a quiet day with good reef visibility, you could try leaving by this route.

When leaving the Cays to go north: the safest route is to sail from the anchorage to the north end of Mayreau, then head northwards after you have passed Baline Rocks.

There is also a channel to the east of Baline Rocks about a quarter of a mile wide. From the Cays you have to head just south of the rocks until you reach the channel and then turn north, or you are in danger of hitting the western edge of Horseshoe Reef.

DIVING IN THE SOUTHERN GRENADINES

When the water is clear the diving in the southern Grenadines can be wonderful, though currents can be strong and many dives have to be done as drift dives. There are two dive shops to chose from, and there is no need to go to the shop – the dive boat will come by and pick you up from your yacht in the Tobago Cays, Mayreau or Union.

Grenadine Divers [T:458-8138, 458-8122, F:458-8398, VHF:16,68] is a pleasant, relaxed dive operation run by Glenroy Adams from Bequia. Based in Union, it is linked to Dive St. Vincent, Dive Bequia and Dive Canouan, and certification courses or dive packages can be arranged which work for all these dive shops. Glenroy or one of his instructors will collect you from your yacht in Union, Mayreau, PSV or the Tobago Cays. If you are short of ice or have run out of bread, they will happily bring some along on their way out.

Palm Island has an active dive station called Scuba Shack run by a certified diver who has learned the local waters really well and is a first rate guide. You can call them for a rendezvous [T:458-8824, VHF:68, Scuba Shack].

One of the easiest dives to find for yourself is just west of Mayreau – the wreck of the first world war gunboat, Purina. It is marked on our chart. The depth is 18-40 feet and the current out on the wreck can be ferocious. The wreck is small but pretty and the fish life fantastic. This is a perfect place for some underwater photography. Under no circumstances should you anchor your yacht on the wreck as the tug of the anchor will damage it.

There is a spectacular area for diving in some cuts among the reefs between Mayreau and the Cays. Discovered by Glenroy, this area is called Mayreau Gardens. If you manage to dive one of these in clear visibility, it could turn out to be the dive of your holiday. There is usually lots of current here, so we are talking drift dives, sometimes so rapid that you surface over a mile from where you went down. You hardly need to fin. The current does all the work while you get wafted through a delightful garden of hard and soft corals, sponges and fish. My favorite part is on the southern side of the gardens coming out along the southern edge of the reefs. A sloping reef drops to a sand bottom in 40-60 feet. The reef has a wonderful texture made up of all kinds of corals. Boulder, pillar and plate corals rise in a variety of intricate shapes. There are areas of huge sea fans, so large you can play hide and seek behind them. The special luminous quality of the light typical in the Grenadines seems to extend below the waves. Massive schools of brown and blue chromis engulf you from time to time, swimming inches from your mask. A few yards away schools of snapper and jack swim by purposefully, creating a flurry of nervousness in the chromis. Angelfish, trumpetfish, large boxfish and brightly colored parrotfish are all there as well.

Diving is good outside Horseshoe Reef on either side of the small boat passage. These are best done as drift dives as the currents can be very strong.

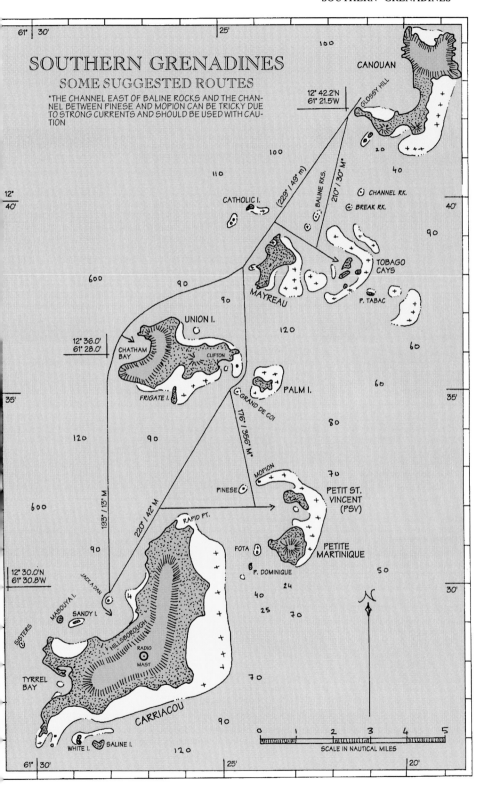

SOUTHERN GRENADINES
SOME SUGGESTED ROUTES

*THE CHANNEL EAST OF BALINE ROCKS AND THE CHANNEL BETWEEN PINESE AND MOPION CAN BE TRICKY DUE TO STRONG CURRENTS AND SHOULD BE USED WITH CAUTION

CANOUAN

12° 42.2'N
61° 21.5'W

GLOSSY HILL

100

100

110

CATHOLIC I.

(229° / 49° m)

210° / 30° M*

BALINE RKS.

(C) CHANNEL RK.
(C) BREAK RK.

20

40

90

TOBAGO CAYS

MAYREAU

P. TABAC

600

90

90

UNION I.

120

60

12° 36.0'
61° 28.0'

CHATHAM BAY

CLIFTON

PALM I.

GRAND DE COI

60

FRIGATE I.

176° / 356 M°

80

120

90

MOPION

PINESE

PETIT ST. VINCENT (PSV)

70

193° / 13° M

220° / 42 M

RAPID PT.

FOTA

PETITE MARTINIQUE

JACK A DAN

P. DOMINIQUE

50

12° 30.0'N
61° 30.8'W

24

MABOUYA I.
SANDY I.

40

25

70

SISTERS

HILLSBOROUGH

RADIO MAST

70

TYRREL BAY

CARRIACOU

90

WHITE I.   SALINE I.

120

SCALE IN NAUTICAL MILES

0   1   2   3   4   5

600

600

120

MAYREAU

Mayreau is a one-road island, rimmed with pristine beaches and affording spectacular views from up on the hill. Most islanders are happy to see you and it is well worth exploring on foot.

Salt Whistle Bay

This beautiful bay has a sweeping half moon beach, and Salt Whistle Bay Club is tucked away behind it. The resort is so well hidden in the trees that people who sail in the bay often question whether it is really there.

Enter right in the middle of the bay as there are reefs to the north and south. The northern reef is about six feet deep, and not usually much of a problem. The southern reef is dangerous; both wind and swells will help drive the inattentive navigator hard onto the coral. Boats often come to grief here, so take care. The holding in the bay is good in sand if you avoid the weed patches. If there is a northerly swell, anchor bow and stern to cut the roll.

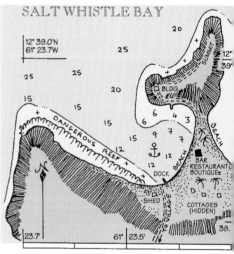

Ashore

Salt Whistle Bay Club [T:458 8444, VHF:16, 68, $B] has a whimsical woodland atmosphere where the appearance of the Mad Hatter at tea would not be out of place. The unique dining area is set in the open

mong the trees and each table is built of
tone with its own thatch roof. You can be
ure of a top quality meal here with a set
hree-course dinner and a choice of fish or
neat dishes. Lunch is a la carte, with soups,
andwiches, salads and local dishes. For a
change from the boat, start the day ashore
vith one of their full breakfasts.

There is also a little boutique and beach
oar. Manager Undine Potter speaks Ger-
nan and English and is nearly always on
and and very helpful.

Just across the low land there is another
oeach on the windward side where shells
and driftwood wash ashore. Snorkeling on
he reefs and rocks in the bay is fair but
sometimes murky. A pretty trail leads up to
he village from near the hotel dock.

Saline Bay

As you sail round to Saline Bay keep to
seaward of the black and yellow beacon that
narks the long reef off Grand Col Point. It
is placed right on the edge of the reef, so do
not cut it too fine. The large Saline Bay

anchorage offers good holding in sand if
you avoid the weedy areas. A stern anchor
may be advisable to cut the roll in northerly
swells.

Sometimes cruise ships anchor and Saline
Bay does a quick imitation of Coney Island.
However, they are always gone before
nightfall.

Ashore

Basic supplies (and sometimes fish) are available in several small groceries. The biggest is part of the Dennis's Hideaway complex and another is just across the road. A few handicrafts are available in small shops tucked in people's houses and Curtis St. Hillaire often exhibits his goat skin and banana art by the roadside.

A few years ago the only businesses ashore were a couple of very basic stores. Now yachting visitors support three Mayreau-owned restaurants and a few handicraft and t-shirt outlets. All good for the local eonomy.

It all began when an enterprising young man called Dennis was working as a charter skipper and realized the potential of the island for yachts. You can see the arches o Dennis's Hideaway [T&F:458-8594 VHF:68, $B-C] as well as his guest house from the anchorage. It is just a few minutes up the only road and is a grand spot to stop to take in the view and a beer or two. Late afternoon is the best time to meet other yachtsmen. Dennis offers tasty local cooking, using fish and lambi from the surround-

SALINE I

Dennis's Hideaway

Telephone:458-8594

VHF:68

Seafood Restaurant and Bar, 5 minutes up the hill from Saline Bay, Mayreau, with a perfect view of the bay. We can arrange transport from the beach. Supermarket with fresh produce, fish, liquor and soft drinks. Call us for delivery to the dock. Water sports and water taxi service with snorkeling and fishing trips. Enjoy the fish you catch at a beach barbecue. Our pleasant new guest house is now open.

Everything for those on yachts in Mayreau

ing reefs, or livestock from the hillside. On Wednesdays and Saturdays he does a large seafood buffet with live music. Dennis's Hideaway also has a modern guest house and a traditional pizza oven for cooking lunch is planned.

J & C Bar and Restaurant (T:458-8558, VHF:68,16) is just beyond Dennis's hideaway on your left. It has the best view of the harbor. It is owned by Jean and Claude. Their music is soft, so it is good for those

who want to chat, and it is large enough to take a huge group. Jean and Claude are very friendly, they make a big effort and their large portions of lobster, fish and lambi are excellent value. Their lambi is especially delicious and they often have whelks and curried goat. They also have a small boutique behind the restaurant.

It is hard to meet a more engaging and friendly pair than James Alexander and Robert Lewis who have opened Island

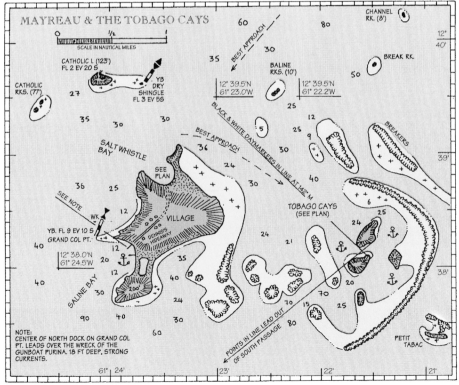

Paradise Restaurant [T:458 8068, VHF:68, $C]. It is well up the hill with bird's eye view. This is not a place to come if you are in a hurry as everything is cooked from scratch, but their creole fish and curried conch are well worth the wait. Best of all if three or more come up to eat, the captain's meal is free. They have the biggest sound system on the island and for those who want to groove to some sounds, this is the place. They have a nightly happy hour from 1800-1900 with half-priced drinks, and on Fridays they offer a barbecue with a local string band. They offer free rides up the hill for anyone who does not want to walk.

A walk eastwards from Saline Bay along the salt pond will bring you to some long pristine beaches on the windward side.

Water sports

Snorkeling on the reef coming out from Grand Col Point is good. Dennis has a 39-foot charter yacht and takes yachtsmen fishing the local way and for large groups will organize a traditional Caribbean beach party.

MAYREAU VIEW: UNION IN THE BACKGROUND, CARRIACOU BEHIND

THE TOBAGO CAYS

The Tobago Cays are a group of small deserted islands protected from the sea by Horseshoe Reef. The reef colors are a kaleidoscope of gold, brown, blue, turquoise and green. There are small sand beaches and clean water. On clear nights the stars are cast across the sky like wedding confetti thrown in an excessive gesture of bonhomie. Even squalls can be dramatically beautiful as they approach from afar. The anchorage is, however, open to the full force of the ocean winds which are occasionally strong. The Tobago Cays are a national park.

The approach to the islands is helped by black and white day markers. Petit Rameau and Petit Bateau look like one island for most of the approach. It is important to avoid cutting corners lest you land on a coral head.

You can anchor just west of Petit Rameau, in the cut between Petit Rameau and Petit Bateau, or to the south of Baradel. There are strong currents in the cut anchorage, so bow and stern anchoring is necessary.

Several moorings have been put down and more are planned. These are available for a fee. Some are in just a few feet of water and suitable only for shoal draft boats. Always check the state of a mooring for yourself.

When heading south out of the Cays it is safest to pass round the lee of Mayreau, though the Cays do have a southern channel which is okay as an exit for the experienced when the light is good. Avoid using this southern route as an entrance as it is hard to find and many charter yachts have gone aground in the attempt.

Regulations

Fish and reef are all protected in the Tobago Cays. Please help keep it wonderful. Fishing is not allowed, jet skis are not allowed, and when you anchor your dinghy

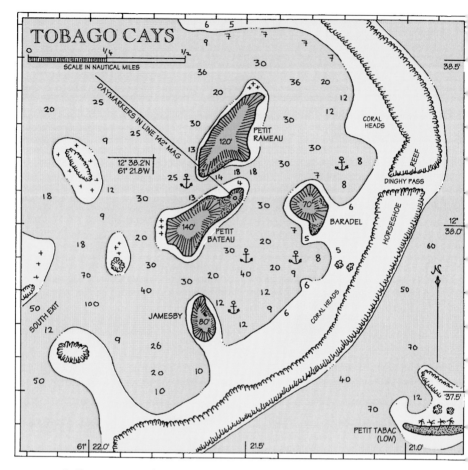

to go snorkeling, you must do so on the sand and not on the reef. (Dinghy mooring buoys may be added.)

Ashore

The Tobago Cays is probably the last place you would expect high fashion. But French designers Paul and Cecile and their two children live here from Christmas to Easter on Boreal, a catamaran. They design their own distinctive fabrics and have them printed in the far east. These are then shipped to Trinidad where Paul and Cecile oversee the transformation into smart, top quality casual and bathing wear and dresses. They offer their line for sale exclusively in the Tobago Cays. Prices are reasonable since there are no middle men. Designs change every year which keeps many of us running back to get the latest. They are kept very busy so it is best to call them for a viewing soon after you arrive in the Tobago Cays (VHF:16).

Local boats hang out in the Cays during the season offering everything from ice, bread and lobsters to jewelry.

Water sports

The snorkeling on Horseshoe Reef is superb, though it can be choppy out there, and in some places you will meet current. If you have beginner snorkelers on board, the east beach on Petit Bateau (facing Baradel) has good snorkeling that starts in calm shallow water. The Tobago Cays is also an excellent place for sailboarding with miles of fairly protected water and a constant wind. Experts can sail out through the small dinghy passage into the ocean.

To go scuba diving, contact Grenadines Dive or Scuba Shack who will come and collect you from your yacht. Currents can be very strong for scuba and most dives are done as drift dives.

228

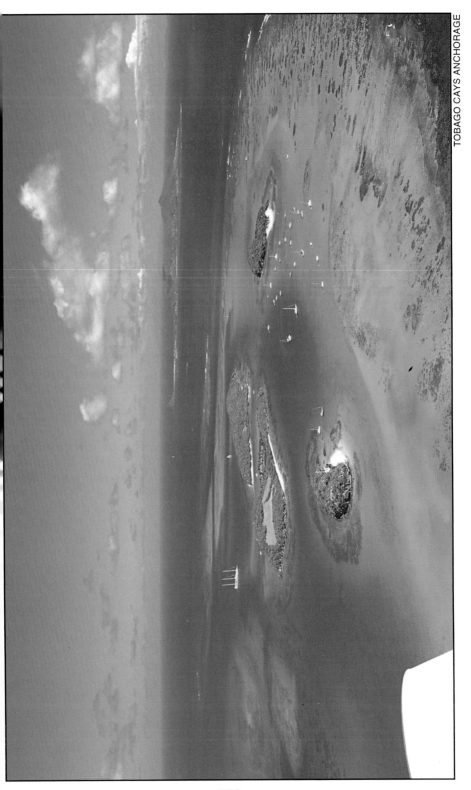

TOBAGO CAYS ANCHORAGE

PALM ISLAND

CASUARINA BEACH, PALM I.

Palm Island [T:458-8824, F:458-8804 VHF:68, $A, cc:V,A] is a lovely little resort that was created on an uninhabited island by John and Mary Caldwell and their local friends. After the Second World War John decided to sail from the U.S.A. to Australia so he could get back with Mary, despite the fact he had never sailed in his life before. His journey was a total disaster. He ran out of food and had to eat the slime off the bottom of his boat, he lost his mast and was finally wrecked on a Pacific island. This is all described in his book "Desperate Voyage." (I recommend it to everyone – especially those learning to sail.) He did better on his trip from Australia to the Caribbean, where he became known for planting palm trees wherever he went. He finally dropped anchor in Palm Island.

The anchorage is off the docks and holding is fair in 15 to 20 feet with a sand bottom. The anchorage can be rolly, so check it out for lunch and if you feel comfortable there, stay overnight.

Services

This is a good place to buy water. Come stern to the southernmost dock, using the buoy provided. There is a small general store which sells ice and a variety of food and household items. There are two docks you can use for your dinghy, but you should use a stern anchor to keep it from riding underneath.

Ashor

You step ashore on Casuarina Beach, gorgeous expanse of golden sand lapped b translucent turquoise water: the ultimat picture-perfect Grenadine beach. The fin new Sandy Feet Boutique [cc:A,V] ha light clothing and gifts, and a few step away the great new Sunset Bar and Restau rant [T:458-8824, VHF:68, $B-D, cc:V,A is run by John's son, Roger. The Sunset Ba was designed for the yachting trade after i was found that the main hotel facilities wer getting overcrowded. The atmosphere i casual and friendly, the prices reasonabl and the sunset view perfect. Hamburgers sandwiches and hot dogs are always avail able and if you want to have a more elabo rate dinner, make a reservation a little whil in advance. They offer fish, steak and chicken and sometimes have Saturday nigh barbecues with a steel band.

It is fun to walk over to the windward sid and explore some of the other five beache and perhaps find one to yourself. You ca run or walk John's mile and quarter lon "Highway 90," a jogging or walking trai marked by hand painted signs. A local div master is available for those who want t scuba dive [T:458-8824, VHF:68, Scub Shack] and snorkeling on the surrounding reefs is good. The hotel part of Palm is kep private, but those interested in seeing a room should ask in the main office.

PALM ISLAND
BEACH CLUB

Phone:809 458 8824, Fax:809 458 8804, VHF:68

Probably the most beautiful place on earth.

John and Mary Caldwell's Palm Island, known as the Grenadines' most spectacular hideaway resort, is now offering yachtsmen:

THE SANDY  BOUTIQUE
For elegant casual wear and quality gifts

THE SUNSET BAR AND RESTAURANT
A relaxed meeting place for smart and salty sailors
(we sell water too - come stern to our dock)

SCUBA SHACK
For high adventure under the waves

and for your next dream holiday, ask about our rooms.

UNION ISLAND

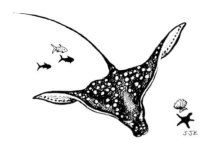

With its dramatically mountainous outline Union stands out from afar. Clifton, the main harbor, is protected by a reef which shows off its brilliant kaleidoscopic colors and patterns as you sail in.

Clifton

Clifton is a bustling small port with a cosmopolitan atmosphere and is the center of yachting in the southern Grenadines. It has a thriving day charter industry, with tourists flying into the small airport daily to tour the Grenadines. Do not anchor close to any of the innocent looking empty mooring buoys. Come 1600, the large day charter boats will return and pick them up regardless.

You may see Red Island on older charts. This is no longer. It has been bulldozed and connected by a causeway to Union which now forms the new airport runway.

When approaching Clifton from the north it is necessary to sail half way over to Palm Island to avoid Newlands Reef (keep well outside the two red beacons on its outer edge). When approaching from the south, give Grand de Coi a wide berth.

Clifton Harbor is protected by Newlands Reef and has a small reef in the center. The main entrance is just south of this center reef and marked by red and green beacons. It is also possible to sail to the east of the center reef and up behind Newlands Reef toward Green Island.

A pleasant anchorage is just behind Newlands Reef, but if you prefer to be nearer the action, anchor anywhere off the town.

Regulations

Clifton is St. Vincent's southern port of entry for customs clearance. Check with customs and immigration at the airport. Office hours are weekdays 0900-1500. Officers are also on hand on weekends whenever a plane comes in. It is also possible to clear customs in the customs building in town, but you still have to go to the airport for immigration.

Services

The Anchorage Yacht Club [T:458-8221, F:458-8365, VHF:68,16, cc:V] has a 12-berth marina where you can tie stern to a floating dock, and they offer water, laundry, ice, mechanic, card telephone, fax, mail pickup and showers. The marina office is right on the dock and opens daily from 0730 to 1800. The Anchorage is an agent for Mustique Airways and Air Martinique, as well as private charter companies. They offer inexpensive transport to the airport. There are two rough, ready and inexpensive railways for hauling your yacht. Check them out before you decide and be prepared to bring everything you need. The Anchorage has a complete sail loft run by Gilles Griot who sailed to the Caribbean 12 years ago in a 24-foot yacht. Gilles worked as a sailmaker in France, runs a complete loft and can repair your old sails or awnings or build you new ones. You will find Star Voyage and Star Dust at the Anchorage. Gilles Griot manages Star Dust and whenever possible they will help passing yachtsmen.

Clifton Beach Hotel [T:458-8235, VHF:68, $B-C cc:V,A,Ds] is the base for Captain Yannis's fleet of charter boats and there is about nine feet at the end of their dock. You can come in here stern-to and take on water, buy ice and get your laundry done. Clifton Beach Hotel is also the home of Island Marine Special, a first rate mechanical shop run by Earl Allen. He has worked on boats, generating plants and other machinery for several big hotels over the last 25 years and he can repair all makes of diesel engine, outboard, gear box or generator. If he doesn't have parts on hand, he can arrange to get them through his agent

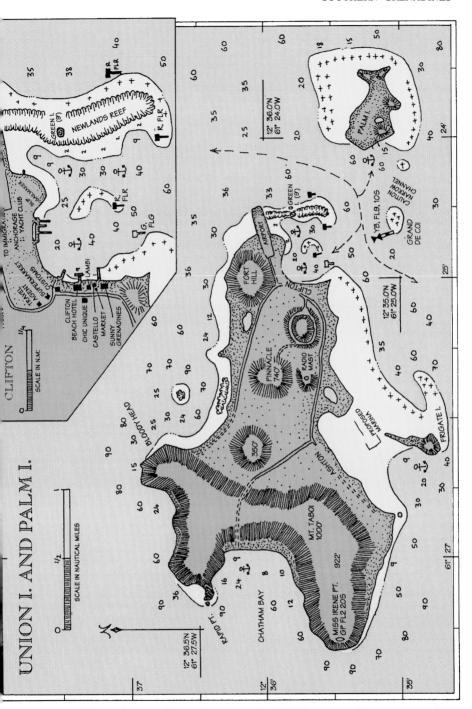

UNION I. AND PALM I.

CLIFTON

in Miami and, if the gods are smiling, they take about three days to arrive.

Diesel and gasoline are available at Eillon near the market. You have to bring jugs. Some form of dinghy transport to your yacht might be arranged at extra cost, but for large quantities it would be easier to go to Petite Martinique, PSV or Carriacou.

If you need to fly out, Eagle Travel [T:458-8179, VHF:68] can help book tick-

CLIFTON HARBOR

ets. Ice is available at The Anchorage Yacht Club, Park East, Grand Union, Lambi, and many rum shops.

Ashore

Everyone and his brother seems to own a "supermarket" in Clifton. Do not expect gleaming aisles and push-round carts, but most essentials are available. Grand Union is a good place to start and they have a fine new little bakery where you can sit and drink a cup of coffee. They will deliver to their dinghy dock at the Clifton Beach Hotel. The Lambi Supermarket and the open market carry fresh produce, and you should also check out Park East which often has lettuce and other vegetables in season, as well as fish and conch. There is also a small Rasta market near the customs office.

Union is becoming quite the place for boutiques. The Anchorage Boutique [cc:V] has an impressive selection of casual wear, toiletries, books, and they even stock current overseas newspapers in season. Chic Unique has some good buys in clothing and books and handicrafts. Costello is the art gallery and studio of Jutta Hartmann. It is in a pleasant Caribbean style building just beyond the market. You can watch Jutta at work and buy paintings or hand-painted garments. The Clifton Beach Hotel has the Art Shop with a wide range of both batik and silk screened casual wear. There are several other small stalls and shops for local handicrafts.

234

Anchorage Yacht Club

Telephone:
809-458-8221
Fax: 809-458-8365

VHF Ch 68 or 16
telex: St.Vincent
7595 AYC VQ

The Anchorage Yacht Club is the true center of the Grenadines

***12 BERTH MARINA *WATER *ICE
*MECHANIC *SAILMAKER *LAUNDRY
*BREAD *FISH * TELEPHONE, TELEX AND FAX.**

**Best French/Creole restaurant and bar in the Grenadines
Jump up and dinner on Mondays and Fridays in season**

Air conditioned beach bungalows and rooms
Nearby airport with daily flights to the rest of the Caribbean
Free ferry service for our customers to and from their yachts in season

BAKERY
Open from 0700, with croissants and fresh coffee. Fresh bread, sandwiches, baked goodies and ice cream.

If you are planning to go snorkeling you can frighten yourself by counting the sharks in the pool in front of the Anchorage Yacht Club. (If it is any comfort they are only nurse sharks.) After that you may need a stiff drink and a bite to eat.

The Anchorage Yacht Club [T:458-8221, F:458-8365, VHF:68, $A-B, cc:V] is the smartest and prettiest of the Union Island hotels with a delightful view of the harbor and is the only place to go if you want to dress up (but you don't have to). They have a good dock for tying up the dinghy and a pleasant bar for relaxing. Their bakery counter opens at seven a.m. with fresh coffee and croissants. They also sell sandwiches, snacks, excellent bread to take away and delicious ice cream straight from Martinique.

The hotel is ably managed by Charlotte Honnart who is French and you will find good French and creole cuisine. On Mondays and Fridays in season they have a steel band, with occasional piano and guitar entertainment on other nights. On special oc-

casions the chefs prepare a grand buffet dinner. They are well known for their large parties at Christmas and New Year's Eve. To make life really easy, they offer a free water taxi between their bar and your boat in the evenings. Last boat leaves when the bar closes.

Lambert is smiling these days and why not? His Lambi emporium [T:458-8549, VHF:68, $C-D], consisting of a supermarket and two-story, two-dining room restaurant is going well. Each time I come his building seems to have crept farther out to sea. The conch shell walls give plenty of rough and ready atmosphere. Lambi often has steel bands.

The Clifton Beach Hotel [T:458-8235, VHF:68, $B-C cc:V,A,Ds], run by Marie Adams, is small and appealing with a perfect open waterfront location and its own dinghy dock, which is the most convenient one to use to visit town during the day. After you have finished shopping try one of their first rate sandwiches. You can also visit for dinner and they have the occasional jump

up.

The Boll Head Restaurant and Bar [T:458 8657, $C-D] is owned by Anthony "Boll Head" Frederick. His hair fell out at an early age, earning him a nickname which has stayed with him. It is opposite the Clifton Beach Hotel with outside seats where you can watch the activity in the street outside. Informal and inexpensive with local food, and a convenient place to get chicken, mutton, beef or lambi rotis for lunch.

T&N [T:458-8348, $B-D], is a cute, intimate upstairs restaurant. Excellent rotis, and first class local food.

Jennifer's Restaurant and Bar [T:458-8689, $C-D] is on Clifton's main road beyond the turn off to the Sunny Grenadines. Jennifer offers west Indian food at a reasonable price and turns up the music for dancing on the weekends.

In the other direction, Sydney's Bar and Restaurant [T: 458-2965, VHF:68, $C-D] is just before the airport. It is a new clean building owned by Sydney from Union who paints t-shirts and sells them in the Tobago Cays. It is run by Maria from Munich. Maria offers good local meals and snacks, as well as seafood crepes and pasta. There is a popular happy hour from 1800-1900, two for the price of one.

At the airport, Lorna serves very inexpensive local dishes and snacks.

Any walk in Union away from Clifton will be rewarded with peace, quiet and panoramic views. The view from the hill behind town shows up the reefs and water colors.

Water sports
You will find information on the dive shops and some dive sites under the southern Grenadine diving section. Clifton is the base of Grenadines Dive [T:458-8138/8122, F:458-8398, VHF:16,68].

OTHER UNION ANCHORAGES

Frigate Island
Frigate Island, although just over a mile from Clifton, is generally deserted and reasonably well protected. You can anchor in the lee of the island but enter carefully as the bottom shelves quickly. A large development, including a 300-berth marina, is planned for this area.

Chatham Bay
Chatham Bay, on the lee side of Union, is a large protected anchorage. The best spot to anchor is in the northeast corner. (You may have to move if the fishermen are seine netting.) The wind tends to come over the hills in shrieking gusts. There is a long beach to explore and some good snorkeling around the rocks off Rapid Point. The fish life here is particularly rich and attracts all kinds of birds, including pelicans. Paths lead over to Ashton. A development is planned.

PSV AND PETITE MARTINIQUE

PSV (Petit St. Vincent) and Petite Martinique lie just a short sail southeast from Union. PSV is part of St. Vincent and Petite Martinique is part of Grenada.

PSV

The main anchorage is shown on the chart. There is current in the anchorage and if the wind drops the yachts can swing about. The reef off the dinghy dock extends farther than some think.

Ashore

PSV [T:458-8801, F:458-8428, $A] is one of the Grenadines' great success stories. Back in the late 50's Haze Richardson and Doug Terman quit flying for the Air Force and with what little money they could

beg, borrow and scrape, they bought an old wooden yacht called Jacinta and set sail for the Caribbean. They chartered and one of their clients was Willis Nichols who thought it would be fun to buy a Caribbean island and build a hotel. Haze and Doug were asked to build it, and started together, though eventually Doug went his own way and is now the highly successful author of spy novels. Haze got the hotel finished and tried to find a manager. This proved harder than he thought and he is still there holding the fort, though now as owner. PSV is a very quiet and exclusive resort where the guests get pampered in secluded stone cottages. Each cottage has a flagpole, used to summon room service, which soon appears in a

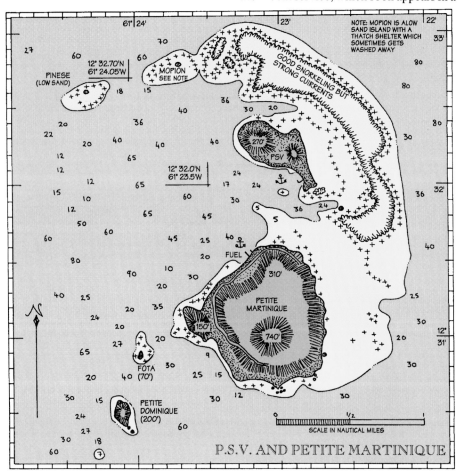

Petit St.Vincent Resort
The Grenadines, St. Vincent, West Indies.

We welcome yachtsmen to visit our private island hideaway for special people. We pride ourselves on seclusion. No crowds, cruise ships, or calypso fire-eaters. Just superb food and fine wines in a secluded romantic atmosphere. We reserve just a few tables for visiting yachtsmen, so please book as early as possible.

Our bar has a perfect sunset view, and our boutique abounds in exotic clothes and gifts from all over the world. We can help out with ice, bread, and phone calls during office hours. Many of our customers made their first visit by yacht and fell in love with our secluded cottages on the slopes and by the sea. Outdoor patios with glorious views provide a perfect setting for breakfast delivered by our "mini-moke" service. If you would like to see a cottage while visiting our island, please ask at the office.

Tel:809-458-8801, VHF:16
in USA: P.O.Box 12506, Cincinnati, Ohio 45212
Tel:800-654-9326/ 513-242-1333

mini moke. The hotel usually keeps full with rates at over $500 a night for a double cottage in season. Water and fuel are sometimes available by arrangement from the main dock if you call in advance. Cube ice is normally available from the bar, as is homemade bread. The hotel has an excel-

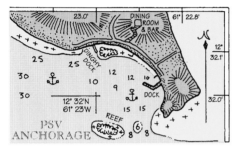

lent boutique, right next to the bar. They are happy to accept yachtsmen as dinner guests, but limited space means they can only take three or four groups each day, so book well in advance. They occasionally have live background music.

Water sports

The snorkeling on the surrounding reefs is good. Mopion makes an exciting destination for a picnic by dinghy. The northern side of the reef surrounding Pinese makes a fair dive.

Petite Martinique

The last outpost of Grenada, Petite Martinique (PM) is small and enchanting for those who like something off the usual tourist path. It is a great place to take on water and fuel and have a stroll and a meal. The inhabitants live by boatbuilding, seafaring and fishing, and in days of old, by smuggling. There are usually several cargo

vessels at anchor. The wooden, pitched roof houses are photogenic, especially at the eastern end of the island. PM is a lot larger than it looks. If you turn right off the dock, the road winds right round to the south side of the island.

If you are coming north from Carriacou you can clear out and visit PM on your way to Union. Those in PSV technically should clear into Carriacou before visiting PM, but there is no customs in PM and the inhabitants have never been noted for worrying too much about technicalities. Anchor anywhere off the fuel dock among the other boats. Watch out for the shoals close to shore further to the west. PM can also be visited by dinghy from PSV. You can leave your dinghy on the fuel dock.

Services

Glen Clement and Reynold own B & C fuels [T:443 9110, VHF:16 Golf Sierra], a convenient fuel dock where Dexter will be ready to serve you. You can easily approach the dock into the wind and it has about 14 feet of water alongside. They sell diesel, gasoline, water and cube ice. If you ask around you can also get good buys on cases of beer or liquor. A beach bar is planned

Ashore

Peterson and Augustina Clement have just built PM's first serious restaurant, The Palm Beach (T:443 9103, $C-D). The setting is perfect, a pretty garden shaded by palms right on the beach. Fresh seafood from the local fishing fleet, cooked local style, with chicken for those who don't like fish or lobster. Immanuel Clement is the manager and they have showers so customers can freshen up after the beach.

There are several small supermarkets, rum shops and snackettes dotted around the island. These include Petronilla Caesar's Miracle Mart [T:443-9118, $D], a local supermarket, rum shop and restaurant. Snack foods from rotis to chicken and chips are always available and Petronilla will cook more elaborate local seafood meals with a little bit of notice.

PSV ANCHORAGE

241

GRENADA AND CARRIACOU

TRADING SLOOPS, TYRREL BAY

Regulations

Carriacou is part of Grenada and if you are coming from another country you must anchor in Hillsborough and clear with the customs facilities at the foot of the jetty before visiting any other port. Those going on to Grenada should tell the customs officers who will hand over a stamped crew list to show the Grenada customs. If you arrive on a holiday, ask a taxi driver to take you to Mr. Decoteau in Belmont. Bring your own crew lists (4 copies) or pay for photocopies. Those clearing outside normal office hours (0800-1145, 1300-1545 on weekdays) will pay a reasonable overtime fee. There are modest entry charges. For rates, see Hillsborough.

Spear fishing is not allowed around Sandy Island or on the reefs around White and Saline Islands, which are all underwater parks.

Holidays

See Grenada.

Shopping Hours

Shops and offices normally open from 0800-1200 and 1300-1600. Saturday is half day and most places are closed by noon. Banks normally open weekdays till 1300, and on Fridays 1500-1700, as well.

Telephones

Card and coin phones may be found all over the island. You buy cards for the phone in post offices and selected shops. For U.S. dial 1+number; other overseas calls dial 011 +country code + number. For collect and credit card calls, dial 0+country code+number. When dialing from overseas, the area code is 809 followed by a 7-digit number.

Transport

There are inexpensive ($1.50-$6 EC) buses running to most villages. Taxis are plentiful. Sample taxi rates are:

	$EC
Hillsborough to Tyrrel Bay	20
Tyrrel Bay to Airport	15
Half day tour	150
By the hour	60

Rental cars are available (check our directory). You will need to buy a local license which costs $30 EC. Drive on the left.

CARRIACOU

"This is an island with over a hundred rum shops and only one gasoline station." Frances Kay, Carriacou.

Carriacou is the only place where I have frequently seen a pelican sitting on a buoy, with a seagull sitting on the pelican's head, both appearing content in the afternoon sun. Somehow this symbolizes the relaxed, easygoing nature of the island. As a Carriacou man said to me: "People does like it here, we move nice wid dem as we does wid each other – no corruptions or hatreds, all is like one."

Carriacou is enchanting, as anyone who takes a taxi ride or hike inland will find. The inhabitants live by farming, fishing and seafaring and must number among the friendliest in the Caribbean. The last few years have seen the emergence of several new restaurants and Carriacou now offers the widest choice in the lower Grenadines for those wishing to eat out. Just about everywhere in Carriacou is of interest, but Windward should definitely be part of your tour, as should the road running from Windward to the north end of the island.

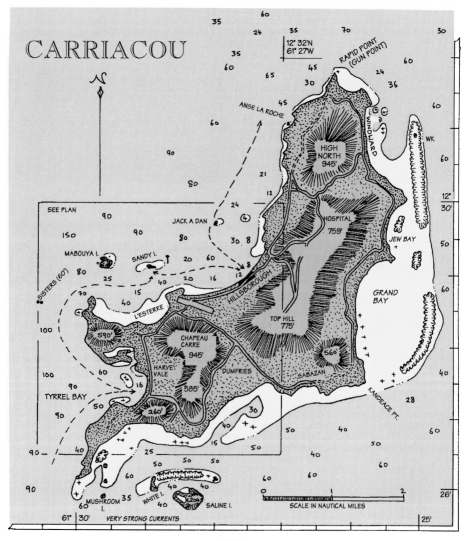

Windward is the traditional center of boat building and it is here you can see the fishing fleet arrive under sail. If you cannot afford a taxi, then take a bus over to Windward and hike. Another destination for a spectacular view is the hospital which sits high on the mountain overlooking the harbor.

HILLSBOROUGH

Navigation

Carriacou is a Carib word meaning "island surrounded by reefs," but do not worry: the approach down the western coast is simple enough. When sailing from the north it is safest to pass to the west of Jack a Dan before heading up into Hillsborough. If you take the trickier route east of Jack a Dan, watch out for the shoal patch about one third of the way between Craigston Point and Jack a Dan. Favor the Jack a Dan side of the channel (but not too close). You can anchor almost anywhere off the town, or better still, save yourself the bother by calling the Silver Beach Resort to see if they have moorings available. You are welcome to use their dinghy dock. Hillsborough is a good anchorage except in bad northerly swells, when you would be better off in Tyrrel Bay.

There is a flashing red light, which occasionally works, on Jack a Dan and another on a red beacon to the east of Sandy Island.

Regulations

See "Regulations" at the beginning of the Carriacou section. Hillsborough is a port of clearance. Port entry fees are $10 EC up to 50 feet and $15 EC over 50 feet. In addition, vessels carrying passengers will pay $2 US per passenger. Less expensive yearly fees are available to Grenada-based charter boats. All departing vessels pay $15 EC.

Services

The Silver Beach Resort [T:443-7337, F:443-7165, VHF:16] offers telephone, fax, laundry, complimentary showers,

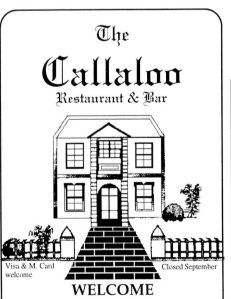

block and cube ice. They don't even mind getting rid of well wrapped garbage for restaurant customers.

Ashore

There are several small supermarkets, including Bullen's and the new Ade's Dream, a bakery and a small produce market. Some of the best buys (especially liquor) are to be found at Franky's Supermarket [T:443-7310]. This tiny bustling shop will be expanded soon. Frankie and his sister Phyllis also own Millie's Guest House and the shop called M&M underneath, which is one of the better general hardware and appliance stores in town.

The museum is worth the short walk and is open Monday through Friday 0900-1545, with an eclectic collection, from Arawak pottery to the first telephone exchange.

Silver Beach Resort [T:443-7337, F:443-7165, VHF:16, $C, cc:V,A,Ds] is making a big effort to encourage tourism in Carriacou and they will try to help you in any way they can. They arrange island tours

and rent cars. A boutique and food store should be open by the time this book comes out. They have a charming open restaurant on the beach, specializing in freshly caught seafood. Oliver Bullen will arrange a complimentary car to bring parties of four or more over from Tyrrel Bay for dinner. Happy hour is 1700-1800.

Eddie, Carriacou born but raised in England, was an electrical contractor in Birmingham. A holiday to his homeland made him realize life could be better, so he created his own little heavenly corner, The Hillsborough Bar [T:443-7932, VHF:16, $C-D, cc:A,V,Ds], where he is the perfect "mine host." It is an English pub style establishment with bold modern decor. This is a great place to relax, eat inexpensive meals on a table overhanging the water and, if your party so inclines, let Eddie switch on his disco so you can dance the night away. Unlike its British counterparts, the Hillsborough bar is open from breakfast to dinner.

The Callaloo [T:443-8004, $C, cc:V,Ds, closed Sunday and all September] is Carriacou's most fashionable restaurant. It is upstairs in a charming old historic building which is painted green and white. Glenna Bullen makes sure that everything, from the local soups, seafood and meat to the homemade bread, are cooked to perfection. The Callaloo only seats 25 and has an intimate atmosphere, so reservations are essential for the evening meal. The Callaloo also opens for lunch when reservations are not necessary.

The ambience at the Roof Gardens [T:443-8919, $D] is early 60's plastic, but don't let that put you off. Jean Bullen, the owner, serves excellent conch, rotis, fried fish and chicken any time of day at a very reasonable price.

A reader recommends Kayak Restaurant on main street. He says the owner Cynthia is from Venezuela and does great paella, salads and rotis.

Should you happen to arrive on the first weekend in August, you will witness the famous Carriacou Regatta. It is no secret that the best trading and sailing sloops in the islands are built right here in Carriacou. Once a year they get together to race on this festive weekend. What amazes me is not just their tradition of boatbuilding, which is all done by eye on the beach, but the way they have managed to refine and speed up their designs so that now they can keep up with modern yachts to windward. The boats they build today are unbelievably fast and sweet, and if you are lucky enough to see one sailing into harbor, it is a joy to behold.

Water sports

Silver Beach Resort was the first to take the plunge with the introduction of Silver Beach Diving [T:443-7337, VHF:16]. The diving is new and very good with excellent visibility most of the time. The dive shop is efficiently run by Max from Germany who is a CMAS and PADI instructor. He will be happy to arrange to collect you from your yacht in any of the Carriacou anchorages. Those diving on their own can try The Sisters off Tyrrel Bay, or the reef to the east of Sandy Island. Start by the red beacon. Both are excellent dive locations. Keep an eye on the current (see also below).

SANDY ISLAND AND L'ESTERRE BAY

SANDY ISLAND

Sandy Island is nothing but a flawless strip of sand, decorated by a few palms and surrounded by perfect snorkeling and diving reefs. Pelicans and seagulls will be your neighbors in this wonderful day time anchorage, and okay for overnighting in settled conditions.

Long and thin for over a 100 years, Sandy

Island is slowly changing and no one knows why. The middle of the island is now awash, making two islands, while the western end grows larger. You can carry seven feet quite close to the middle of the island, but watch out for the reefs north and south. There is also one dark spot toward the western end of the anchorage that is made up of dead coral. It is a little under six feet deep and seems to be getting shallower. There is not much room to drag in Sandy Island, so make sure you are well anchored, preferably with two anchors.

L'Esterre Bay has a long flawless beach and is right opposite Sandy Island, well within dinghy reach. Here you will find Tanki's dive shop and his wife Ali's bar and restaurant [T:443 8406, VHF:16, $C-D, cc:A,Ds] Ali is the daughter of the famous local "naive" artist Canute Caliste. The restaurant is right on the beach, a relaxing place to hang out and drink beers or eat Ali's inexpensive creole cooking. A Carib happy hour is planned. For a break you can wander up the hill and visit Canute Caliste. His paintings catch the local spirit and will probably cost you less than the frames you put them in.

Water sports

The dive off the reef at the eastern end of Sandy Island is quite delightful with a healthy coral slope full of angelfish, spadefish and many other reef creatures. While there are excellent dives in Carriacou, there are superb ones down off Round Island and Kick em Jenny. Here the fish life is outstanding with sharks, rays and big pelagic fish. There are 200 foot walls, caves and many reefs. Since it is a long way it is done as a two-tank dive in fair weather.

Tanki's Watersports Paradise Dive Shop [T:443 8406, 443 8391, VHF:16, cc:A, V,Ds] is happy to help. Tanki is a CMAS instructor from Germany who has been diving in Carriacou for years. If you contact him he will be happy to come by and pick you up from your yacht to go diving, fill your tanks, or bring a group over to Ali's restaurant for lunch. Anchorage for yachts drawing less than six feet is possible off Tanki's shop, but the way in is tricky so best get him to come and guide you.

TYRREL BAY

Tyrrel Bay is deep and well protected, but you must take care to avoid the following hazards. A reef off the southern shore extends about a hundred yards out. Many people hit this reef, so do not hug this coast tightly. A reef in the middle of the bay is about four feet deep and marked by two large red buoys on the northern side. As if this isn't enough, we also have an unmarked wreck about 100 yards south of the reef, close to the middle of the bay. This wreck has about six feet of water over and is a danger to deep draft yachts. The easiest way to come in is between the wreck and the southern shore. There is plenty of room. Stay in the southern part of the bay, but still give the southern shore plenty of room.

Holding is good in sand.

It is very peaceful here. Occasional sounds drift out; a bleating goat, a far away shout, the thump of dominoes, and closer by: "Hey, Skip, how about some oysters?" These salespersons refer to the local delicately flavored "mangrove oyster." Make sure opening them is included in the price. If you have run out of limes for your oysters they can also supply you with these. You may be offered jewelry and calypso music as well. John Bedeau has been at it the longest. He has long harbored ambitions to make adventurous cruises. He owns a 100-year old Carriacou sloop on which he sets out on great voyages for adventure and profit. John has a slow and thoughtful man-

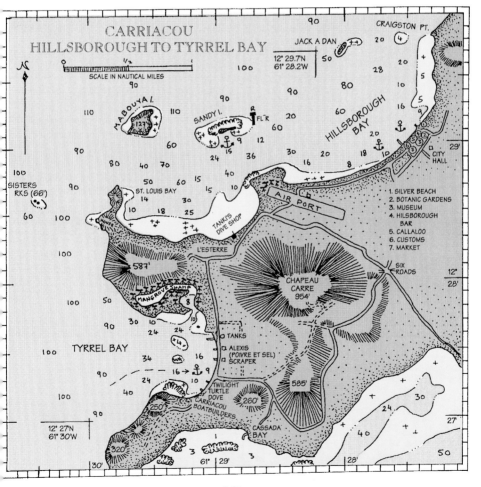

give them a call or wander over and ask. Basic supplies of International paints are in stock and more can be brought in at fairly short notice.

You can arrange fuel (duty free if you have cleared out) by the big storage tanks at the head of the town dock. It is piped down the dock (currently being rebuilt).

Bubbles and Vena Alexis at the Turtle Dove [VHF:16] are helpful to visiting yachtspeople. They offer a laundry service, and when they have enough water, you are welcome to fill jerry jugs or come close enough to get a very long hose on your boat. They also run a first rate taxi service in a minibus for island tours or trips to town and they have a water taxi for snorkeling and offshore island trips. They have a small multilingual book swap.

Both Barba [T:443-7454] and Alexis [T:443-7179] have fleets of fine self-drive rental cars and are happy to rent to yachtspeople.

Ashore

There are two good little supermarkets that stock a supply of liquor and beers, along with bread, canned and packaged food, eggs and chicken. You can find onions but fresh fruits and vegetables are scarce. Both stock some clothing, radios, and other electronic appliances. If you don't see what you want, it is worth asking. Alexis Supermarket [T:443-7179, cc:V] is run by the Alexis family who own a fleet of boats, including some of the ferries that run to Grenada. The Twilight Supermarket [T:443 8530, VHF:16, cc:V] is run by La Qua and Diana Augustin. They sometimes

ner which does not always keep him out of trouble. He has single-handed to Bequia, and he once cornered the banana market and spent days frantically trying to sell a huge heap of bananas before they went ripe. John can sometimes supply lobsters.

Services

Carriacou Boat Builders [T:443-5742, VHF:16/09] is a relaxed and pleasant place to haul out. Their railway can take three yachts at a time, up to 70 tons and 8.5 foot draft. They have a high speed wash off with wet sanding facilities. This is one of the better places for getting work done in the Windwards. They have a first rate machine shop with equipment for cutting and welding steel, stainless steel and aluminum. Gitta runs the yard, Dominique [T:443 8175] does wonders in aluminum, from building a new dinghy to fixing a broken mast. Uwe [T:445-8572] runs the machine shop. There is a woodworking shop, electric and electronic repair service. They can probably help arrange other services if you

have block ice on hand, and if they don't you can get them to order you a block for the next morning.

Along with their supermarket La Qua and Diana Augustin run the Twilight Restaurant and Bar [T:443 8530, cc:V, VHF:16]. It is in an authentic little local building with just a couple of tables. You get good local creole cooking, featuring lobster, fish, chicken and pork at reasonable prices.

Poivre and Sel [T:443 8390, $B-D, VHF:16] introduces a little Gallic flair to the Carriacou restaurant scene. It is run by Patrick and his ebullient chef/wife Magoly, both from the south of France. The imaginative menu makes good use of wine and creme-fraiche and will probably raise your spirits and make you loosen your belt. Specialities include lobster crepe, and a dish from Lyon called Quenelle of Fish. Consider also the fish in aurore sauce (onions, mushrooms, white wine and cream). You won't find a better chocolate mousse on the island. Poivre et Sel is open for lunch

and dinner. Breakfast can be arranged by request.

Bubbles and Vena Alexis's Turtle Dove [T:443-7194, VHF:16, $C] is a good, friendly, down home style restaurant. Bubbles goes out and catches fish and lobster; Vena cooks it so well that she has won two prizes in the Carriacou World Food Day competition. Her lambi, fish with mustard sauce and puff lobster are all excellent. The Turtle Dove is on the water front with a dinghy dock, though you will need a stern anchor or an extra line to tie onto Bubbles' workboat. They have a small boutique featuring Vena's tie dye clothing and dolls at very reasonable prices and a horde of clay "wild ting" men.

Yachtspeople on a budget will enjoy Estamie's Constant Spring Guest House. [T:443-7396, $D] Estemie is delightfully warm and friendly. She runs a cheap and cheerful bar where you can get deep fried fish and chicken. Apart from that, Estamie is happy to pass on phone messages and she

has a fresh water well so you can take a shower or bring jerry jugs to fill. Estamie's is popular as a hang out with some of the expatriate community. Everything is very inexpensive and on a good night you have to keep count of the number of beers you drink, as by the end of the evening Estamie may have completely forgotten.

The Mighty Scraper, one time calypso king of Carriacou, used to come out and sing to the boats. He recognized the different charter companies and if it was a Stevens yacht he would add "I am also Bill Stevens' personal representative in Carriacou." Of course Scraper did not know Bill from Adam. One day he gave a group this same old line, and one of them leaned over and said "Pleased to meet you. I'm Bill Stevens." Today Scraper is one Tyrrel Bay's most ambitious businessmen with his big new Scraper's Restaurant, boutique, Rum Punch Bar and Apartments

[T:443-7403, VHF:16, $C, cc:V]. It is a family run affair with Scraper's wife Iris cooking and making handicrafts and their four youngsters helping out. They have put a dinghy dock right outside the restaurant and they sell both cube and block ice. Yachtsmen are welcome to use the dock as long as they patronize the bar from time to time. The boutique features Scraper's t-shirts and Iris's dolls along with other souvenirs. The wide ranging menu includes Scraper's spicy chicken, grilled fish and roast pork. They can even arrange a plate with all three on it at once. Happy hour is 1700-1800 in season, with a dollar off all drinks.

There are several other inexpensive local hangouts. Liz's Place [T:443-7425, $D] is a friendly hang-out where you can get good local food at bargain basement prices. Al's Place [T:443-7179, $D] is owned by the Alexis family. You can get a very inexpensive lobster and chips along with other local specialties. They have a table across the road right on the beach. A Carib happy hour is planned.

Just a pleasant twenty minute walk away lies the Cassada Bay Hotel [T:443-7494, F:443-7672, VHF:16, $B-C, cc:A,V,Ds] whose bar and restaurant surely has one of the island's most impressive views. The view south over a carpet of blue-green sea is decorated by swirls of turquoise and brown reef from which several knobby islands rise. On a clear day Grenada looms in the distance. The view makes it one of

Cassada Bay

Carriacou + Grenadines + Grenada

The Hide Away of Carriacou ...*and the Caribbean*

Throw away your tranquilizers. You won't need them here. Sit at our open air bar or restaurant and enjoy our panoramic view of five islands. Try one of our Piña Coladas or one of "Spud's Specials" made with fresh fruits. Speak English-Italian-Spanish? No problem.

Hot in town? We have cool, ocean breezes 365 days a year. Come to visit us or come and stay in one of our sixteen cabins set on a gentle hill sloping to the sea. Each has an ocean view with a private balcony where you may sit and watch the sunset. Speedboat trips to fabulous White Island are free for our guests and cost only EC$25 (roundtrip, per person) for our visitors. Enjoy this secluded island with its white sand beaches and coconut palms. Take along our cooler filled with drinks. We only charge for what you actually use.

Let us arrange a special tour for you: day charters (or longer) on sailing yachts; speedboat trips to nearby islands or around Carriacou; fishing trips for dolphin fish, barracuda, kingfish; and much more....

We accept credit cards. For reservations or information, please give a call or send a fax. For visiting yachtsmen, we monitor VHF channel 16

Cassada Bay Resort
Carriacou, Grenada, West Indies
Tel: (809) 443-7494 Fax: (809) 443-7672
Telex 3425 GA
Yachting frequency VHF 16

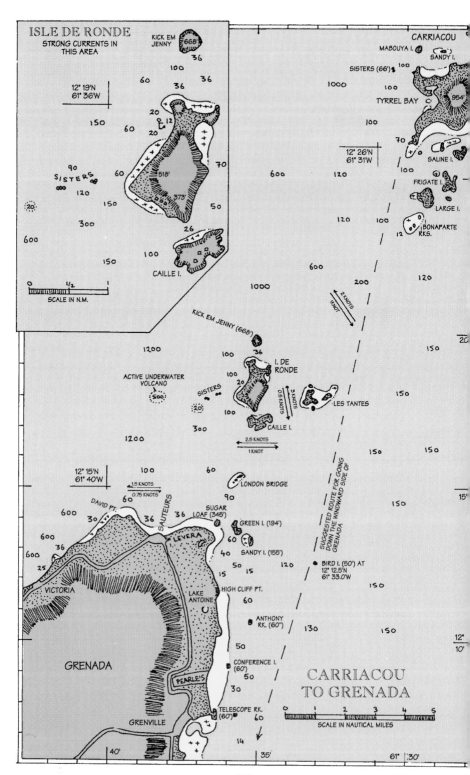

ISLE DE RONDE
STRONG CURRENTS IN
THIS AREA

KICK EM JENNY 668'
36

12° 19'N
61° 36'W

CARRIACOU
MABOUYA I.
SANDY I.
SISTERS (66')
TYRREL BAY
954'

12° 26'N
61° 31'W

SALINE I.
FRIGATE I.
LARGE I.
BONAPARTE RKS.

SISTERS
CAILLE I.

SCALE IN N.M.

KICK EM JENNY (668')

ACTIVE UNDERWATER VOLCANO
SISTERS
I. DE RONDE
LES TANTES
CAILLE I.

2 KNOTS
1 KNOT
3 KNOTS
0.5 KNOTS
2.5 KNOTS
1 KNOT

LONDON BRIDGE

12° 15'N
61° 40'W

1.5 KNOTS
0.75 KNOTS

DAVID PT.
SAUTEURS
SUGAR LOAF (345')
GREEN I. (194')
LEVERA
SANDY I. (155')

VICTORIA
LAKE ANTOINE
HIGH CLIFF PT.
BIRD I. (50') AT
12° 12.5'N
61° 33.0'W

ANTHONY RK. (60')

GRENADA
CONFERENCE I. (60')
PEARLE'S
TELESCOPE RK. (60')
GRENVILLE

SUGGESTED ROUTE FOR GOING DOWN THE WINDWARD SIDE OF GRENADA

CARRIACOU
TO GRENADA

SCALE IN NAUTICAL MILES

256

the more enchanting places to eat out and the food is good. Go for a drink while it still light, stay for dinner, or drop by for lunch. For large groups dinner reservations are helpful.

The mangrove swamp in Tyrrel Bay is protected by fisheries and well worth a visit by dinghy. Switch off the engine and listen to the peace (take insect repellent). Yachts are not allowed in except during times of a hurricane warning. Dinghies must go at less than four knots and taking oysters is forbidden.

There are plenty of hiking possibilities, including a hike up Chapeau Carre. For anyone wanting some shore time in this area, rooms are available at Constant Spring Guest House, Alexis apartments, Scraper's apartments or Cassada Bay Resort.

Water sports

Snorkelers can check out the two reefs in the bay and the new wreck. There is plenty of good diving. Right off the Sisters rocks is another excellent dive where you find a sloping reef of soft and hard corals decorated with many sponges. Lots of fish gather here. You are bound to see angelfish, and sting rays and turtles are likely. Call Tanki's Paradise Diving [VHF:16] or Silver Beach Diving [VHF:16].

PASSAGES BETWEEN CARRIACOU & GRENADA

Unfortunately none of the islands between Carriacou and Grenada affords good shelter. Isle de Ronde can be used in a pinch. The anchorage is in the bay on the northern side of the west coast, but it is likely to be rolly, even for lunch. This is a shame as the snorkeling is excellent and the island has some good walks. Only about 20 inhabitants live on the south coast and on the smaller Caille Island.

It is impossible to anchor at either Kick 'em Jenny or the Sisters, but both are interesting and may be approached reasonably closely, weather permitting. Both have large nesting bird populations and you can see boobies and pelicans, particularly on The Sisters. Beware of the strong currents, eddies and rip tides in this area.

Cautious sailors might prefer to steer about six miles west of Isle de Ronde to avoid the underwater volcano nearly two mile west of The Sisters rocks off Isle de Ronde. This volcano is active and erupted in both 1988 and 1989.

Kick 'em Jenny has the reputation of kicking up a nasty sea as you go north and this is particularly true if the tide is running east.

When sailing from Grenada to Carriacou, the fastest way to go (if you are willing to take a chance on the volcano) is to hug Grenada's lee coast right to the north before heading to Carriacou. If the wind is in the northeast, it is even worth putting a tack into Sauteurs, as the west going current is weakest close to the Grenada coast.

AIRLINES OF CARRIACOU

♦ Six Scheduled flights a day to connect you with the international airlines of Grenada

♦ Charter and Air Ambulance services

♦ Ideal for day trips

♦ Fly with the experienced. Over 40 years flying to Carriacou, Union Island, Bequia and St. Vincent.

♦ Contact your travel agent or call us at Telephone: 444-2898/3549, Fax:444-2628

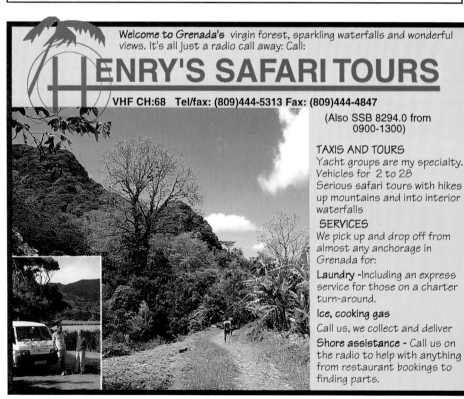
258

Regulations

Grenada, Carriacou and Petite Martinique are one country which has ports of clearance in Hillsborough, St. George's and Prickly Bay. Port charges are $10EC up to 50 feet and $15 EC over 50 feet, with all departing vessels paying $15 EC. However, these charges are only being collected in Carriacou as the port authority is not yet organized to collect in Grenada. Passenger carrying vessels currently pay $2 US per passenger. There is no restriction on how long you stay. If you do not come with your own crew lists, you may be charged a small fee for their photocopied ones. It is best to clear during normal office hours (0800-1145, 1300-1545 on weekdays), as otherwise you will be charged overtime fees which always seem higher in Grenada than Carriacou. If you have any questions about yachting contact Liz Gorman in tourism, 440-2872.

Collecting or damaging corals or buying lobsters out of season are strictly forbidden. (Lobstering season is 31 October to 31 April.) Spearfishing in Grenada, Carriacou and their surrounding islands will probably be banned by the time this book comes out. Those wanting to take dogs ashore will need a valid rabies certificate.

Holidays

Jan 1st - New Year's Day
Jan 2nd - Recovery Day
February 7th - Independence Day
Easter Friday through Monday
First Monday in May - Labor Day
Whit Monday (7 weeks after Easter)
Corpus Christi (Thursday, 12 days after Whit Sunday).
First Monday and Tuesday in August (Carriacou regatta, Carnival)
Dec 25th - Christmas
Dec 26th - Boxing Day

Shopping Hours

Shops and offices normally open 0800-1200 then 1300-1600. Saturday is half day and most places are closed by noon. Banks normally open weekdays till 1300, and also on Fridays 1500-1700.

Telephones

Card and coin phones may be found all over the islands. You buy cards for the phone in post offices and selected shops. For overseas calls dial 1 for the U.S.A., 011 plus the country code for other countries. For collect and credit card calls, dial 0 then the whole number. From some public phones you can get a USA direct line by dialing 1-800-872-2881. When dialing from overseas, the area code is 809 followed by a 7 digit number.

Transport

In Grenada there are inexpensive ($1.50 - $6 EC) buses running to most towns and villages. If you are going a long way check on the time of the last returning bus. Taxis are plentiful. Sample taxi rates are:

	$EC
Prickly Bay - St. George's	25
Airport - St. George's	40
Airport - Prickly Bay	25
Prickly Bay - Grand Anse	15
By the hour	52
Short Ride	10

Rental cars are available (check our directory). You will need to buy a local license which costs $30 EC. Drive on the left.

GRENADA

YACHTS IN PRICKLY BAY

Grenada, a spectacularly beautiful island, has lush green mountains, crystal waterfalls, golden beaches and the fragrant spice trees that give the island its epithet "Isle of Spice." Come from late January to early March to get the added bonus of seeing the hills ablaze with hundreds of bright orange flowering immortelle trees: pure magic. Grenada's recent history has been lively. Much of it started with the transition to full independence in 1974. Most Grenadians felt this premature and instead of jubilant celebrations, the island was on strike and in protest. Nonetheless independence was thrust upon her and Grenada came of age under the rule of Sir Eric Gairy, a flamboyant and controversial figure who had a very divisive effect on the population, resulting in the 1979 left wing coup by Maurice Bishop, who greatly admired Fidel Castro. Bishop attempted to turn Grenada into a socialist state, improving medical care and education, but he did so at the cost of freedom: anyone who opposed him was thrown in jail, and all independent papers were banned.

However, this didn't insulate him from opposition within his own ranks. Second in command, Bernard Coard, his wife Phyllis Coard, and members of the army took Bishop prisoner. After a massive crowd freed him, an army group executed him along with half his cabinet. At this point the U.S.A., along with Grenada's eastern Caribbean neighbors (the Organization of Eastern Caribbean States), launched a "rescue mission" and were welcomed with open arms. Grenada is now again a full democracy. Grenadians are a warm and hospitable people, exceptionally so once you get off the main tourist route.

The interior

Grenada is picturesque with beautiful waterfalls where a swim will leave you feeling wonderfully refreshed, your hair and skin seemingly extra soft. Annandale is the most accessible waterfall. You can drive almost all the way, but then so can all the tour buses, so it is sometimes crowded. Concord Falls are in beautiful countryside and anyone with a spark of adventure should hike the extra half hour to the upper falls for a swim. Seven Falls are the best, most secluded and difficult to get to (a one hour muddy hike) and you need a guide. The most spectacular road in Grenada is the road which runs from Gouyave over to St. Andrew called the Belvedere road. It runs right across the middle of Grenada through verdant agricultural land with spectacular mountain views. Stop by Edmond Morrel's colorful stand near Clozier for a friendly welcome and great buys on local fruits and flowers.

Grand Etang is a crater lake and the Forest Center is close by. Trails are laid out so you can wander into the forest. There are wonderful hikes, including one half way across the island (four hours). For a meal out on your tour, try lunch at Betty Mascoll's old estate house at Morne Fendu

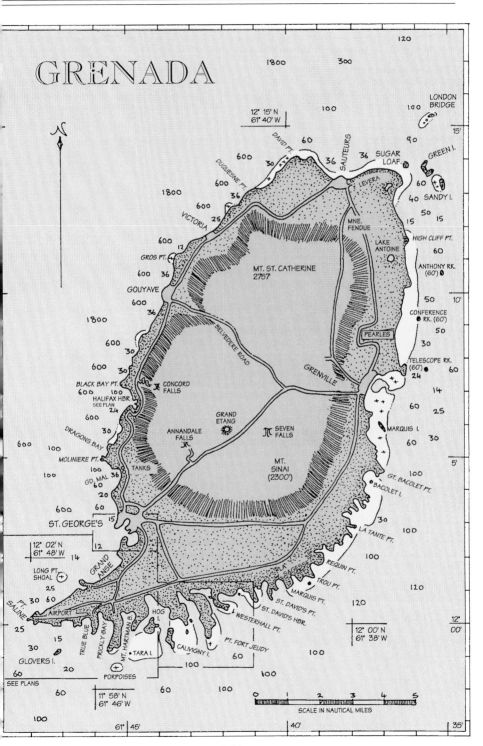

GRENADA

near Sauteurs. This is a great experience though you need to book in advance and the meal will take some time. Alternatively, the Victoria Hotel [T:444-9376, $D, cc:A,V] in Victoria on the west coast does excellent local food at very reasonable prices and the service is good.

For hiking, Henry of Henry Safari Tours [T:444-5313, VHF:68, SSB:82921] is the best man to contact. He runs a taxi service, specializes in hikes and knows the trails well, including Seven Falls. Most other taxi drivers are reluctant to get their feet muddy, but there are a few exceptions including Selwyn Taxi, Rock Taxi and Funseeker Tours (see section on Prickly Bay).

A great day tour for those planning to rent a car is to drive up the west coast to Concord falls then hike to the upper falls for a swim. Drive on to Victoria for lunch, return to Gouyave and take the Belvedere road across the island. Take your time; this is a great drive. You eventually join the main road over Grand Etang. Stop at the crater lake and follow the short circular hike which takes you into the rain forest and then back down to the Grand Etang lake. This should leave you time for a leisurely drive back down the mountain.

In reading about Grenada, keep in mind that Prickly Bay, Grand Anse and St George's are all within an easy taxi ride, so wherever you anchor, read about all three.

There is often an informal cruisers net which meets on VHF CH:72 at 0800 daily. These cruisers often hold a picnic at Hog Island on Sunday afternoons.

Navigation

There is a major light on Point Saline visible for 18 miles both to the north and south, flashing (2 + 1) every 20 seconds. There is a lower elevation quick-flashing light on Glovers Island, and another at the western end of the airport runway. The lights have not always proved reliable.

Grenada uses the IALA B (red right returning) rule. Unless you draw more than 10 feet you will not have to pay attention to the two big ship channel buoys outside St George's or use the leading marks.

The west coast of Grenada is steep-to; a quarter of a mile offshore clears all dangers except Long Point Shoal.

Some yachtspeople like to sail down Grenada's east coast to Prickly Bay. It can be rough, but trolling for fish is usually rewarded. It is only advisable in settled weather. Stay well off Grenada's east coast. Pass close inside Bird Island, but outside all other islands. Keep well away from The Porpoises as you come along the south coast. They can be difficult to see, especially in the afternoon with the sun in

your eyes. There are not many landmarks along the south coast, but you can look out for the development at Westerhall. Prickly Point has a distinctive saddle shape, and a conspicuous house that looks like a lighthouse.

GRENADA'S WEST COAST

Grenada's west coast has several anchorages, useful as a last stop for northbound yachts. They are all susceptible to northerly swells. Halifax and Grand Mal are acceptable in most conditions, Dragon's Bay and Happy Hill will get very uncomfortable in moderate swells, and be dangerous in large ones.

Halifax Harbour is a quiet spot enclosed by hills. It is a small bay without a village and easily missed unless you follow closely along the coast. A few landmarks help. Dragons Bay is about two miles up the coast from St. George's and Halifax Harbour is about two miles beyond that. Between them, but much closer to Dragon's Bay, is a tall red and white striped aerial, and closer to Halifax is a village. There is a white house which stands on the hill to the north overlooking the harbor. You have to tuck well in the harbor as the water in the middle is very deep. A nearby refuse depot sometimes causes a fly problem, and occasionally creates bad smells. However, if you arrive an hour or so before sunset the flies will have already gone to bed on someone else's boat. Note the spectacular large silk cotton tree at the water's edge in the southern bay.

Happy Hill, just north of Dragon's Bay is more open but can be very peaceful. There is a narrow beach backed by a hill, and on the hill is another large old silk cotton tree. Avoid the southern part of the bay which is strewn with coral heads and anchor in the middle or closer to the northern headland. If jacks are running the fishermen may ask

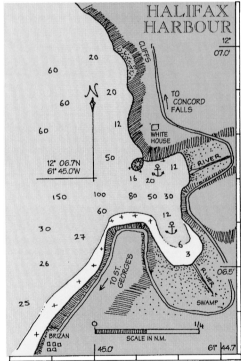

BLACK BAY PT.   Low cliffs   HALIFAX HARBOUR   Conspicuous cluster   ST. GEORGE'S,   Pt.. Saline
                                                                of houses   2 miles further down   just visible
                                                                                   the coast, is hidden

Moliniere Pt.

View from 1.5 miles west of Halifax Hbr.

263

you to clear out at the crack of dawn, which will give you a good early start for Carriacou. There is good snorkeling in the southern part of the bay around the rocks.

Dragon's Bay is a delightful anchorage with a palm-lined beach, but too small to allow more than two or three boats. Avoid anchoring in the south part of the bay as it is full of coral heads which make for good snorkeling. You can find a good sand bottom for anchoring in the middle of the bay. Both the snorkeling and the diving are first-rate around Moliniere Point just south of Dragon's Bay. Do not be tempted to anchor your yacht off Moliniere Point as you will damage the coral. If you dinghy round, you can anchor your dinghy in the odd patch of sand in shallow water.

Grand Mal is a well protected anchorage most of the time. The water is usually clean and the long beach attractive. There are gas storage tanks in Grand Mal, and two buoys offshore which are used for unloading tankers. Pipes run out from the small dock to the buoys so avoid anchoring in this area. You can anchor just north of these buoys, between them and the headland, or south of them just outside the fishing fleet.

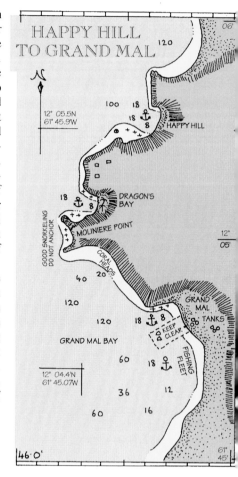

ST. GEORGE'S

St. George's is built on a ridge, with the sea on one side and the protected Carenage on the other. The houses mingle with shrubs and trees, giving splashes of bright color against a background of dark green. From afar it is as neat and pretty as a picture book illustration. The old brick buildings are capped with antique "fish scale" tile roofs, a reminder of long ago when the profitable journeys were outward bound, laden with rum, spices and fruit and returning sailing ships would arrive "in ballast" of bricks and tiles.

When approaching from the north, the harbor entrance remains hidden until you reach it. On your left as you enter, you will see Fort George. This fort spent a few socialist years as "Fort Rupert" in memory of Prime Minister Bishop's father. When Bishop was imprisoned by members of his own party and later freed by thousands of his followers, they came here in a euphoric mood. The army sent in armored cars, shot some civilians (several more hurt themselves jumping off the walls of the fort), and executed Prime Minister Bishop and half the cabinet. The ruins you see over on your right-hand side are those of a building that started life as a hotel and was used by the socialist government as a main office building, Butler House. The damage is due not so much to the American assault forces as it is to a desperate attempt by the communists to destroy documents. Although

Mamma's

THE place for good local food.
No trip to Grenada
is complete without a night here!
(see write up in this book)
Phone: 440-1459

1994 Certificate or Ac-
creditation *for quality &
Value* by Interactive
Travelvision Network.

(Also Mamma's Lodge –
the brand new
inexpensive place to stay)

managed by Cleo.

Mamma

10 GOOD REASONS ◄
► TO VISIT 1 LOCATION
in Grenada

1. THE BEST LITTLE LIQUOR STORE IN TOWN
From climate controlled cellars we offer the widest selection of fine wines in
these parts and great prices on all kinds of liquors and liqueurs, bottled
water, ice, tobacco, film and cold drinks.

DINGY TIE UP – WATERFRONT SEATING

2. DUTY FREE – delivery to all marinas

3. the fastest way to receive money – WESTERN|MONEY UNION|TRANSFER *The fast way to send money worldwide*

4. DHL – worldwide express courier service
WORLDWIDE EXPRESS

5. Fabulous beach cruises by – *Rhum Runner*

6. **Havadu** – snorkel excursions and game fishing

7. Shoreside excursions with a difference – *Grenada Safari*

8. Xerox – photocopy service

9. Boat and marine supplies by – *RUSH ORDER*

10. and most of all **WE CARE** about our customers

Telephones: 1-809-440-2198/2625/3422
VHF RADIO CHANNEL 16 RHUM RUNNER BASE"
Fax: 1-809-440-4179

RENWICK & THOMPSON BUILDING, CARENAGE, GRENADA

the damage looks impressive, over three tons of paper were recovered. This building may soon be rebuilt as a hotel. Straight ahead on the hills above the lagoon you can see Fort Frederick, from which the attack on Bishop was launched, and the prison, where all the culprits, including the Coards, now sit.

The main anchorage is in the lagoon between Grenada Yacht Services (GYS) and the Grenada Yacht Club. Expect depths of 15 to 20 feet in soft gooey mud. The channel into the lagoon is about 13 feet deep and marked by unlit buoys and stakes. Many people find it confusing, but it is easy if you do the following: when entering the harbor, head straight for the right hand (southern) end of the big ship dock, only turning into the channel when you clearly see all the markers lined up.

The harbor master has been discouraging anchoring or tying up in the Carenage. However, if you wish to do so, call the Grenada Port Authority on VHF:16. No town in the Windwards is completely free of theft and St. George's is no exception. Always lock up the boat and dinghy and if possible leave someone on board. Every

few years, St. George's has outbreaks of petty boat theft that go beyond the normal. You can find out the current situation by calling Liz Gorman, the tourism officer in charge of yachts and cruise ships, at 440-2872.

Regulations

The customs office is located in the GYS complex. Normal office hours are weekdays 0800-1200, 1300-1600. When you clear in tell the customs officers which ports you plan to visit.

Services

GYS [T:440-2508, VHF:16] has been dreadfully dilapidated for many years. It is supposed to have changed hands and a multimillion dollar rebuild is planned. However, expect it "just now." Meanwhile most services still operate. There is a 250-ton synchro lift and a screw lift dock, a machine shop and wood shop. There are security guards (though there have still been a few break-ins) and a telephone. Fuel and water are available, and for those moments when rain destroys your still-wet varnish, there is a bar.

The Grenada Yacht Club [T:440-3050,

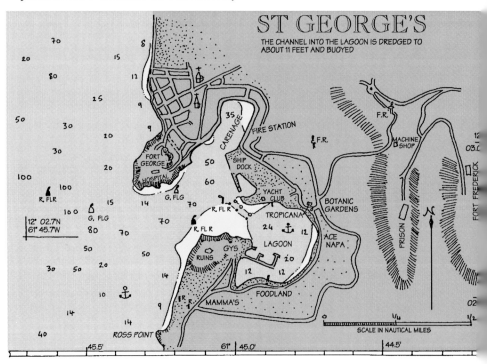

266

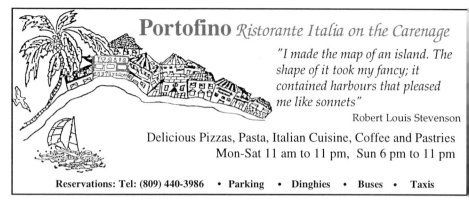

Portofino *Ristorante Italia on the Carenage*

"I made the map of an island. The shape of it took my fancy; it contained harbours that pleased me like sonnets"

Robert Louis Stevenson

Delicious Pizzas, Pasta, Italian Cuisine, Coffee and Pastries
Mon-Sat 11 am to 11 pm, Sun 6 pm to 11 pm

Reservations: Tel: (809) 440-3986 • Parking • Dinghies • Buses • Taxis

VHF:6, 16] is an inexpensive place to drink beers and watch others run aground as they try to come in the cut. Snacks are available, as are showers, water and a card phone. Dockage is sometimes available and there is a hand crank railway suitable for the smaller cruising yachts (up to 10 tons, 35 ft.). The yacht club organizes the Grenada Sailing Festival, a week of racing and social events which is held in January. All entrants are welcome, from serious racing boats to live-aboards. The first festival was a great success with 39 boats, including a sizeable contingent of Canadians who chartered bareboats for the event. Also featured in last year's festival was a series of match races between Buddy Melges and Terry Neilson.

Albert Lucas [T:440-1281] runs an excellent machine shop and is usually there every day including Sunday. He will often do small jobs while you wait. Finding him is more of a problem as he has no sign. At the Tropicana roundabout, turn right away from the sea. At the main road turn left and you will see a roundabout in front of you. Turn right up the hill at the roundabout. Eventually you will come to the Blue Danube bakery/supermarket, easily seen as lots of cars park outside. Albert is on the right-hand side of the road on the corner, just before you reach the Blue Danube.

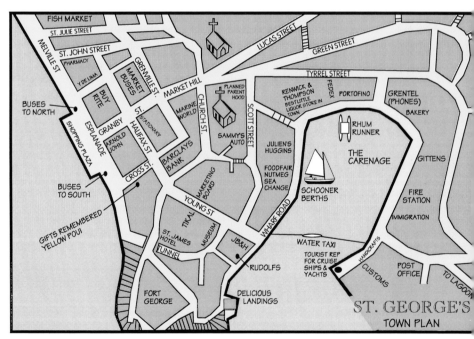

ST. GEORGE'S
TOWN PLAN

ST. GEORGE'S HARBOUR

You will see steps going up forever, but you only have to take a few to reach Lucas and you will see his workshop on the left.

Clifford Bascombe at C.B. Stove and Small Engine Repair Shop [T:440-9559] fixes all manner of gas stoves, and carries parts that will fit almost any model. If you give him a call he will visit in any of the main anchorages.

Ross's workshop, just down the road from GYS, will have a go at welding anything.

Henry's Safari Tours [T:444-5313, VHF:68] offers a collect-and-deliver laundry service from any of Grenada's main anchorages. Henry also sells block ice, collects garbage, passes on dinner reservations at no charge and fills cooking gas tanks. Otherwise to fill cooking gas bottles you have to take a taxi to the filling depot in Mt. Gay, which is a fair way outside town. Henry will also find you cut flowers or organize anything else you might need.

Basil St. John at Lagoon Marine Refrigeration Services [T:440-3381] is a first class refrigeration repair man. You can call him up and he will pay a boat visit either in St. George's or in Prickly Bay.

Walker & Sons [T:440-1756] have been in the sail repair business for many years. Their operation is on River Road on the far side of town, so best call them to come and discuss the job. (See also Johnny Phillips in Prickly Bay.)

Outfitters International [T:440-7949, F:440-6680] have an office and dinghy dock on the opposite side of the lagoon from GYS. Their famous Priority Parts Service is well known throughout the Caribbean. They will find whatever part or piece of equipment you need and deliver it to your yacht and they handle all the customs work. The price you pay depends on how quickly you need the part and what it is. You can get many chandlery items at around the U.S.A. list price. For large thirsty yachts, Outfitters run a duty free fuel bunkering service. They also act as a mail drop (c/o Outfitters International, Box 581, St. George's, Grenada, W.I.).

Water taxis are available in town and will drop you back to your boat for about $2EC, but they are hard to find at the GYS end. There are plenty of hopeful laborers looking for a job, but it is best to get a local recommendation.

If you need a survey you can contact Mike Forshaw or Alan Hooper through GYS, Spice Island Marine or call 440-3693 or 440-2881.

Ashore

You can take your dinghy from the lagoon over to town. If you take this guide with you, our town map will help. Tie up outside Food Fair or Delicious Landings which is less dusty. An alternative is to walk to town from the Yacht Club, and return by water taxi.

St. George's is a busy place with plenty of traffic including large colorful buses laden with people and goods, smaller mini buses with loud music, cars, trucks weighed down with building material, and sometimes it seems like they are all honking at once. People will shout "taxi" at you and vendors may offer fruits from baskets.

Most shops open from 0800 to 1200 and then from 1300 to 1600 on weekdays. Banks are open only till 1300, except Friday when they also open from 1430 to 1700. The post office moved near customs after the old post office building on the Carenage burned down in 1990. It is open over lunch, but closed all day Saturday. Most shops are closed Saturday afternoon and everything is closed on Sunday.

St. George's is a first rate place to provision, with comfortable air-conditioned supermarkets. The newest is Foodland [T:440-1991/4496, VHF:80] in the lagoon. It has its own dinghy dock and is

270

often open quite late at night. Foodland has an excellent selection of regular items and a pleasing delicatessen section. It offers a 5% discount to yachtsmen on orders over $150 US. In town, Food Fair [T:440-2558/5035/6] is conveniently close to the water and you can tie up nearby. They are open weekdays till 1730, except Friday when they are open till 2045. On Saturdays they close at 2000. For sizeable orders ask Mr. Harris about a discount.

Those wishing to buy wine or liquor should visit the Best Little Liquor Store in Town [T:440-2198/3422, F:440-4179, VHF:16 Rhum Runner Base, cc:A,V]. You can tie your dinghy close to the shop. Their selection includes over 125 different wines. If you are buying by the case, duty free prices are available. It is best to allow 48 hours for processing. On large orders delivery to Prickly Bay is a possibility. You can also buy block and cube ice here, send your DHL packets, organize money through Western Union, and ask them about bringing you spares via Rush Order.

Visit the local market, preferably on a

Saturday morning. It is a riot of color where determined ladies under big umbrellas sit amid huge heaps of vegetables. You can get fresh produce, spices and handicrafts. If you feel peckish, try a freshly cooked fish cake. The Marketing Board on Young Street (opposite Tikal) has the best prices on fresh produce, although the range is limited.

When GYS is restored it may feature a chandlery. Meanwhile there are several good hardware stores. Arnold John [T:440-3412] is on the Esplanade/Granby St. corner. Jonas Browne and Hubbards Hardware [T:440-2087] and Huggins [T:440-2031] are on the Carenage. Marine World [T:440-1748] on Grenville St. has a good selection of fishing gear, snorkeling gear and charts. In the lagoon, on the opposite side to GYS, you will find a well stocked Ace Hardware and NAPA agent [T:440-5265].

Other auto parts type shops include Sammy's and Hubbards.

Some things are not where you expect them. For some sizes of watch battery you

have to go to the Anglo American Funeral Parlor.

Souvenir items range from baskets of spices to large woven mats, batik, art, perfumes and pottery. The Rolls Royce of the boutiques in town is Jeanne Fisher's Tikal [T:440-2310, cc:V,A] on Young Street. It is stacked with quality arts and crafts, including the local Art-Fabrik batiks. You will also find paintings, maps, hammocks, ornaments, casual shirts, and much more. Spice Island Perfumes (near Portofino on the Carenage) sell their own herbal products: sun care lotions, perfumes, skin care creams, teas and pot pourris. A wonderful smell fills their shop. They also sell batiks, colorful shirts and sunglasses. Next door, Creation [T:440-0570, cc:A,V] carries a wide range of handicrafts, clothing and art items.

There are two duty free shops. Gittens [T:444-4101, cc:A,V] sells all the top names in perfumes and beauty care products and close by Bon Voyage [T:440-4217, cc:A, V, Dn, Ds] sells crystal, bone china, jewelry and leather goods. When cruise ships visit, the craft stalls by the cruise ship docks come alive.

On the other side of town, visit Gifts Remembered [T:444-2482, cc:A,V] on Cross Street. They have a large range of handicrafts suitable as gifts. If you like art, visit Jim Rudin's Yellow Poui Art Gallery [T:440-3878/3001] above Gifts Remembered. He has wonderful local paintings, but his selection goes beyond this to antique maps, objets d'art and artistic postcards.

St. George's is best viewed when you have plenty of time and nothing you have to do. There are wonderful views wherever you go; the more panoramic are around the fort, and up by the cemetery (up Church Street and keep going). There are plenty of steps and narrow alleys to explore and the museum is well worth a visit for the $1 US entrance fee. If the heat gets to you, pull up for a cold drink.

Rudolf's [T:440-2241, $B-D] is an excellent pub style restaurant with a cozy atmosphere and draft beer. They serve delectable seafood and steaks. They also of-

fer a large range of tasty snacks. It is popular among the local business community for lunch, and as a dinner restaurant it is wonderful value and usually uncrowded.

Grenada is the land of the unexpected, so it should come as no surprise to find Patrick, a friendly Irishman running an Italian restaurant he took over from Goh, a Malayan, and running it very well. It is called Portofino [T:440-3986, B-D, cc:A,V] and it is upstairs on the Carenage with a view over the Carenage to Grand Anse. The service is good and you can get crisp salads and appetizing pizzas and pastas. For fancier tastes there is lobster and steak. Patrick also offers a takeout service.

The Nutmeg [T:440-2539, $C-D, cc:V] is inexpensive with a bird's eye view from their perch above Food Fair. Although it is sometimes crowded at lunch, there is usually plenty of room at dinner.

Delicious Landing [T:440-9747, $B-C, cc:V], has a prime location right over the water with a superb harbor view. It is open from breakfast to dinner every day. Owner Grace Raymond specializes in seafood and offers a good variety of lobster dishes as well as fish, shrimp and lambi. They also have meat and vegetarian meals. For lunch they also have sandwiches and specials. Quality is good, prices are reasonable, and there is a convenient dinghy dock right outside which you are welcome to use even if you are just passing through. Occasional live entertainment is put on during the season.

The adventurous should try to find the Ye Olde Farmhouse Kitchen [$D] behind Gifts Remembered where you can eat a hearty local lunch.

There are also two good restaurants in the lagoon.

Horatio Brizan's Tropicana [T:440-1586, $C-D, cc:V] is Grenada's best inexpensive restaurant; cheap enough to eat at any time cooking seems too much of a chore. The food is Chinese and local with good rotis, fish and lambi dishes. You can tie your dinghy somewhere on the shore opposite the restaurant. Excellent value for lunch or dinner with a separate and speedy takeout section. Horatio has completely renovated the building and put in some clean modern and inexpensive rooms upstairs.

Mamma's [T:440-1459, $B], run by Cleopatra, serves a very wide variety of local dishes all at the same time. About 16 dishes including chicken, fish, beef, rabbit, conch, octopus, lambi and lots of different vegetables are all prepared in local style, making a fine feast. During the hunting and lobster season (September 30th - March 31st) lobster, turtle, monkey, tatoo (armadillo), iguana, manicou and monkey are

often offered. The taste of these "wildbeasts" are only for the very adventurous. Since Mamma's is by reservation only and you eat a set meal, you should discuss your tastes when you book. Cleo will certainly accommodate you. Although Cleo faithfully sticks to the hunting season, it would better for the environment if you asked that turtle, iguana and tatoo are left off your menu, as these are all under considerable human pressure. Mamma's is just up the road from GYS in a neighborhood which is not safe. If you are walking, go in a group.

Water sports

The Rhum Runner [T:440-2198/3422, F:440-4179, VHF:16, Rhum Runner Base], is probably not most yachtsmen's idea of entertainment. However, besides their tourist trips, they do full moon barbecue runs which are mainly for the local population, are inexpensive and can be fun.

GRAND ANSE

Grand Anse is what most people have in mind when they think about the Caribbean: a generous two-mile sweep of white-gold sand, backed by shady palms and almond trees. Although it forms the center of the Grenada Hotel Industry, strict laws protect it and no hotel can be higher than the tallest coconut tree.

Anchoring is currently forbidden at Grand Anse, though this restriction may be lifted. Meanwhile you can anchor just south of St. George's and dinghy down. There is currently no dock here which means dragging your dinghy up on the sand. The beach closest to the Coconut's Beach French Restaurant is calmest.

Ashore

Food Fair at Grand Anse is air conditioned and spacious, making it a comfort-

EDMOND MORREL'S STAND AT CLOZIER

able place to provision. It is set in a pleasant shopping center where you will find Imagine [T:444-4028, cc:A,V], a terrific handicraft store with batiks, woodcraft, hand painted t-shirts, Spice Island cosmetics, books and much more. Other shops include Hubbard's Home Center[T:444-3232, Rick's Cafe [T:444-4597, $D], Chantilly [T:444-2554] for lingerie, Mitchell's Pharmacy [T:444-4845 open till 2100], a men's clothing store, a bank and more. Upstairs in the same center is Dr. Mike Radix [T:444-4855/440-4379, in emergency: T:443-5330], who is very good and used to dealing with people from yachts.

Just down the road, Gittens Drugmart is a full pharmacy, with everything from prescriptions to newspapers. A few doors down, the Grenada Bank of Commerce can take care of your money matters. There is also a travel agent and liquor store. On the other side of the road is the Marquis Mal, where anyone with a computer will find disks, print heads and ribbons at Onsite Software Support [T:444-3653]. Toothache? Sunsmile Dental Clinic run by Dr. Roxanne Nedd [T:444-2273], is in Marquis Mall and has been recommended by cruising people.

All the major hotels have boutiques.

There is a good bus service to town.

Coconut's Beach French Restaurant [T:444-4644, $A-B] has a superb location right on the water's edge on Grand Anse Beach. You can drive up to it in your dinghy or come by car. Good French cuisine adapted to local foods, well managed by Grenadian "Scratch," and very romantic on a full moon night.

Lawrence Lambert is a Grenadian who spent some years in Canada and then returned to buy The Flamboyant Hotel and the Beachside Restaurant [T:444-4247, $B-D, cc:A, V]. It is at the western end of Grand Anse beach with a sweeping view to St. George's. The restaurant has good West Indian and continental food, with a big buffet and steel band on Wednesday nights in season. There is also crab racing Monday nights and a calypsonian Friday nights. They have a good, very cheap Sunday barbecue brunch which is geared toward families who come to enjoy the beach and the pool – so bring your kids.

Cot Bam [T:444-2050, $C-D, cc V,Ds] on Grand Anse Beach is open to the breeze and serves an excellent lunchtime shrimp roti. It is managed by Leroy who inherited the recipes from his father Papa Hall. They have live entertainment most nights in season.

Determined gourmets should make time to visit Eric and Gina's Canboulay [T:444-4401, $A-B, cc:V], one of the Windward's finest restaurants. It is on a hill behind Grand Anse with a panoramic view over to St. George's. The food here is excellent; an imaginative contemporary cuisine based on local fresh fruits, vegetables, herbs and spices. Come with a large appetite because the price includes several courses and a delightful sorbet to clean your palette between the starter and main course.

The Bird's Nest will satisfy those with a hankering for Chinese food.

There is entertainment at both Spice Island Inn and Ramada Renaissance most nights. While in Grenada, try to listen to a good steel band. You may have listened to one or two farther north and come to the mistaken conclusion that, while steelband is fun, it is repetitive and best listened to from a distance. Good "pan" sound is fantastic and there are very good groups in Grenada. Ramada Renaissance has one on Sunday and Monday nights, Beachside on Wednesday nights in season, and Spice Island Inn on Friday nights with their barbecue.

A short ride or healthy walk from Grand Anse is the beautiful but shallow Morne Rouge Bay. There is a complex here called the Gem Holiday Beach Resort [T:444-4224/1189, F:440-4124], managed by Julia Moore. Apart from rooms for a night ashore they run the Fantazia 2001 disco which is open on Wednesdays for Oldie Goldie night, and on Fridays and Saturdays with live music. They have the inexpensive restaurant, Sur La Mer [T:444-4224, $C, cc:A,V,Ds,Dn], which makes a pleasant lunch destination for anyone who wants a walk from Grand Anse (also open for dinner).

Water sports

There are several dive shops in Grenada, all keenly competitive and happy to take yachtsmen. If you call one they will probably arrange to send a car to collect you from your anchorage. All dive shops are Padi or Naui establishments with all kinds of

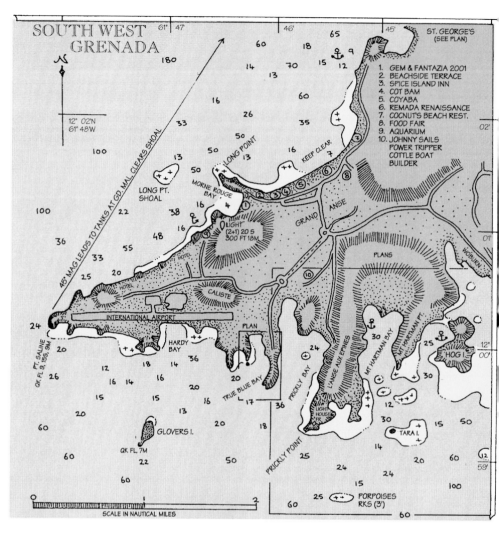

SOUTH WEST GRENADA

1. GEM & FANTAZIA 2001
2. BEACHSIDE TERRACE
3. SPICE ISLAND INN
4. COT BAM
5. COYABA
6. REMADA RENAISSANCE
7. COCNUT'S BEACH REST.
8. FOOD FAIR
9. AQUARIUM
10. JOHNNY SAILS
    POWER TRIPPER
    COTTLE BOAT
    BUILDER

ST. GEORGE'S (SEE PLAN)

SCALE IN NAUTICAL MILES

courses, including introductory resort courses.

Randi Bolt at Grenada Aquatics [T:444-4219, ext 144, F:444-4808, VHF:16] is based at the Coyaba Hotel. Randi will rent equipment by the day and is happy to point out some dive sites. He runs dives at 1000 and 1400 and for a real adventure he does two tank dives at Isle de Ronde.

The Ramada Renaissance has a dive shop, currently undergoing some changes.

David MacNaughten at Dive Grenada [T:444-4334, T/F:444-5875, VHF:16] has a shop at the Calabash, but hopes to open a new base at Grand Anse soon.

Grenada has the Caribbean's most dramatic dive. The wreck of the Bianca C, a 600-foot cruise ship, sits upright on the sea bed. The Bianca C caught fire while in St. George's Harbour. Everyone in town rushed to rescue the passengers in small boats, and the cruise ship was towed out into deep water and sunk. There are lots of fish, including big schools of curious barracuda. The wreck lies in about 160 feet of water; the top deck is at 90 feet. This is an exciting and dramatic dive, but it is deep and local knowledge is necessary, both to find it and cope with the currents. You have to go straight down on a line, sometimes with some surface current. This is not always easy so the dive shops will want you to do one other checkout dive with them first. You could try one of their reef dives

278

such as Wibble Reef off Grand Anse which slopes from about 50 feet deep to 170 feet. You swim in and out of forests of soft corals, there are large sponges, black coral, big angelfish, lobsters, groupers and often eagle rays. For a shallower dive, there is Bass Reef which goes from the red buoy off St. George's Harbour toward Point Saline. As there are currents here, this is generally done as a gentle drift dive. The reef varies in depth from 20-90 feet. You float through massive schools of brown and blue chromis and there are plenty of colorful parrotfish, groupers, and banded coral shrimps.

NORTH SHORE OF POINT SALINE

Coast hoppers may want to explore this shore which has several pretty beaches. You must, however, be very careful of Long Point Shoal and only approach when there is good light and you can see the reefs. (Or see our "Sailing to Prickly Bay" section.) It is possible to eyeball your way inside Long Point Shoal, but don't cut too close to Long Point as there are some shoals that come out about 150 feet from shore. As you round Long Point heading west, you will see the beautiful Morne Rouge Bay, which, unfortunately, is only about four feet deep. You can usually find lunchtime anchorage just outside Morne Rouge Bay or off the Aquarium Beach Club, but anchor a couple of hundred feet offshore as there are reefs close to the shore along most of the coast. This can also be an acceptable overnight anchorage in settled calm conditions when there is little chance of northerly swells.

Uli and Rebecca's Aquarium Beach Club [T:444-1410, $B-D, cc:A,V,Ds] is an away-from-it-all spot in a garden setting on a deserted beach. The fresh seafood is excellent and this is a great place to come for a quiet romantic seafood lunch or dinner, or bring a group and make it what you will. The Aquarium Beach Club is popular

279

on Sundays when people come to swim, play volley ball and snorkel. Rebecca is an artist and if you ask she will show you some of her work. If you are driving here, take the airport road and look for the signs.

Leaving the island and looking for an inexpensive hotel near the airport? No problem. Try Godfrey Ventour's No Problem Apartments [T:444-4634].

PRICKLY BAY

PT. SALINE TO PRICKLY BAY

When sailing between St. George's and Point Saline, keep well clear of Long Point Shoal. This may be done by heading west from St. George's and continuing till you are on the line between Pt. Saline and the tanks at Grand Mal before heading for Pt. Saline. Reverse this procedure for returning.

As you sail round Pt. Saline and head toward Glovers Island, Prickly Point will be the farthest headland that you see. As you get closer, Prickly Bay is easily identified by all the yachts inside and the handsome houses on the hill. There is plenty of water for most yachts to sail inside Glovers Island. There is one good anchorage just before Prickly Bay called True Blue.

TRUE BLUE

True Blue is the bay just west of Prickly Bay. It is pretty, peaceful and conveniently placed as an overnight spot for charterers who want somewhere near their base for a first or last night.

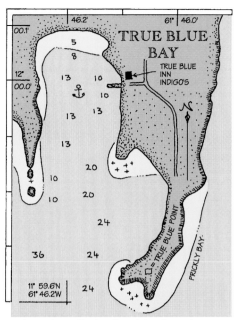

There is a distinctive island at the entrance to the bay, often used as a roost by cattle egrets. Enter in the middle of the bay between this island and True Blue Point. Go straight up into the bay and anchor

inside or take up one of Indigo's moorings. The water is about 25 feet deep at the entrance to the bay and there is 13 feet all the way up almost to the end of the bay. As with Prickly Bay, a surge can enter from time to time. If you find it rolly, try using a stern anchor.

Ashore

Indigo's Restaurant [T:444-2000, F:444-1247, $B, cc:A,V] is run by Trinidadians Tony and Gillian Potter. True to their nationality, they are excellent hosts and run a first rate kitchen. They have a dock with 10 feet of water at the end and can provide water. Telephone and fax services are available. You are welcome to use one of the moorings they have put opposite their restaurant. Indigo's Restaurant has an intimate open atmosphere with a perfect sunset view over the bay. The food is a delightful blend of West Indian and international dishes with offerings from the sea, including dolphin fish, lambi and lobster. True Blue Inn behind the restaurant is under the same management and rooms are available.

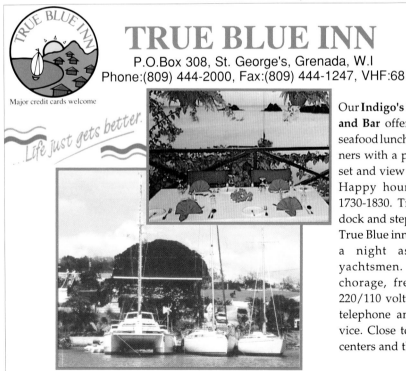

PRICKLY BAY

(Also known as L'Anse Aux Epines, pronounced "Lans O Peen")

Prickly Bay is a delightful spot. The land is a tapestry of attractive gardens which form a background of green, speckled with bright flowers. Lovely homes and all kinds of roofs peek out over the vegetation. At the head of the bay is a palm fringed beach. You feels very much in the country here, with the sound of birds by day and tree frogs by night. Yet St. George's is only 15 minutes away by car and the airport and Grand Anse are even closer. The facilities of Spice Island Boatyard are close by, as are several hotels, restaurants and even a disco. It is an ideal place for those who want to have truck with civilization, yet feel apart from it.

Thomas, publisher, yacht restorer and currently realtor and builder, has built a prominent house at the end of L'Anse aux Epines Point, part of which looks just like a lighthouse. He shows a fixed red light when there is mains electricity. This makes Prickly Point very easy to recognize.

While Prickly Bay is easy to enter, don't get too careless. There is a reef marked by a nondescript buoy in the middle opposite the boatyard which is just deep enough to be hard to see. Reefs also extend nearly all the way up the eastern shore and one should give the True Blue headland reasonable clearance. Occasional southerly swells can make the bay uncomfortable, though a stern anchor will do much to restore a sense of calm.

Regulation

Prickly Bay is a port of entry with the customs at the boatyard. Anchoring is forbidden within 300 feet of the beach as it is reserved for swimmers.

Services

Spice Island Marine Boatyard [Box 449, St. George's Grenada, T:444-4257/4342, F: 444-2816, VHF:16, cc:V] is a charming small marina where fresh green lawns are dotted with palms and almond trees. It has

PRICKLY BAY

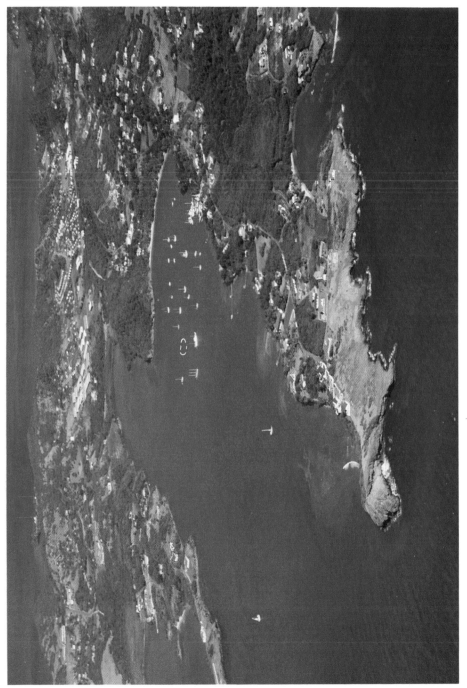

an informal atmosphere and docks for about 25 yachts. It is managed by ex-charter skipper and yachtsman Champie Evans. Showers, laundry, electricity, fuel, water, ice, and cooking gas can be found here. There is a 35-ton travel lift and you can do your own work or hire their labor. Mechanics and electronic repairs can be arranged. There is a chandlery which offers many items duty free. Michael runs an efficient sail loft, and Spice Island are agents for Offshore Sails. Snagg will sell you fuel and help in any way he can. You can have your mail sent here and post your outgoing letters. Buy telephone cards at the chandlery for the card phone. You will also find a fax and an uncertain bus service to town which leaves about 0930 in the morning. Confirm the time with the boatyard before you pack your shopping bag. Within the boatyard Shirley's Essentials [T:444-4662, VHF:16, (cc:V, boutique only)] is a convenient mini-market and boutique. What Essentials lacks in size it makes up for in service and Shirley will bring in anything you want that is not on the shelves. Or you can call on the radio for special orders or a full provisioning service. Spice Island Boatyard is the home of Seabreeze Yacht Charters and the Boatyard Restaurant (see below).

Jeff Fisher [T:440-2556] is an agent for Neil Pryde sails, made in Hong Kong. These sails are of good quality and reasonably priced. Jeff says he can arrange for new sails to reach Grenada within six weeks. He is often around the boatyard, so if you cannot get him on the telephone, ask around for him.

For mechanical problems there are several possibilities. Power Tripper [T:444-1351, F:444-4638, VHF:16], run by Richard Herrera, is a high-tech mechanical shop located between Prickly Bay and True Blue on the side road known as Dusty Highway. He fixes all kinds of pleasure boat engines and outboards, including alternators and electrics. Richard is set up for testing injectors. He has a very fast spares service for just about any make of engine and can supply new units. He is agent for Mercury, Northern Lights and Yanmar. Ben [T:440-

YOU'LL BE OVER THE MOON WHEN YOU SHOP AT

The best of
CARIBBEAN HANDICRAFTS
in natural materials
**dolls*ceramics*straw
clothing*great gifts**
at
Grand Anse Shopping Center
*Open daily (except Sunday)
9 am-5 pm
Tel:809-444-4028*

*Elizabeth Belingy and
Shirley Hooper*

Credit cards welcome

Visit also our other shops:

IMAGINE AT THE REX GRENADIAN
For creative t-shirts, mens' shorts, and ladies clothing

CHANTILLY (At the Grand Anse Shopping Center)
For Lingerie, men's underwear, gifts soaps, wraps

OCTOPUS GARDENS AT RAMADA RENAISSANCE
(Just across the road from Grand Anse shopping center)
For swimwear, beach games, toys and t-shirts

ESSENTIALS (At Spice island Boatyard, Prickly Bay)
*The complete mini-mart for visiting yachtsmen with
fresh and frozen foods, liquor, soft drinks and much
more including a good range of essential handicrafts,
books, postcards, clothing and souvenirs. Tel:444-3466
Open Monday to Saturday 0900-1800,
Open Sun & Holidays 0900-1200*

5360] is a good general mechanic who is reliable and reasonable.

McIntyre Bros [T:440-2044, F:440-4125] are on the airport road. They are agents for Yanmar, Lehman and Cummins, have qualified diesel mechanics, and will try to help with parts for other engines. They are also the sales and service agents for Yamaha outboards and can arrange sales to yachts duty free at good prices. McIntyre also rents cars.

In the same building as Power Tripper, down the dusty highway, Johnny Sails and Canvas [T:444-1108, 441-9619, F:444-1108, VHF:16/66] is a good sail loft. Johnny, a Grenadian, trained in Canada at Boston Sails for four years and for a time was charter manager at The Moorings. Johnny can repair and make new sails. He carries and can bend stainless tube so biminis are a breeze, as are awnings, covers, interior and exterior cushions. Johnny is also the man to see for rigging problems. He aims to stock stainless rigging and Staylock fittings.

Also in the same building you will find Cottle Boat Works [F:444-1108/444-2090, VHF:72 from 0800-0900], a full marine joinery and carpentry shop. Owner Jim Cottle has over 20 years experience in the business. He sailed to Grenada on his Yacht J. Jeffrey. Jim keeps one foot on the sea by living aboard. He can often be found at The Moorings Rum Squall Bar after the sun has gone over the yard arm. Teak decks are one of Jim's specialties, and when business is a bit slack he builds handy cruising dinghies.

Anyone wishing to leave their yacht here and have someone reliable keep an eye on it should contact Selwyn Maxwell [T:444-1653, VHF:68] or ask for Errol at Seabreeze Yacht charters.

Tangey's Laundry and Dry Cleaning Service [T:444-4747] is reasonably priced. It is about a mile down the road, but if you call they will collect and deliver to Prickly Bay or St. George's.

There are some excellent taxi drivers around. Selwyn Maxwell [T:444-1653, VHF:68], spent some years as a charter skipper so he is well acquainted with the

whole yachting scene. He is charming, reliable and has a mini-van. He is willing to hike and can do the Seven Falls trip. Funseeker Tours [T:444-1342 441-9443, F:444 4847, VHF:16] operated by Russ, Trevor and Janet, is another good operation. They offer all kinds of tours geared at showing how things are done in Grenada. They do hiking tours, offer a taxi service and rent good, but not brand new, jeeps.

It is very easy to call Boatyard Taxi [VHF:16, 444-1703]. This is a taxi drivers' association with a small office in Spice Island Marine, there is nearly always a good driver available.

Ashore

The Boatyard Restaurant [T:444-4662, VHF:68, $B-C, cc:A,V, closed Mondays] is right in Spice Island Marine. Run by Brits Cleve and Carol, it is a favorite yachty haunt. Everyone gathers at happy hour (1730-1830) for cut-price drinks. Stay for dinner and enjoy first rate seafood, steaks and straightforward fare at reasonable prices as you look out over the yachts and the harbor. There is early evening entertainment (1900-2200) on Wednesdays and Fridays, and on Friday it usually continues and becomes a late night jump up. They also have a satellite TV which is dusted off and turned on for important ball games or yachting events.

The gourmet will hone up his appetite by taking the five minute walk to the Red Crab [T:444-4424, $:A-B, cc:A,V]. Owner/ Chef George Mueller is a German who speaks English with a Scottish accent. However, you will not be offered haggis. George is a professional chef with impressive credentials. He worked for many years with Hilton International as executive chef. At the Pan American Culinary Olympics he not only won gold, but was awarded honorary citizenship of New Orleans. In Trinidad he had his own TV program. The Red Crab offers such delights as "Crepe Pottare" – shrimp rolled in a thin French pancake capped with sauce chablis, and filet of pork sauteed in butter topped with mushrooms in cream and wine. They also have first rate steaks (try the filet Wellington) and lobster.

Distinctive dining in a relaxed environment - only 5 minutes from Prickly Bay Marina.

The ingredients we use must be fresh and the best available on the market.

Because of changes in season, weather and catch, we adjust our fantasy and fine art of cooking accordingly in order to be able to offer our guests a vibrant and interesting menu.

Our courteous, efficient staff will be happy to serve you in the best Grenadian tradition.

THE RED CRAB RESTAURANT

L'anse aux Epines, Grenada, West Indies,
P.O.Box 356. Telephone 444-4424
Open Monday through Saturday
from 11 a.m. to 2 p.m.and from 6 p.m. to 11 p.m.
Major credit cards welcome

Next door the Choo Light [$C-D] is an informal Chinese restaurant. The staff welcomes you warmly, the service and food are good and the prices won't put to much of a dent in your wallet.. They also offer a full takeout service.

Other restaurants in the area include the Calabash [T:444-4334, $A, cc:V,A], where a pianist is frequently present, and there is a steel band on Friday nights and for Sunday buffet lunch. A jazz and pan band plays on Wednesday nights.

If the tree frogs fail to lull you to sleep, you can hit the Sugar Mill Nightclub (Wednesday to Saturday) about a mile down the road by the roundabout. However, take a care; it can be a pretty rough.

You will find tennis courts at the hotels and the Calabash has a snooker table.

Water sports

David MacNaughten at Dive Grenada [T:444-4334, T/F:444-5875, VHF:16] has a shop at the Calabash Hotel. He likes working with yachts and will negotiate the price for large groups. David is happy to fill tanks, but he does not normally rent gear. He usually dives at 1000 and 1400.

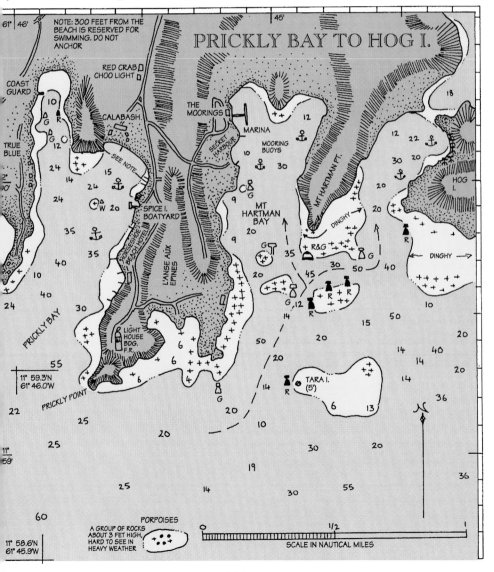

THE SOUTH COAST BEYOND PRICKLY BAY

The south coast of Grenada offers beautiful, secluded and protected anchorages. A mass of reefs provides interesting if somewhat murky snorkeling. The area should be treated with caution and in places eyeball navigation is essential. On our charts we have marked as "too shallow" several areas of relatively shoal water (12-15 feet) which extend well offshore. In normal conditions you can sail over these, but when the going gets rough, seas start breaking on them and they are best avoided. The Porpoises, about half a mile off Prickly Point, awash and hard to spot, are as nasty a group of rocks you could find to get wrecked on. Navigation into Mt. Hartman Bay and Hog Island has been greatly simplified by the new buoys put down and privately maintained by The Moorings. From Prickly Bay, pass about midway between Prickly Point and the Porpoises. Look out for Tara Island, a small coral island about five feet high. Leave Tara to starboard, passing half way between it and Prickly Point. From here follow the buoyage system into Mt. Hartman Bay or Hog Island.

MOUNT HARTMAN BAY

Mt. Hartman Bay is a deep and well protected harbor (see chart "Prickly Bay to Hog Island"). It is a large scenic bay with a modern marina, the luxury Secret Harbour Hotel and a charter base, all operated by The Moorings. This is a great area for dinghy sailing or sailboarding as there is protected water all the way to Hog Island. By land, it is a 20 minute walk from Prickly Bay.

Services

The Secret Harbour Marina [T:440-4548/9/4439, F:444-4819, VHF:16/71, cc:V,A] is first rate. There are 50 berths in the marina and 24 moorings off the hotel. Fuel, water, cube ice, showers, laundry, telephone, fax, and electricity (110/220V, 50 cycle) are available. There is a night watchman on the premises and long term storage can be arranged. Two taxi drivers, LeRoy and Rock, are willing to look after yachts left in Secret Harbour Marina. Charter manager Sarah will try to help in any way she can.

Ashore

The Moorings Marina have managed to combine a low-key welcoming atmosphere for the cruising yachts along with their up-market sophisticated charter fleet. Much of the activity revolves around the Rum Squall Bar, open daily from 1100-1900, with a happy hour from 1700-1800. Inexpensive snacks are available most nights. They have a mini-mart open from 0800-1600 daily except Sundays and holidays, when it closes at 1500. A fresh vegetable van visits on Friday mornings. They have a book swap, and you can leave your laundry here for Henry Safari Tours laundry service. You can use The Moorings as a mail drop: c/o The Moorings, Secret Harbour, P.O. Box 11, St. George's, Grenada, W.I.

Secret Harbour [T:440-4548/9/4439, F:444-4819, VHF:71, $A-B, cc:V,A] is Grenada's most impressive hotel, with brick arches, carvings, heavy wooden ceilings and Italian tile floors. The rooms have four poster beds and sunken tile bathtubs. The main building is up the hill, and you can take a drink in a secluded little alcove looking out across the bay. A visit will give rise to some "ohs" and "ahs" and impress

your friends. It is a great setting for a special night out. An exotic menu caters to local and international taste. Lunch is served on the terrace with a wide choice which will satisfy the hungry or appeal to the weight conscious. They offer entertainment about twice a week. Call for details.

Buses run a couple days a week to town and there are some good reliable taxi drivers. Rochel (Rock) Charles [T:444-5136, VHF:16] has spent some years as a charter skipper so he is well acquainted with the whole yachting scene. He is charming, willing to hike and can do the Seven Falls trip. Keith Alexander of K&J is very pleasant and has a special interest in agriculture

and herbs and their medicinal and other traditional uses. Leroy Taxi [440-4803, 444-3640, VHF:16/68 also does driving and hiking tours, including Seven Falls, the Hot Springs and Fedon's Camp. Leroy has a particular interest in Grenada's history, so you can be sure of getting some good information.

Water sports

Bob Dunn's Scuba World [T:444-3333 ext 584] has bases at both Secret Harbour Hotel and the Rex Grenadian. He has excellent dive boats and is happy to take yachtsmen diving. Bob does many gear rentals to yachts.

HOG ISLAND

Behind Hog Island is a huge protected bay. When you anchor, there will be just a finger of horizon to remind you the sea is still there. Spiky mangrove roots stick upwards like bristles from a witches broom, their leaves bushing out in the form of a huge green Afro. A cow walks on the beach as though to say hello to the little blue heron who spends her day patrolling the shore, watching for little flurries of fish. The heron strides forwards with huge but delicate steps, like a fastidious matron trying not to step on something unpleasant. Sometimes she grabs a wriggling silver catch, other times the fish churn the water into a frightening foaming hiss and she runs back to the safety of the sand.

Follow the buoys in from Tara Island and anchor anywhere that takes your fancy.

You can leave the same way or take the south route into deep water. Pass close by the reef just south of Hog Island and head out on a bearing of 170° magnetic. Make sure the current is not setting you to the west. Hog's resident goats and cattle are owned and under no circumstances should they be hunted.

Ashore

You can buy vegetables from the farmers by the water tank on the mainland side or dinghy over to Woburn for ice or a bus to town. Hog Island is owned by a large family, two of whom, Rock and Vibert, have been local yacht skippers. Cruising yachtspeople have a tradition of a large pot luck Sunday barbecue on the beach, starting at 1400. Everyone is welcome.

MT. HARTMAN BAY AND HOG ISLAND. TARA ISLAND SHOWS CLEARLY IN THE FOREGROUND

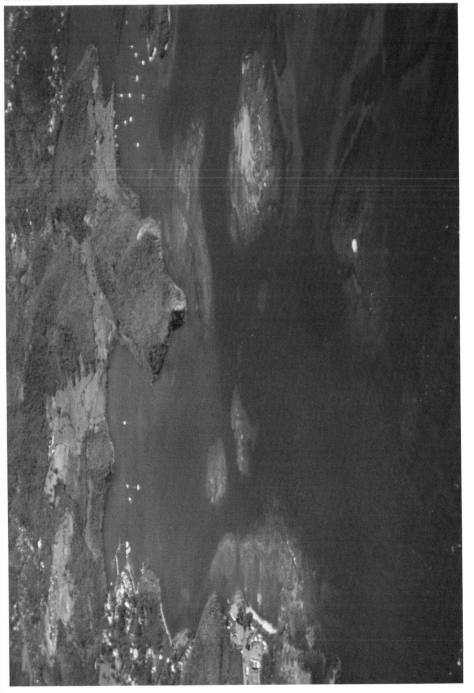

This large and sheltered bay offers enough anchoring possibilities to delight the confirmed gunkholer and you can explore and find your own spot. In the old days big sailing ships would anchor here to take on rum which was brought down the river to the head of the bay by small boat. Enter fairly close to Calivigny Island to avoid all the reefs and shoals that extend south of Hog Island. There are a few ruins on Calivigny Island. The most popular anchorage is just north of the island, off the beach. The bottom shelves steeply, so make sure you are well hooked.

Both Calivigny and Hog are dotted with hardy little frangipani trees. Their leaves fall in the dry season, leaving only sweet smelling, delicate white flowers.

There are tracks all over Calivigny and it is delightful to explore to the southern tip where rough waves try to pound down massive black rocks, and spume fills the air, forming little tide pools.

Ashore

You can anchor off Woburn or dinghy there and tie your dinghy to the village dock. Wander up to the road and turn left and you will find a little corner store called Nimrod and Sons Rum Shop. Nimrod is a part-time professional sign painter, but while there are plenty of other signs lying about, his own store is unposted. You can buy a little ice here along with bread, fresh chicken, lettuce, a few cans, beer and rum. This store is patronized by cruising people and there is a visitors book to prove it – along with the Chin Up Tree Thinking Club (or should it be drinking club?). On the other side of the road a small bar serves fresh fish sandwiches and other goodies. The road here looks so rough and rural, with the odd chicken wandering over it, that it seems impossible to imagine a bus hurtling by, full of smiling faces and big shopping baskets, but it happens all the time. Whichever way it comes you can catch it to town. On the return run ask for a bus going to "Lower Woburn." Boats left unattended have occasionally been robbed in the Calivigny/Woburn area.

PORT EGMONT

Port Egmont is a completely enclosed lagoon surrounded for the most part by mangroves. It is quite pretty and makes a first class hurricane hole. Enter the outer inlet fairly close to Fort Jeudy, keeping an eye out for the reefs which lie near the shore. Fort Jeudy is being developed and there are several prosperous looking houses on the hill. Anchor anywhere in the inner harbor. You can also anchor outside, off the little beach at the inner end of Fort Jeudy, but keep an eye out for the shoal off the northern end of the inlet.

CALIVIGNY HARBOUR

This harbor (not to be confused with Calivigny Island) is another enclosed harbor with a fine palm shaded beach. It makes an acceptable hurricane hole, though heavy rains can create currents which cause boats to lie sideways to the wind from time to time. The entrance to the outer harbor is between Fort Jeudy and Westerhall Point. You must have good visibility to see the reefs off Fort Jeudy. The shoals coming out from Westerhall Point are deeper and harder to see, though they often cause breaking seas. Stay with the devil you can see. Find the reef off Fort Jeudy and follow it into the outer harbor. This entrance can be hairy in heavy winds and large swells and I would only recommend it to sailors with a lot of experience in reef navigation in rough conditions. When passing into the inner harbor, favor the Fort Jeudy side as a

HOG I. TO WESTERHALL

shoal extends from the sand spit. Anchor anywhere in the inner harbor.

There is a shop at the entrance to Westerhall Estate where you can catch a bus to town.

WESTERHALL POINT

Westerhall Point is an attractive housing development with well tended grounds. You can easily see it by walking up from Calivigny Harbour. Westerhall Bay offers a protected anchorage if you tuck up in the southeast corner of the bay behind the mangroves. In rough conditions the entrance is tricky and the exit straight into wind and sea. I would suggest anchoring in Calivigny Harbour and walking over to take a look before you attempt this

POINT FORT JEUDY. PORT EGMONT SHOWS, PARTLY HIDDEN.

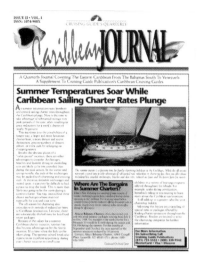

The Pages of Cruising Guide Publications' *Caribbean Journal* Are Your Window to Adventure.

You are invited to join sailors throughout the islands for Caribbean cruising adventures. The quarterly *Caribbean Journal* is a publication designed to keep you abreast of happenings and news that will be important to your next vacation, charter or voyage.

You will learn about new marinas, boatyards, charter operations, resorts and restaurants that cater to the cruising sailor. Navigational updates, including sketch charts, anchorage information, cultural events, travel tips, diving and snorkeling, cooking recipes, features on people and places, and a host of other topics will be covered in coming issues.

The *Caribbean Journal* is published in full-color and is packed with news, features and photos. It is the ideal companion update to our Caribbean Cruising Guides.

Join us in our cruising adventures by subscribing at a special introductory rate of $14.95 annually. Call **(800)330-9542** to subscribe.

Caribbean Journal is published by:
Cruising Guide Publications, P.O. Box 1017, Dunedin, FL 34697-1017, Phone: (813) 733-5322, Fax: (813) 734-8179

AIRLINES & COMMUNICATIONS

Notes on the charter scene and airlines

All the main Windwards except St. Vincent have large international airports with direct flights to the USA and Europe. One can also hop between the islands. The biggest inter-island airline is LIAT. Although this has been nicknamed "Leave Islands Any Time" and "Luggage In Another Terminal," LIAT does run a quite good service and since computerization you can often get an instant reservation. Air Martinique runs 14-seater planes between Martinique and Union, stopping in St. Lucia and St. Vincent. They run two round trip flights, one in the morning and the other in the afternoon; the afternoon flight also takes in Mustique.

If your charter starts and finishes in St. Vincent and the Grenadines, Grenadine Tours (U.S. booking agent is Anchor Travel: 800 526 4781) can book you on Mustique Airways. They fly daily between the islands of Barbados, St. Vincent,

Mustique, and Union, increasing the number of flights to meet demand.

Chartering a plane for a group of four or six is often an economical way to go and gives great flexibility. Charters are available from Eagle Air, Helenair, Mustique Airways, Tropic Air, Air Martinique, LIAT, and St. Vincent Grenadines Air. Your travel agent may not have heard about some of these, so you may need to give them the telephone numbers listed in our directory near the back of this book. (Air Martinique can be booked through all Air France offices.)

St. Lucia has two airports: Hewanorra is the big international one in the south and Vigie is the smaller inter-island one close by Castries. It takes a good hour to reach the north end of the island from Hewanorra. In the other islands the airports are within a few miles of the main towns and charter companies. In most islands you will need to keep some local currency to pay a departure tax. If you are transferring from a large carrier onto an inter-island air line, it is safer to retrieve your baggage when you switch (time permitting) rather than checking it through.

The sail from St. Lucia to St. Vincent is a long hard day's sail. The return trip is often worse. If you are starting a charter in St. Lucia or Martinique, it makes a lot of sense to sail one way and finish in Union Island or Grenada. This is especially true if you only have a week or so. For those without much experience, the easiest sail is from St. Vincent to Union or Grenada. Most charter companies will be happy to arrange one way

charters for an extra fee, and most skippered yachts will pick up and drop off at ports of your choice for no extra charge.

Bareboating

I had the pleasure to run one of the first Caribbean bareboats - a little 31-footer called Rustler. When we said "bareboat," we meant it. Rustler came with a hand start diesel that would barely push her out of the anchorage, a small ice box full of ice and 40 gallons of water which were pumped up by hand. Mechanical complexities consisted of a massive British marine toilet, with endless valves and pumps. This antiquity was almost impossible to clog, but at the same time, however much you worked on the packing gland, within a couple of days it tended to squirt you in the eye. The outboard was a close relative - all chrome and stainless with no cover. You had to wind the cord round the flywheel for every start and go through an elaborate system of switching valves and vents and bleeding for exactly the right number of seconds. The only thing to be said in its favor was that even the roughest of mechanics could do a major overhaul with a screwdriver, hammer and pair of pliers.

When I look at some of the bareboat ads these days it seems that people want to take it all with them when they get away from it all. Freezers, fridges, hair driers, microwave ovens, TV and video are all on offer.

One thing that years of sailing has taught me is that anything mechanical, electrical or electronic, when installed on a well-used yacht, will eventually go wrong. Bareboats are particularly susceptible because of all the different people using the gear. In practical terms this means that breakdowns are part and parcel of a modern sophisticated yacht, and not necessarily a reflection on the efficiency and ability of the charter company. The charter people realize this, they all help each other's yachts and do their best to have some kind of breakdown and back up service, despite the problems posed by the Windwards, which are well spread out. But I think it is important that bareboaters appreciate the essentially adventurous nature of a bareboat holiday and not let it be ruined by a malfunctioning hair drier.

I still have the log book from Rustler and there is an entry I am specially fond of. At the beginning it is written in the hand of the group's self-appointed leader, Dr. Smith, who was not in the least bit happy. Each day was another disaster. He couldn't make the outboard start, he couldn't find the boat hook, one of the navigation lights malfunctioned, he was "very disappointed" in the condition of the boat. Then the handwriting changed and the new entry said: "Dr. Smith had to return home for pressing personal reasons. Rustler is now a fine yacht, the weather is perfect, the sailing fantastic. We are having a marvelous time."

A good thing about chartering is that those occasions that are terrible at the time make great stories later. Not very long ago a bareboat was on a reef in the middle of nowhere and on the radio to the company's local representative who was trying to assess the situation.

"We are hard aground, the rudder is broken and we cannot steer," lamented the charterer.

"Ok. I've got that," said the rep. "Now tell me, are you taking on water?"

There was a pause of a few seconds, then back came a very definite answer, "Oh no, we did that yesterday in St. Vincent."

Crewed Charters

Having spent years both running bareboats and skippering charters, I can

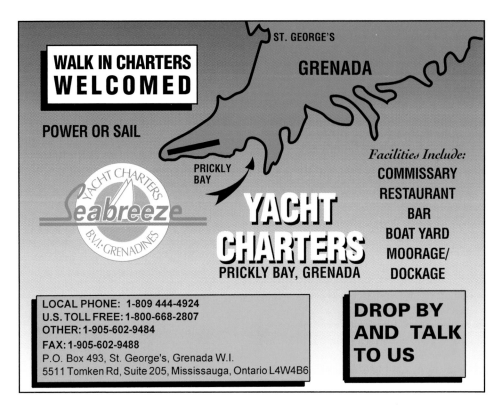
attest without any question that skippered charters produce more glowing praise. A crewed charter is also a real holiday for everyone, with no galley and cleaning chores.

Many agents talk a lot about matching charterers to crew. In fact most charterers are

"It's a pro-rated refund from the charter company!"

happy, easy to please and good company, and good professional skippers can adapt themselves to all kinds of people. Cooks develop a sensitivity to produce the right kind of food.

It is worth keeping in mind that, although yacht crews really enjoy what they are doing and genuinely like their guests, there is some strain to always being on one's best behavior and there are a few things that can make life a lot easier. It is a huge help if all the charterers go ashore for a couple of hours each day, either to shop, walk, or go to the beach. At this point the crew can put on their favorite music full blast and clean the boat with much banging and gay abandon. The charterers will return to a clean boat and a much refreshed crew.

Cooks hate to be watched while they work. It makes them nervous and upsets their concentration. There is no way you would know this, because they are well trained to smile and answer a string of questions. Much better to leave them alone in the galley and give them the attention

they deserve when they produce their final works of art.

The cook usually works much harder than the skipper so it is a great break if the guests decide to eat out, even if it is just a matter having a sandwich ashore instead of returning for lunch. Unfairly, the best cooks get the fewest breaks, as no one can bear to miss a single meal.

It is a tradition that at some point the guests take their crew out for dinner. For the crew the break is more important than the dinner, and if you are on a budget, they don't mind if it is somewhere quite simple.

Tipping is a big item for most crews as this makes up a large part of their income. Unless otherwise stated, 10% of the total charter fee is the norm and an appropriate figure for good service. With the current costs of maintaining a yacht, owner-skippers are delighted to accept tips. However, if you feel embarrassed about tipping an owner, give it all to the cook, especially if the owner is a man and the cook is his wife or girl friend. If they have a good relationship she will split

it with him and if they don't, she probably deserves all of it.

303

Types of charter available:
C=fully crewed, BB=bareboat, SB=Semi Bareboat (skippers available), Ck= cooks available, OW=One way charters available, A= All of the above.

MARTINQUE

Caraibes Yachting, 4 Rue de la Liberte, 97290 Marin, Martinique T:74 95 76, F:74 95 60, A

Catana-Antilles, Port de Plaisance, Marin, 97290, Martinique, T:74 88 87, F:74 70 09, Catana Catamerans, Maire Lloret, A

Kiriacoulis Antilles, Port de Plaisance, Marin, 97290, Martinique, T:74 86 51, F:74 73 41, Consantin Christou, A

Bambou Yachting, Port de Plaisance, Marin, 97290, Martinique, T:74 78 05, F:74 82 77, Alain Hesnard, A

Sunsail, Port de Plaisance, Marin, 97290, Martinique, T:74 77 61, F:74 77 80, Gilles Loucif, A

Petit Breton, Port de Plaisance, Marin, 97290, Martinique, T:74 74 37, F:74 74 43, Claude Thonet, A

Tropical Yacht Services, Port de Plaisance, Marin, 97290, Martinique, T:74 82 22, F:74 78 19, Philippe Leconte, A.

The Moorings, Port de Plaisance, Marin, 97290, Martinique, T:74 75 39, F:74 76 44, In USA: 19345 US Hwy, 19 North, 4th Floor, Clearwater, FL 34624-3193, T:800 437 7880/535 7289, A

Stardust Marine, Port de Plaisance, Marin, 97290, Martinique, T:74 98 17, F:74 88 12, A

Star Voyage, Marina Pointe du Bout, T:66 00 72, also Port de Plaisance, Marin, 97290, Martinique, T:74 70 92, F:74 70 93, BB, SB, OW

Tropic Yachting, Marina Pointe du Bout, T:66 03 85, F:66 06 33, BB, SB

Chimere Yachting, Port de Plaisance, Marin, 97290, Martinique, T:74 78 56, F:74 78 57, A

ST LUCIA

Destination St. Lucia, Box 2091, Gros Islet, St. lucia, W.I. T:809-452-8531, F:809-452-0183, BB, SB,Ck OW

Sunsail, Box 928, St. lucia, W.I. T:809-452-8648, F:809-452-0839, In USA, 3347 NW 55th St, Fort Lauderdale, FL 33309, T:800-327-2276/305-484-5246, F:305-485-5072, A

The Moorings, P.O. Box 101, Castries, St. Lucia, West Indies, T: 809-451-4357, F: 809-451-4230. In USA: 19345 US Hwy, 19 North, 4th Floor, Clearwater, FL 34624-3193, T:800 437 7880/535 7289, A

Tradewind Yachts,, P.O.Box 1186, Court Circle, Gloucester, VA 23061. T:800-825-7245/800-6940881, F:804-693-7245. Locally Box 2158, Rodney bay Marina, Gros Ilets, St Lucia, W.I. T:809-452-8424, F:809-452-8442, A

ST. VINCENT

Barefoot Yacht Charters, Box 39, St. Vincent, W.I. T:800-677-3195, 809-456-9526, F:809-456-9238, A, also air charters.

Tradewind Yachts,, P.O.Box 1186, Court Circle, Gloucester, VA 23061. T:800-825-7245/800-6940881, F:804-693-7245. Locally Blue Lagoon, St. Vincent, W.I.

GRENADA

The Moorings, P.O. Box 11, St George's, Grenada, T:809-444-4439. F:809-444-2090. In USA: 19345 US Hwy, 19 North, 4th Floor, Clearwater, FL 34624-3193, T:800 437 7880/535 7289, A

Seabreeze Yacht Charters, Box 493, St. George's Grenada, T&F:809-444-4924

CHARTER COMPANIES AND YACHTS

W.I. In Canada: 5511 Tomken Rd, Suite 205, Mississauga, Ontario L4WB6, T:800-668-2807, F:905-602-9484.

INDIVIDUAL YACHTS

Nirvana (also through agents), Spacious 50 ft trimaran, very stable and comfortable. Kurt Bartz, Box 826, St. Vincent, WI. C,OW

Secondo, O'Day 37. Johnny Olliviere, Bequia, St. Vincent, T:458-3695. SB,Ck

Touch of Time, Edson Hazell, c/o Frangipani, Box 1, Bequia, St. Vincent, WI. C,OW

LOCAL AGENTS

Anchorage Yacht Club, Union Island, St. Vincent, WI. T:809- 458-8221/458-4848/8328

Spice Island Marine, Box 449, St. George's Grenada. T:809-444-4342

U.K. AGENTS

Camper and Nicholsons, 31, Berkeley St, London, W1X 5FA. T:01 491 2950.

The Moorings, 188 Northdown, Cliftonville, Kent CT92QN T:0 84 322 7140.

Sun Days Charters, Linden House, Crapstone, Yelverton, Devon PL20 7SP. T:0 822 85 3375, F:0 822 85 4485

World Wide Yachting Holidays, Liz Fenner, 35 Fairfax Place, London NW64EJ. T:01-328-1033.

Yacht Connections, The Hames, Church Road, South Ascot, Berks SL5 9DP, T:0344 24987, F:0344 26849, C, OW.

Tropic Sail, Jo Cronk, 23 Stray Park, Yealmpton, Nr Plymouth, S.Devon. PL8 2HF. T:0752 88 1570

W&G Yachts, Tony Gould, 103 Banstead Road South, Sutton, Surrey SM2 5HL. T:01 642 3788, F:01 661 7326

U.S.A. AGENTS

Anne-Wallis White, 326 First Street, Annapolis, MD 21403. T:301-263-6366

Catamaran Charters, (Privilege) 1650 SE 17th St. Ft Lauderdale FL 33316, T:800-262-0308/305-462-6706, F:305-462-6104

Caribbean Yacht Owners Ass. P.O.Box 9997 Yacht Haven Marina, St. Thomas, USVI 00801 T:809-774-3677, F:809-774-6910.

Ed Hamilton, Box 430, N. Whitefield, ME 04353, T:207-549-7855, F:207-549-7822

Joanne Russell, Ste 15, 2750 Black Rock Turnpike, Fairfield, CT 06430. T: 203-372-6633

Lynne Jachney Charters, 1 Townhouse Square, 2nd floor, Marblehead, MA 01945. T:617-639-0787 or 800-223-2050, F:617-639-0216

Nicholson's Yacht Charter, 432 Columbia St, Cambridge, MA 02138, T:800-662-6066/617-225-0555, F:617-225-0190. Nelsons Dock Yard, Post Office, English Harbour, Antigua. T:809-463-1530, F:809-463-1531.

Ocean Voyages, Mary Crowley, 1709 Bridgeway, Sausalito CA 94965. T:415-332-4681.

Privilege Yacht Charters (see Catamaran Charters)

Stardust Marine, 2280 University Drive, Suite 102, Newport Beach, CA 92660, 800-634-8822/714-650-0889, F:714-642-1318

Yacht Connections, P.O. Box 3160, Coos Bay, Oregon 97420, T:800-238-6912, F:503-888-5582, C, OW.

VHF radio

Nearly everyone and his brother has a VHF radio these days, and it is necessary to observe a few rules to stop the airways sounding like the Mad Hatter's tea party.

Channel 16 is for emergency and raising other stations only. As soon as you have made contact, switch to another channel. (Note: on some radios you have to push a connect/disconnect button as well as switching channels on the channel selector.)

In St. Vincent and the Grenadines channel 68 is also designated for making contact only. It is used by all the shore stations and channel 16 is for marine stations only. So in this country use 68 only for calling shore stations and not for chit chat.

Let us suppose you are on yacht Argo calling Basil's Bar. First you would go to channel 68. (If it was another yacht rather than a shore station, you would use 16.) Proceed as follows: "Basil's Bar, Basil's Bar.....Argo." If you do not get a reply within a few seconds, repeat. But if you don't get any reply after the second try, wait half an hour before trying again.

They should answer: "Argo Argo...Basil's Bar." You should then say "Basil's Bar this is Argo, can we go channel..." (choose a channel not 16 or 68). They

should confirm the channel before you switch. There is no need to say "over" on VHF as you can hear the mike keying on and off.

Distress calls

If you hear one, keep off the radio unless you can assist. This is no time to order a pizza.

Should you have a problem, please note that **Mayday** is used only when grave and imminent danger threatens (i.e.: sinking, on fire, crew member turning purple). Use **Pan** for lesser emergencies such as aground, but not sinking or a crew member sick enough to need taking off as soon as possible. Be sure it is an emergency. Someone once gave a Mayday call on seeing a yacht on a reef that had been wrecked there three months earlier. Having the engine conk out on a sail boat or running out of water are not normally marine emergencies, even if they seem dire at the time. Contact an appropriate station, such as your charter company.

A **Security** call is used for warnings of a navigational kind. For example if you see a derelict container floating, or if you are drifting with no means of control in a channel.

The distress call consists of: "Mayday" or "Pan" repeated three times. Then the name of the yacht in distress repeated twice. Then give the particulars of position: latitude and longitude or bearing and distance from a known point, repeated twice. Then state the nature of the distress and kind of assistance required, plus any other information which would help the answering station identify you, such as the size and color of yacht and the number of masts, also give the number of people on board. Finish by saying: "This is yacht... standing by on 16."

If you do not get an immediate reply, keep trying.

If you hear a distress call it is your obligation to end any transmission with any other station which might interfere, and to render assistance if possible.

Phonetic alphabet for spelling out words on the radio

Alpha Bravo Charlie Delta Echo

Foxtrot Golf Hotel India Juliet

Kilo Lima Mike November Oscar

Papa Quebec Romeo Sierra Tango

Uniform Victor Whisky X-ray

Yankee Zulu

Telephone country codes:

USA........... 1	Grenada...........1*
UK 44	Martinique.....596
Australia... 61	St.Lucia.......... 1*
New Zeal... 64	St.Vincent....... 1*
Austria.......43	Barbados......... 1*
Germany....49	Antigua........... 1*
Denmark....45	St. Martin......590
France...... 33	Dominica.........1*
Italy.......... 39	St. Kitts........... 1*
Sweden......46	* All these countries
Switzerland..41	have an 809 area code.

Shoreside telephones

Under services in each anchorage we mention the location of convenient public telephones. If calling within an island, dial the number: 6 digits for Martinique, 7 digits for the rest of the Windwards. Telephone companies in the islands have frequently changed the numbers you dial for overseas calls. So if you have no luck with the following instructions, look in a recent phone book or call an operator.

If calling overseas out of Martinique: dial **19+country code+number.**

For overseas calls from St. Vincent you have to dial **0+country code+number.** For example to call the USA you dial 0+1+10 digits. To get the UK dial 0+1+44 followed by the number (if the area code in the UK starts with a 0 leave the 0 out). When calling other Caribbean islands dial 0 + 809+ seven digits. I suspect this system may soon change to become more like St. lucia and Grenada below.

To get the the USA from St Lucia and Grenada dial 1+10 digits. For operator assistance dial 0+10 digits. To get another

THEY'RE HERE... UH, ... HOW LONG DID YOU SAY THIS CHARTER IS?

Caribbean 809 area code outside the island dial 1+809+7 digits (St. Lucia), or 809+7 digits (Grenada). To get any other country dial 011+Country code+number. For operator assistance dial 01+country code+number. If your overseas area code starts with a 0 leave it out.

To call Martinique from abroad dial 011+596. To call other Windwards dial 1+809+7 digit number.

Boatphone

Nearly all charter yachts in the Windwards are now fitted out with a phone on board which you use just as you would a normal house phone. Making a phone call can be a lot easier and less frustrating than using the VHF. To find out the number that will be allotted to your yacht, contact your charter company or Boatphone [T:809-452-0361]. Other yachts can use their own cellular phones to hook into the service (just dial 0) or you can buy or lease from Boatphone. The service extends throughout the Lesser Antilles.

The system of codes for the boatphone is the same as for St. Lucia.

Courier Services

In the old days, Caribbean bars were full of people who had run into some mechanical disaster, like the engine's rear end thrust widget had stripped its sprocket. They seemed to get consigned for months to some kind of limbo between the telephone, the bar and post office while the offending spare vanished into the ether. Nowadays the advent of fast and efficient courier services such as Federal Express and DHL has made it very easy to move spares, checks and documents fast and efficiently. Outfitters International, a procurement service, makes even finding the parts easy. We list some of these services in our Directory.

TWO WINDWARD VIDEOS

A personal approach by Chris Doyle & cameraman Jeff Fisher.
Choose the one that suits you best.

SAILING THE WINDWARD ISLANDS WITH CHRIS DOYLE

For the bareboater. Lots of navigation and harbor
shots, from Martinique to Grenada. (70 minutes)

ISLAND PORTRAITS: ST. VINCENT AND THE GRENADINES

From the Falls of Baleine to the Tobago Cays, this video will
show you what 's in store or bring back memories of these
charming islands. (45 minutes)

USA, Cruising Guide Publications, Tel:800-330-9542
Available in most boutiques in the Windward Islands

One of the best ways to experience local foods is to eat out. This way you don't have to slave over the stove and best of all – no dishes to wash up. In this section we are going to introduce you to some of the wonderful local fruits and vegetables, as well as some ideas about sea food and locally obtainable meat. Those who cook for themselves will find recipes. For those who prefer to eat out, we will make some suggestions. But you cannot start without a drink in your hand, so why not make:

SKIPPERS RUM PUNCH. Mix: the juice from 3 limes, ¼ cup of Grenadine syrup, 1 cup of brown rum with one liter of juice (orange, pineapple, or maybe local passion fruit). Serve with a lot of ice and liberally grate some fresh nutmeg on top.

We are not going to be delving much into drinks, but for those who have a blender we should mention "smoothies." These are made by taking the flesh of any suitable local fruit (try mango, banana, guava, pawpaw, pineapple or soursop), adding a good slosh of rum, a good measure of ice, then blend. You can add lime or orange juice for flavor and you can try combinations. An evening of research should produce your favorite concoction and leave you so contented and full of fruit you will probably be able to skip dinner.

We should also mention the Caribbean's very own natural soft drink: coconut water. If you are driving around the countryside, or even wandering around town, you will probably see a home made barrow by the side of the road stocked high with green coconuts. These are "water-nuts" - young coconuts that have not yet developed a hard inner brown husk or firm white flesh, but are full of a delicious tasting liquid. The vendor will slice off the top of the nut for you. It now ready for you to drink, straight from the shell. As with any other soft drink, coconut water works as a mixer and can be spiced with a squeeze of lime.

COMMENTS ON EATING OUT

Eating out, even in the most international of restaurants, will give you some idea of local food because they will almost certainly use the local vegetables, seafood and fruits. But it is also worth trying some of the inexpensive local restaurants. You can be offered amazing fare. My favorite is "Chair broiled SirLion steak." It would be a terrible mistake to eat steak in such a restaurant, though they often do excellent curries, creole style specialties and pepper

pot. I usually go for lambi (conch). This is firm white flesh from a large sea shell and absolutely delicious. Soups are generally excellent in all restaurants, desserts better in the more expensive ones.

Those who go down to the Windwards and eat hamburgers deserve whatever they get. Much better to eat as the locals do and have a "roti" which is the ideal lunch-time snack. A roti is curry wrapped in a wheat flour tortilla-like shell. It usually comes in

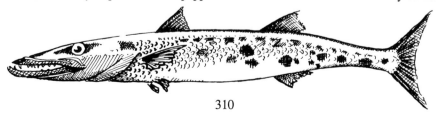

EXOTIC TROPICAL FOOD

three flavors: beef, chicken and conch. The chicken roti is often made from "back and neck" and full of bones; locals love to chew on them, but for others this can be an acquired taste. In the more expensive restaurants chicken rotis may be "boneless."

Mountain streams produce wonderful fresh water crayfish. These will occasionally appear in an inexpensive restaurant, but more often in a really good one. Nearly everyone offers lobster in season. Lobster is delicious, delicate and easy to ruin. Many restaurants parboil lobster, freeze it, then broil to serve. This all too often produces something dry, chewy and tasteless. To be on the safe side only eat lobster at a restaurant where you can select your own alive and fresh from a pool.

311

A FEW THINGS TO KNOW

Grenada is the world's second largest nutmeg producer. Buy some fresh nutmegs as soon as possible. You will find them in the market and in boutiques, not only in Grenada but also in the other Windwards. If possible buy them as a "kit" with a little grater. The outer hard dark brown husk must be removed before grating. Nutmeg is not only essential for rum punch but excellent at spicing up desserts, pancakes, french toast and some vegetables.

In the market and the supermarket you can buy something locally called saffron, which is in fact turmeric – a root which can be brought fresh or grated. It is good in curries and for coloring rice. True saffron (made from crocus) is expensive and only to be found in the bigger supermarkets.

If you are in St. Vincent and the Grenadines, look out for their wonderful peanuts which are dry roasted and packed in recycled beer bottles. In Grenada you will find similarly packed local cashew nuts, also delicious.

Villamar's smoked fish, produced in St. Vincent, tastes wonderful and is available in selected shops through the Windwards.

Grenada's Spice Island Coffee is a superb, dark roast, freshly ground coffee.

TROPICAL VEGETABLES AND STAPLES

We do not mention the many vegetables – e.g. tomatoes, sweet pepper, cucumbers and beans – you will be familiar with from home. Cooking suggestions and recipes assume basic cooking knowledge.

Coconuts are nutritious and cheap. Coconut milk (not be confused with the water) is used in a lot of Caribbean cooking, much as one would use cream where cows are more plentiful than palm trees.

To make coconut milk, you need an older "flesh nut" - one of the brown ones you buy in the market. Grate the flesh, add any water from the nut, and add ordinary water till it is covered. Leave it for a few minutes, then squeeze the flesh into the water. Throw out the flesh, and the liquid you are now left with is the milk.

Breadfruit, plentiful and inexpensive year round, is a savior to the traveller on a budget. It is green, balloon sized, pocked

and hard. Originally from the Pacific, it was imported here by Captain Bligh, but arrived late because of the mutiny. Watch it carefully or it will cause you grief, too. It remains nice and firm for a day or two, but when it decides to go soft and rotten, it can do so almost as quickly as Bligh could order a keel hauling. Best to cook it first and store after. Boil it (40 minutes in an ordinary pot or pressure cook for 10), or bake it in the oven (about 40 minutes). It will now store for quite some days in an ice box or fridge. Treat it like potato: mash it, cut slices off and fry it, use it in salad or stews. Mash it together with an egg and some cooked fish, season then fry to make wonderful fish cakes. Buy one for a barbecue and cook it on the embers of a dying fire till you can slide a thin sliver of wood from opposite the stem up into the center. Cut it open and serve with salt, pepper and lashings of butter. Try making it like mashed potato, but mash with coconut milk instead of ordinary milk, cover with grated cheese and brown.

Calaloo, an elephant ear shaped green leaf, grows on wet ground such as the banks of small streams. Plentiful year round and inexpensive, available as bundles of leaves or in bags chopped and prepared for cooking. If you get the leaves it is necessary to remove the skin from the

312

on each side) or baked whole (about half an hour), they are delicious. Plantains perfectly complement any kind of fish.

Pumpkin. The local pumpkin is green streaked with white, and has an orange red pulp that is more akin to butternut squash than the Halloween pumpkin. It keeps a long time unopened and is both versatile and tasty. Remove the seeds before cooking. Boil or bake till soft and serve with butter, or boil and mash with seasoning and a little orange juice. If you want to make a meal out of a pumpkin, slice it longways down the middle and bake it. While it is cooking fry together onion, christophene, tomato and any left-overs you might have, melt in a quarter pound of cream cheese. and stuff the cooked pumpkin with this mixture. Pumpkin makes a delicious soup. Try it in a restaurant or make it yourself.

West Indian Pumpkin Soup. 1 small pumpkin, 1 chopped onion, 1 Tbs of butter, 1 chicken stock cube, ½ pint of fresh cream (or two cans of cream), ¼ of a glass of white wine, salt, pepper, grated nutmeg. Skin and seed the pumpkin and chop into small cubes. Lightly saute the onions in butter till cooked. Add pumpkin, stock cube and a minimum of water. Boil, using a lid. When soft, blend or sieve. Add the cream and wine, flavor with salt, pepper and nutmeg to taste. If too thick, thin with milk or water.

Avocado. Local avocados are absolutely delicious, and reason enough to come down in the summer (available June to November, but peak season around August and September). Never store them with citrus. They can be eaten as they are, flavored with a little salt and lime juice, or stuffed with mayonnaise and shrimp. If they get a little over-ripe, mash them with

stem and off the center vein. Always boil calaloo for 30 minutes. Eating it raw, under-cooked, or badly prepared has much the same effect on your mouth and throat as one imagines chewing on raw fiberglass would. The discomfort is temporary. Calaloo makes a wonderful soup and if you do not cook it for yourself, eat it in a restaurant at the first available opportunity. To use calaloo as a vegetable just boil it with a little salt for at least 30 minutes. It boils down to very little.

Calaloo Soup– ½ lb chopped bacon, 1 pint of water, ¼ lb peeled shrimp, 2 bunches of prepared calaloo (about 1 lb.) 5 sliced okras, 1 sliced onion, ½ oz. butter, salt, pepper, garlic, thyme and hot sauce to taste.

Fry the bacon and onion in butter, drain off excess fat. Add calaloo, okras, water and seasoning. Boil for 40 minutes then add peeled shrimp. Cook a little longer and serve. For thicker soup, blend, then serve.

Plantains. To the uninitiated these look just like bananas, but try putting one in a banana daquiari and you will soon know the difference. Ask the market ladies to make sure you are getting what you want. Plantains have less sugar than bananas, and taste awful raw, but when ripe, split down the middle and fried (a couple of minutes

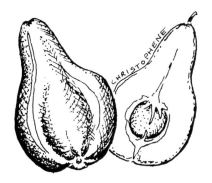

lime, finely chopped onion, garlic and seasoning. This makes an ideal dip to enjoy with your sunset drink.

Okra is a spear shaped green pod with slimy green seeds. Avoid the large ones which tend to be fibrous. They tend to be somewhat slimy if boiled, much less so if sliced and fried. Good in soups.

Sweet potato and yam are sweet and tasty local root crops which take about 30 minutes to cook. Nice with pork. Try mashing it with a little orange juice.

Eddo, tania & dasheen are closely related brown hairy roots. They can be a bit dry, though mashing with oodles of butter and milk helps. Ask the ladies in the market for suggestions.

Christophene is ridged, pear shaped, comes either green or white and grows on a vine. Somewhat delicate in flavor, it makes an excellent vegetable dish or may be added to curries or stews. Peel it and remove the seed. This is best done under water, or with wet hands, otherwise it leaves a mess on your hands that gives the impression your skin is peeling off. It is excellent just boiled with salt, pepper and butter and is even better put in a white cheese sauce. It may also be used raw as a salad ingredient. The seed tastes good raw.

TROPICAL FRUITS
(these may be eaten raw or combined in a fruit salad).

Paw Paw (Papaya), is a lush tropical fruit that contains a digestive enzyme, making it an ideal dessert. It starts green and is ready to eat when it turns yellow and becomes slightly soft. It is available year round but is delicate and hard to store. It must be eaten the same day it becomes ready. Slice like a melon and remove the seeds, add a squeeze of lime to flavor.

Citrus (oranges, grapefruit, tangerines, etc.) occur mainly in the winter. The quality varies from absolutely superb to dry and unusable. When you are shopping, buy one from the market lady to try - she will open it with a knife for you to taste. This is the only way to tell how good they are. Oranges are usually green in color. This is how the local ones come. Despite the outside color the inside is orange and ready to eat. Limes are generally available year round. They are essential for making rum punch, flavoring fish, etc.

Guavas, available July to December, are green-yellow fruits a little bigger than golf balls. They may be eaten raw or are excellent stewed with sugar. They are used to make a sweet called "Guava cheese."

Cashew fruits (French Cashew, Plumrose), are pink fruits with white flesh, available June to August. Do not peel, but remove the stone. Delicious when chilled, good in fruit salad.

314

Pineapples. These are available for most of the year and very inexpensive in Martinique, but harder to come by and more costly elsewhere. Local pineapples can be absolutely delicious. Test for ripeness by pulling on a central leaf. If it pulls out easily it is ready.

Passion Fruit. Available May to November. A small yellow fruit with a slightly crinkly skin and very strong flavor. Makes an excellent drink and locally made passion fruit juice is usually available in the supermarkets.

Bananas are available year round. It is worth mentioning that local bananas, which are naturally ripened, are delicious. As well as the "normal" banana, there are many other similar looking fruits some of which are good eaten raw, and some of which need cooking. Consult your market lady. "Eating" bananas make excellent desserts; try the following:

Skipper's Banana Flambe (for 4). 4 bananas, ½ cup of dark rum, ½ cup fresh orange juice, 2 Tbs brown sugar, a slosh of white rum or vodka, seasoning of nutmeg, cinnamon and allspice.

Split the bananas in two and put in a frying pan, add the brown rum and orange juice, sprinkle on the sugar and spices, simmer for about 5 minutes. Pour on the white rum and ignite. (If vodka, you will have to warm gently in a pan first.)

Bananas Celeste, from Leyritz Plantation (for 4). 6 oz. cream cheese, ¼ cup brown sugar, ½ tsp cinnamon, 4 Tbs unsalted butter, ¼ cup of heavy cream (tinned O.K.), ¼ tsp cinnamon, 4 large bananas peeled and split in half.

Mix the first 3 ingredients. Saute bananas in butter. Lay 4 halves in a buttered baking dish, spread with half of mix and repeat. Pour cream over and bake at 350 for 15 minutes. Sprinkle with remaining cinnamon and serve hot.

Soursop, available year round, is a knobbly green fruit which is ripe when it begins to go soft. It is messy to eat because of all the seeds. It can be blended with a little milk and ice to make an excellent drink.

Sapodilla is a small brown fruit, available in the winter. You need a very sweet

OPENING A MANGO

315

tooth to enjoy these as they are, but they make an excellent addition to fruit salad. **Sorrel** is a flower, available fresh around Christmas and dried the rest of the year. Pour boiling water on a couple of blossoms to make an excellent herb tea with a flavor not unlike "Red Zinger." Or, boil a bunch of the flowers with water, adding a lot of sugar and spices. Serve as a delicious iced drink.

Mangos are delicious and available spring, summer and fall, but only rarely in the winter. They are harder to come by and more expensive in Martinique than the other Windwards. There are many different varieties. Grafted ones are bigger, better and have fewer strings.

SEAFOOD

Although seafood in the Windwards is excellent, you only rarely find it in the local supermarket. The main towns of most islands have fish markets, and the one in St. George's, Grenada, is good, as is the fisherman's coop by Pointe Seraphine in St. Lucia. To get fish you often need to first catch your fisherman. In the Grenadines you can try asking fishermen in camps or those returning from fishing trips. Try asking any of the local people where, and at what time, the fishermen usually bring in their catch. Often it is sold straight out of the boats when they arrive. Calliaqua in St. Vincent has a good little fish market, where the fish generally arrive at about 1600 hours. If you see fishermen untangling a bunch of large fish from a gill

net, be cautious. Sometimes these nets have been left out for some days, and by the time the fish reach shore they are only good for salting. Among other fish you often find:

Barracuda - a delicious white-fleshed fish. It is probably best to try and find ones less than two feet long as ciguatera poisoning is possible, though very rare.

Dolphin – sometimes called "Dorado" or "Mahi Mahi." This pretty fish has white firm flesh, is excellent eating and is absolutely no relative of "Flipper."

Snapper - an excellent white fleshed fish. The red snapper is most common.

Tuna - all kinds of varieties, dark fleshed, excellent flavor.

An easy way to cook most fish is to cut them into steaks or filets, season with salt, pepper and herbs and saute them in butter, or better still, barbecue them. When you get bored with that try the following:

Baked Fish. One whole fish, scaled, finned and gutted, ½ lb butter, 1 onion, 1 tomato, juice of one lime, salt, pepper and garlic.

Make about 4 incisions, ¼ of an inch deep, across the fish on both sides. Take the butter and mash it with a fork into a bowl till soft, add the lime juice, salt, pepper and garlic to taste, rub this all over the fish and get plenty into the incisions and inside the fish. Lay it on a sheet of tinfoil. Thinly slice

316

the tomatoes and onion. Stuff some inside the fish and the rest over the outside. Wrap up in the tinfoil and bake in a medium oven for 20 to 40 minutes, depending on the size of fish.

Shirley's Fish Soup. *(Feeds 4, quantities very approximate). About a 4 lb fish, preferably a whole dolphin or barracuda, cut into pieces. 2 lbs potatoes, 1 lb tania, 2 green figs (cooking bananas) quartered, one big onion (chopped), 1/8 lb butter, juice of 3 limes, coconut milk made from 2 coconuts, salt, pepper, chives, thyme (ask for "Sive and thyme" in the market), 2/3rds of a liter of water and up to a teaspoon of local hot sauce.*

Saute the onion and chives in the butter, along with the thyme and seasonings. Add the water and lime juice and simmer for about 20 minutes. Add the vegetables and coconut milk, boil till just cooked. Cut up the fish, and add, cooking for a few minutes. Serve. To the West Indian the head (eyes and all) goes in, this is the best part, but if you don't fancy it, leave it out. If making coconut milk is too much trouble, try adding cream at the last minute instead.

Seviche. *1 lb very fresh fish, 1 finely chopped onion, 1 chopped tomato, ¼ tsp of local hot sauce, lime juice, salt and pepper.*

Filet the fish and cut into small pieces, put in a non-metallic container with the onion and tomato. Season with salt and pepper. Cover with lime juice into which the hot sauce has been mixed. Let stand in the fridge or ice box overnight, drain before serving.

Conch or Lambi. This mollusc lives in a huge spiral shell lined with a beautiful pink. The whole animal is called a conch, and "lambi" refers to the meat. If you are buying from a fisherman, get him to remove the shell. Then hold the conch up by the claw, remove all the thin skin and slime that hangs from the bottom, remove the eyes and mouth, cut open the gut and clean and remove the tough brown skin. Lastly remove the claw. You should be left with a slab of white to slightly pink meat. Chop this up and tenderize by hammering. One of the best ways to cook conch is in a curry.

(With modifications the same recipe can be used for fish, chicken or peeled shrimp.)

Curry. Curries are very popular in the Windwards, due to the East Indian influence. Although simple, a curry can be made into a feast if you serve it with an array of side garnishes in small bowls, to be sprinkled on top, or eaten beside the curry. Side dish suggestions are as follows: grated coconut, crushed peanuts, chutney, chopped onion, yoghurt, chopped mango, chopped tomato, raisins soaked in rum (drain before serving) and chopped cucumber soaked in vinegar mixed with pieces of fresh ginger (remove ginger and drain before serving). Curry should also be served with a bowl of steaming hot rice.

Kristina's Curried Conch.

1 cleaned and chopped conch per person, 1 chopped onion, 2 crushed cloves of garlic, 1 tsp fresh grated ginger, 1 cup of coconut milk or coconut water, 1 can of drained tomatoes or 2 peeled fresh tomatoes, 1 plantain, 1 tsp thyme, 1 tsp turmeric, curry powder.

Saute the onions and garlic till tender and translucent. Add the herbs and spices. Start with 1 Tbs of curry powder and work up from there as strength can vary enormously. Blend them in. Add the rest of the ingredients and let them simmer for about 20 minutes.

This same recipe will work for meat, chicken, fish or shrimp. In the case of the fish or shrimp, cook the other ingredients first and only add them at the last minute. If you wish to fill out the curry somewhat, add the chopped flesh from two christophenes. They will take about 20 minutes to cook.

Lobster (langouste). The local lobster is

a spiny variety without claws. It is illegal to buy lobsters with eggs (they sit in orange clusters under the tail), or during the sum-

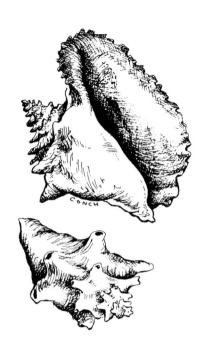

CONCH

mer when they are out of season, or those less than 9" long. Fines of $5000 are not unknown for first offenders.

Lobsters are best boiled alive. Submerge them rapidly in boiling water and they will quickly die. Tie up the legs and tail with string so you don't get splashed with boiling water. Boiling time is 10 to 20 minutes depending on size. We like to buy smaller ones (about 2 lbs) and put them with a pint of cold water in the pressure cooker. Close the lid, bring them up to pressure and cook

for about 2 minutes.

Put the cooked lobster face up on a cutting board and, with a very sharp, tough knife, split it in two from head to tail. Serve with hot garlic-lime butter. Keep the shells and any odd bits; with these you can make an absolutely delicious bisque (you can also use shrimp heads and/or skins). This way you get twice the value for money out of your lobster (or shrimp).

Seafood Bisque. (Serves 4 as a first course or lunch)

Shells from 3 lbs of lobster (or the heads from 2 lb shrimp), 9 Tbs of butter, 1 liter of water, ½ cup of white wine, 2 Tbs of tomato puree.

1 chopped onion, 2 cloves of garlic, 1 bay leaf, 2 Tbs of flour, 1 egg yolk, ½ cup of cream.

Saute the onions, garlic and lobster shells in 6 Tbs butter for about 15 mins. Add water, wine, tomato puree and bay leaf. Bring to the boil and simmer for 20 minutes. Strain. Mix the rest of the butter with 3 Tbs flour, add to the stock and simmer for another 5 minutes, stirring constantly. Adjust seasoning (salt, pepper). Mix egg yolk with cream in a small bowl. Pour a small amount of soup in it and stir. Then pour it back into the soup very slowly beating constantly. Taste again and serve immediately. Garnish with left over bits of lobster or shrimp (if any). Do not reheat as boiling will ruin it. Serve with grated cheese if you wish.

MEAT

The French are very particular about their meat, and you can get first class meats of all sorts in Martinique, both in the supermarkets and the butchers. They tend to sell it fresh rather than frozen, so it is easier to assess what you are getting. In the English speaking Windwards quality meat is a little harder to come by. Local steaks are usually tasty and occasionally tender, but other times you will need to sharpen your teeth. Maison Salaison and Chef's

Choice have good imported steaks in St. Lucia as does Basil's General Store in Mustique. You can usually get good tenderloin in Foodland and Food Fair in Grenada. For those on a budget, kidney and liver are excellent buys, chicken livers being very reasonably priced. Pork tenderloins are less expensive than beef, just as delicious and very tender. In Grenada you can often find them in Food Fair. In St. Lucia you can find them at a farm cooperative on the right hand side of the road between Rodney Bay Marina and Castries. The big standby is chicken. Chicken is imported to all the islands in 5 lb boxes. You can get everything from breasts to backs and necks.

Barbecued Chicken *(for 6). One 5 lb box of chicken parts (whichever kind you like or can afford), ½ lb peanut butter, ½ lb (local) marmalade, ¼ cup oil, ¼ cup of orange juice, 3 oz. of mustard, 1 tsp curry powder, salt and pepper.*

Mix all the ingredients well together except the chicken, and put in a baking pan. Marinate the chicken in the mixture, then bake in the marinade for about 35 minutes in a medium oven. Remove and finish cooking the chicken on the barbecue, basting well with the marinade.

St. Lucian Pork Tenderloin *(Ivan Howell, La Toc). 4 lb porkloin, 1 oz. chopped onion, 1 chopped sprig thyme, 3 crushed cloves garlic, ½ tsp salt, 1 oz. chopped celery, lime juice, 2 whole cloves, dash of Worcestershire, 1-½ lbs chicken, 1-½ lb pork sausage, sprig of parsley.*

Clean, butterfly and flatten pork. Season with next 8 ingredients. Chop sausage and boned chicken, spread over pork. Roll, wrap in foil, and bake for 45 minutes or until done. Remove roll and place pan over flame, add 1-½ cups water, 1 oz. more chopped onion, salt and pepper. Cook 10 minutes. Mix 1 Tbs cornstarch in a little cold water, add to pan and allow to thicken slightly. Serve slices of pork roll in a pool of natural gravy.

 **Your food notes**

319

MARTINIQUE

The area code for Martinique is 596

MARINAS
Ponton du Bakoua T:66 05 45, F:66 09 50, VHF:16, cc:V
SAEPP T:74 85 33, F:74 74 30, VHF:9, cc:V
Somatras Marina T:66 07 74, F:66 00 50, VHF:9

HAUL OUT
CarenAntilles T:74 77 70, F:74 78 22, VHF:16/73, cc:V
Martinique Dry Dock T:72 69 40/72 67 48, F:63 17 69
Ship Shop travel lift T:73 73 99, F:63 85 98, cc:V

SAILMAKERS
Helenon (Voilerie) T:60 22 05, F:63 17 63
La Voilerie du Marin T:74 73 10, F:74 72 22, VHF:67
Nautic Tech Care T:74 74 64, F:74 61 46
Tech Sails Voilerie T:68 03 34
Voilerie Caraibe Martinique T:66 07 24, F:66 09 98, VHF:16
Voilerie Caraibe Martinique T:74 88 09

MECHANICS/ENGINES/SALES/PARTS
Antilles Marine Services T:74 70 78/76 97 93, F:76 78 28
Captain's Shop T:66 06 77/02 72/74 87 55, F:66 01 03/74 96 71, cc:V
Croquet T:71 91 50, cc:V,A
Inboard Diesel T:78 71 96, F:78 80 75
Madia Boat T:63 10 61, F:63 48 70
Martinique Diesel T:51 16 13/51 34 33
Mecanique Plaisance T:66 05 40, F:66 04 08, cc:V

SERVICES
Alphamar T:66 00 89, 66 07 03, F:66 03 29
Antilles Marine Services T:74 70 78, 76 97 93, F:76 78 28
Cadet Petit T:63 79 18
Camaco T:73 70 45
Caraibes Greement T:74 80 33
Carib Electronic Engineering T:60 07 00, F:63 60 14
Chalmesin T:60 03 75, F:63 49 67
Chantier Naval du Marin T:74 89 42
La Survy T:79 70 66
Multicap Caraibes T:71 41 81, F:71 41 83
Nautic Services T:74 70 45, F:74 70 52
Plastic Services T:74 70 37, F:74 70 43
Polymar T:70 62 88, F:60 10 97
West Indies Nautic Distribution T:68 21 28, Fax:68 21 38

CHANDLERIES
Barnett Marine T&F:70 26 69, cc:V
Captain's Shop T:66 06 77/02 72, F:66 01 03, cc:V
Littoral T:70 28 70, cc:V
Puces Nautique T:60 58 48, F:63 73 31, cc:V
Puces Nautiques (Marin) T:74 62 12, F:74 62 22, cc:V
SCIM T:73 54 00/60 63 03, F:71 38 13, cc:V
Sea Services T:70 26 69, F:70 26 69, cc:V,D
Ship Shop T:71 43 40, F:70 13 02, cc:A,V
Ship Shop (Marin) T:74 78 22, cc:A,V

DUTY FREE PROVISIONING
Vatier T:70 11 39, F:60 00 00

SHOPS
8 à Huit, Case Pilot T:78 80 09
8 à Huit, St. Pierre T:77 20 96
Ah!Nanas T:73 60 94, cc:V,A
Armes Levalois T:73 11 96, cc:V
Au Printemps T:71 89 50, cc:V,A,Dn
Azurel T:74 84 14, F:74 99 46
Bora Bora T:66 01 68, cc:V
Boutique Jadis T:73 30 30, cc:V
Bricogite T:63 61 20/61 20, F:60 05 19, cc:V
Cadet Daniel T:71 41 48,
Calypso T:66 08 96, cc:V
Cannelle T:66 05 33, cc:V,A
Caraibes Plaisance T:74 85 73
Caribea T:66 05 33, cc:V,A
Carombole T:63 80 00, cc:V
Crazy T:73 26 68, cc:V,A
Deli France T:66 04 09
Galerie D'Art T:66 09 89, cc:V
Green T:63 27 96, cc:V,A
Jardin Creole T:66 06 78
La Mille Des Isles Boutiques T:76 70 51, cc:V
Maison du Plongeur T:66 02 38
Marine Paint Factory, T:74 84 14
Martine Cotten T:66 05 38, cc:V
Phileas Fogg T:66 07 17, cc:A,V
Phileas Fogg T:66 07 17, cc:A,V
Quick Photo T:71 43 13
Salines Shop T:70 28 28, cc:V,A
Super H T:63 69 69, cc:V
Supermarche Annette T:74 92 73, F:74 90 96, cc:V
Tailame T:71 87 57, cc:V

RESTAURANTS
West Coast
Au Plateau du Theater T:78 11 52
Celeste's Village T:78 80 41, $B-D, cc:AV
Chez Hugo 78 11 00, $C-D, cc:V
La Guinguette T:77 15 02, cc:A,V.
La Mouillage 78 15 09, $B-C, cc:V
La Vague T:78 14 34, $B-C, cc:A,V

Le Central T:78 12 54, $C
Le Maniba T:78 73 89, $B-C, cc:V
Pizzeria du Musée T:78 31 13, $C-D,
Royal Bellevue T:78 10 69, $C, cc:V
Snack Bar de La Plage T:78 81 36
Fort de France
Bmalke Snack T:63 03 10, $C-D
Coco Loco T:63 19 62/63 63 77, $C, cc:V
Dans un Jardin T:60 68 10, $A
L'Abri Cotier T:63 66 46, $B-C, cc:V
La Chacuterie T:63 45 96
La Fontane T:64 28 70, $A, cc:V,A.
La Grand Voile T:70 29 29, $A, cc:V
Le Bristol T:63 66 76, $A
Le Foulard T:61 15 72, $A, cc:A,V,
Le Mayflower T:70 54 45, $D,
Le Planteur T:63 17 45, $C, cc:V,
Marie Saintes T:70 00 81, $C
Pizzarita T:63 17 45, $C, cc:V,
The Crew T:33 04 14, $B-C, cc:V
Trois Ilets to Anse D'Arlet
Anse-Noire T:68 62 82, $B-C
Aux Poisson D'Or T:66 01 80, $B-C, cc:V
Boule de Neige T:66 05 60, $D, cc:V
Calalou T:68 31 67, $B, cc:V,A,Dn,Ds
Chez Desert T:68 61 86, $C
Chez Gaby T:68 65 04, $C,
Chez Jo Jo T:68 37 43, $C, cc:V
Davidiana T:66 00 54, $B, cc:A,V
Delices des Anses T:68 68 33, $C
El Patio T:66 02 70, $B, cc:V
Fanny's T:66 04 34, $C-D, cc:V
L'Abre a Pain $C-D
L'Amandier $C, cc:A
L'Amphore T:66 03 09, $A-B, cc:V,D
La Petite Louisiane, T:66 05 36,$B, cc:A,V
La Reine Hortense T:68 32 92, $B-C.
La Villa Creole T:66 05 53, $A-B, cc:V,Dn
Le Flamboyant des Isles T:68 67 75, $B,
  cc:V,
Le Gommier des Caraibes 68 62 79, $C
Le Marine T:66 02 32, $B-D cc:V
Le Matador T:66 05 36, $A-B, cc:A,V,Dn
Le Nid Tropical T:68 31 30, $D
Pignon sur Mer T:68 38 37, $A-B
Pizzeria Napoli T:66 03 79, $C, cc:V
Quai Sud T:68 66 30, $B-C, cc:V
Reflet de la Mer T:68 32 14, $C
Sable D'Or T:68 62 97, $C-D
Tamarin Plage $C, cc:V
Ti Sable T:68 62 44, $B-C, cc:V
St. Anne - Marin
Anthor T:76 72 93, $C-D, cc:V
L'Outre Mer T:76 91 51, $C-D, cc:V
La Carene T:74 70 22, $C-D, cc:V
Lagon Bleu T:74 80 10, $A-B, cc:V

Le Kaoma T:74 83 62, $C-D
Les Tameriniers T:76 75 62, $B
Poi et Virginie $A-B, cc:A,V
Sunny T:76 76 74, VHF:16, $B-C, cc:V
The Last Resort T:74 83 88, $C-D

TAXIS
Julien Alexander T:41 22 41/76 45 10
Taxis T:63 63 62

OTHER
Aquarium de La Martinique T:73 02 29
Cyparis Express T:77 18 51
Change Caraibes T:60 28 40/73 06 16
American Express Agent, Roger Albert, T:71
  44 44. 7, Rue Victor Hugo
For Visa Cash, Credit Agricole, Blvd General
  de Gaulle
Martinque Change T:63 80 33

CAR RENTAL
Avis T:51 17 70, cc:A,V
Budget T:63 69 00, F:63 51 35, cc:V,A,Dn
Funny (scooters) T:63 33 05, cc:A,V,D
Thrifty T:66 09 59, cc:A,V,D
St. Pierre
Jean Baptiste's T:77 22 91, cc:A,V
Eugene Garage T:77 13 21/77 15 89
cc:A,V
Pop's Rentals T:78 14 46
Marin
Pop's Car Rentals T:51 02 72, cc:V

EMERGENCY
Police emergency T:17
Police headquarters T:63 00 00
Ambulance T:51 51 52/ 71 59 48
Hospital T:50 15 15
Clinic T:71 82 85
Dr. Jacquesson T:68 42 41

AIRLINES, CHARTER, COURIER
Air Canada T:51 29 81
Air France T:63 75 52/ 63 69 97
Air Martinique T:51 09 90
American Airlines T:51 12 29
Eastern Airlines T:51 11 26
Federal Express T:75 56 56
LIAT T:51 10 00
Nouvelles Frontieres T:70 59 70

ST. LUCIA

The area code for St. Lucia is 809.

MARINAS
Bistro (The) T:452-9494, F:452-0453 VHF:16, cc:A,V
Jalousie Cove Marina T&F:459-7666, VHF:68, cc:A,V,Ds
Moorings (The) T:451-4357/4256, VHF:16, 85
Rodney Bay Marina T:452-0324 F:452-8363, VHF:16
St. Lucia Yacht Services T:452-5057, VHF:16, cc:V
Steak House Marina T:452 9800, F:452 9974, VHF:16/17

HAUL OUT
Castries Yacht Center T:542-6234/5348, F:453-2653, VHF:16
Rodney Bay Marina Boatyard T&F:452 9725, VHF:68

CHANDLERY
Johnson's Hardware T:452-2392, cc:A,V
Rodney Bay Chandlery T:452-9973 F:452-9974, VHF:16

SAILS/CUSHIONS
B&L Uphostery Clinic T:452-7644
Blue Water Holdings T:450-0688, F:450-9697, VHF:16
Marine Covers T&F:452-0186
Sunsail T:452-8848/8648, F:452-0839, VFH:16
Trevor Joseph T:450-8864

MECHANICS/REFRIGERATION
International Diesel and Marine Services T:453-1311, F:452-2523
Quick Fix Refrigeration T:484-9016/450-0587
Ray's Refrigeration T:452-4462
Rodney Bay Ship Services T:452-9973 F:452-9974, VHF:16

SERVICES
Andrew Tyson T:452-5794
Cay Electronics T:452-9922, F:452-8524, cc:V
Christopher Kessell T:452-4499, VHF:16 "Chrisalis"
Outfitters T:452 8360, F:452 0722
Remy and Parris Enterprises T:450-1037
Richard Cox T:453-2361
Sunsail T:452-8848/8648, F:452-0839, VFH:16
Windward Island Gases T:28514, 20339

SHOPS
Artsibit Gallery T:452-7865
Bagshaws Factory T:452-2139, cc:A,V
Bagshaws, Marigot T:451-3437, cc:A,V
Brydon and Partners T:452-2811
Caribbean Chateaux T:451-7421, F:451-7413
Chateaux des Fleurs T:451-7422
Chef's Choice T:453-0086, 452-4433
Choice Meats and Delicatessen T:451-7117
Choiseul Craft Center T:459-3226, cc:A,V
Colleta II T:452-3534, cc:A,V
Doolittles T: 451-4357, cc:A,V
Drug Store cc:V
Elliot's Mini Mart T:450-8721, F:450-8577
Erma's cc:A,V
Eroline's Foods T:459-7125, cc:A,V
Glace Motors & Supermarket T:452-8814, F:452-9699
J. N. Baptiste T:452-1139
J.Q.Charles T:452-2721
Maison Salaison T:452-6599
Marche De France T:452-8484
Mariner Market T:453-4357, cc:A,V
NAPA agency T:542-5034
Noah's Arkade T:452-2523, cc:A,V,Dn
Pieces of Eight T:452-0896, F:452 9806, cc:V
Rain's Boutique T:452-3022, cc:A,V
Sea Island Cotton Shop T:452-3674, cc:A,V
Snooty Agouti T:452-0321
Valmonts T:452-3817/8 ext 62
Windjammer Clothing Shop T:452-1041, cc:A,V

RESTAURANTS
A Pub T:452-8725, F:452-9073, VHF:68, $B-D, cc:A,V
Anse Chastanet T:459-7000, $A-C, cc:A,V
Bang Between the Pitons T:459-7864, $C-D
Bistro (The) T:452-9494, $B, cc:A,V
Bread Basket T:452-0647, $D
Capone's T:452-0284, $A-B, cc:A,V
Captain Hook's T:459-7365, $C-D
Charthouse T:452-8115, $B-C, cc:A,V
Chez Paul $B-C, cc:A,V
Club Caribe T:452-0580, $D
Coal Pot T:452-6811, $B, cc:V
Dasheene Restaurant T:459-7850/7323, $A-B cc:A,V,Ds
Dolittles T:451-4761, VHF:16/68/85, $B-D
Eagle's Inn T:452-0650, $C-D, cc:A,V
Fedo's New Venture T:459-5220, $C-D
Ginger Lily T:452-8303, $C-D, cc:A,V
Green Parrot T:452-3399, cc:A,V
Hummingbird T:459-7232, F:459-7033 VHF:16, $B-C, cc:V
Hurricane Hole Hotel T:451-4357, VHF:16,85, $A, cc:A,V,
Il Pirata T:454-6610, $B-C
Islander T:452-8757, $B-D,cc:V,A
Jalousie Plantation Resort T:459-7666, $A, cc:A,V,Ds,Dn
Jimmie's T:452-5142, $B-C, cc:V
JJ's T:451-4076, VHF:16, $B-C, cc:V
Key Largo T:452-0282, $D
Kimatrai T:454-6328, $C-D

ST. LUCIA (cont.)

Lime (The) T:452-0761, $B-D, cc:A,V
Mama Sheila's $D
Marina Yacht Club $C-D
Marine House T:452-8515, $C-D
Mortar and Pestle T:452-0336/8756, F:452-8677, $B, cc:A,V
Natural Cafe (The) T:452-6421, $D
O'Reilly's T:452-8830, $C
Odin's Ship Shop T:451-4098, $B-C
Paul's Place T:453-1588, $C-D
Pepino's Pizza, T:450-9778
Pink Elephant T:453-2847, $D, cc:A,V
Rain T:452-3022, $B-D, cc:A,V
San Antoine's T:452-4660, $A, cc:A,V
Spinnaker's T:452 8491, $B-D
St. Lucian Hotel T:452-8351, $A-C, cc:A,V
Steak House T:452-9800, $B, VHF:16/17, cc:A,V
Still (The) T:459-7224, $C, cc:V
Sunset Bar T:459-7100, $D
Windjammer Landings T:452-1311, $B, cc:A,V

CAR RENTAL

CLT T:452-0732, F:452-0401, cc:A,V,Dn, National Car Rental T:450 8500, F:450-8577, cc:A,V,Dn, Ds

AIRLINE, CHARTER, COURIER

Air Canada T:452-2550
Air Martinique T:452-2463
American Airlines T:454-6777/6779
British Airways T:452-7444/3951
BWIA T:454-5075/5234/5768
DHL T:453-1538
Eagle Air Services (charter) T:452-1900, F:452-8126 cc:V
Federal Express T:452-1320
Helenair T:452-7196, cc:A,V
LIAT T:452-3051/3053/2348
Toucan Travel T:452 0896/9963, F:452 9806, VHF:16, cc:A,V, Ds
World Travel T:452-5574, F:451-7445

OTHER

Barclays Bank T:452-3306, is an agent for the Visa Group
Blue Lagoon T:450-8543
Carib Travel T:452-2151/3176, is an agent for American Express
Home Services T:452-0450
La Panache Guest House T:450-0765
National Commercal Bank T:452-3562, F:453-1604
National Trust T:452-5005
Royal Bank of Canada T:452-2103, F:453-1604
Trims National Riding T:452-8273

EMERGENCY

Dr Soni T:452-6002, out of hours T:452-8116
Rodney Bay Medical Clinic (Dr. Beaubrun) T:452-8621, 452-0179
Kent Glace, Dentist T:452-3840
Police, Emergency T:999
Police, Castries T:452-2854
Police, Gros Islet T:452-8333
Police, Soufriere T:454-47333
Police, Vieux Fort T:454-6333

ST. VINCENT

The area code for St. Vincent is 809

MARINAS

Caribbean Charter Yacht Yard T:457 2178, VHF:68
Lagoon Marina & Hotel (The) T:458-4308, F:457-4716, VFH:68, cc:V

SERVICES AND CHANDLERIES

Aquatic Club T:458-4205, VHF:68, cc:V
Barefoot Yacht Charters T:456-9334, F:456-9238, VHF:68, cc:V
Carlton King T:457-9311
Charlie Tango T:458-4720, VHF:68
Fisherman's Cooperative T:456-2015
Howard's Marine T:457-4328, F:457-4268, VHF:68
Nichols Marine T:456-4118, F:456-5884, VHF:68
Oscar's Machine Shop T:456-4118, F:456-5884, VHF:68
Robert Taxi T:456-4873, VHF:68
Sam Taxi Service T:456-4338/4475, Fax:456-4233, VHF:68
St. Vincent Sales and Service T:457-1820, F:456-2620

SHOPS

96 Degrees T:457-2408, cc:V
Ace T:457-1639
Aquatic General Store T:458 4205
Barefoot Boutique T:456-9334, cc:V
Basil's Boutique T:458-4205, cc:V,A
Combination T:457-1063
Giggles T:457-1174, cc:A,V
Greaves T:457-1074
Jitterbugs T:457-2637
Lagoon Boutique T:458-4308, cc:V
Lime'n Pub Boutique T:458-4272, cc:V,A.
Made in De Shade T:457-2364, cc:V
Noah's Arkade T:457-1513, cc:A,V
Pharmaceuticals T:456-2133
Radio Shack T:457-2504
Rogers Photo Studio T:457-1572
Sprotties Silk Screen Shop T:456-1647, cc:V,

SHOPS (CONT)

Stechers T:457-1142, cc:A,V
T & M T:456-1616, cc:A,V
Y de Lima T:457-1681
Young Island Dock Shop T:458-4826, cc:A,V

RESTAURANTS AND NIGHTLIFE

Aggies Bar and Restaurant T:456-2110, $C-D, cc:V, Ds
Attic T:457-2558
Barefoot Restaurant T:456-9334, VHF:68, $B-C, cc:V
Beachcombers T:458-4283, VHF:68, $B-D,
Bounty T:456-1776
Browne's T:457-4000, cc:A,V
Cobblestone Inn T:456-1937, C-D
Dolphins T:457-4337, F:457-7241, $B-C, cc:A,V,Ds
Emerald Casino T:458-7421/7431
French (The) T:458-4972, VHF:68, $A-B, cc:V.
Heron Hotel T:457-1631
Lagoon T:458-4308, VHF:68, $B-C, cc:V
Lime 'n Pub T:458-4227, $B-D.
Papa Spoon's Rasta Ranch $D
Paradise Inn T:457-4795, $C-D, cc:V,
Petit Byahaut T:457-7008, VHF:68, $B, cc:V
Rooftop Restaurant T:456-1937, cc:A,V
Sid's Pub T:456-2315, $C-D
Stephens Hideaway T:458-2325, VHF:16,68, $C
Wallilabou Anchorage T:458-7270, VHF:68, $C-D
Young Island Resort T:458-4826, VHF:68, $A, cc:A,V

AIRLINE, CHARTER, COURIER

Air Martinique T:458-4528, overseas agent:Air France
Federal Express T:456-1649
Grenadine Tours T:458-4818, overseas agent Anchor Travel T:1 800 526 4789
LIAT T:457-1821, 458-4964
St. Vincent Grenadines Air T:456-5610/4942, F:458-4697

CAR RENTAL:

Johnsons U-drive T:458-4864, cc:A,V
Kim's T:456-1884, cc:A,V
Lucky Car Rentals T:456-2422, cc:V
Star Garage T:456-1743, cc:A,V

OTHER

Barclays Bank T:456-1706, with branches in Kingstown and Bequia, Visa agents.
Caribbean International Travel T:457-1841, American Express agents

EMERGENCY

Police, Coastguard T:999
Botanic Hospital T:457-1747

BEQUIA

The area code for Bequia is 809

MECHANICS

Caribbean Diesel T:458-3191, 457-3201, F:457-3203, VHF:68
GYE T:458-3347, T:458-3696, VHF:16,68

SAILMAKERS, CANVAS WORK

Allick Sailmaker T:458 3992, VHF:68
Bequia Canvas T:458-3369, VHF:68
North Sails T:457-3213, VHF:68

CHANDLERIES

Bequia Marine Supply T:457-3157
Bosun's Locker T:458-3246/3634, F:458-3925, cc:V
GYE T:458-3347, T:458-3696, VHF:16,68

SERVICES, CHANDLERIES

Bequia Marina T:458-3272, VFH:68, cc:V
Daffodil Marine Services T:458 3942, F:458 3369, VHF:68
East Coast Refinishing T:458-3370, VHF:68 "Handy Andy"
Frangipani Yacht Services T:458-3244, F:458-3824, VHF:68
Lighthouse, (The) T:458 3084, VHF:68
Sam Taxi Tours T:458 3686, F:458 3427, VHF:68

SHOPS

96 Degrees in the Shade T:458 3118, cc:A,V,Dn
Almond Tree Boutique T:458-3889, cc:V
Bequia Bookstore T:458-3905, cc:V
Claude Victorine T:458-3150, VHF:16 "Pigeon"
Crab Hole T:458-3290, cc:V,A
Creative Universe cc:A,V
Dieter's Deli T:457-3213, VHF:68
Doris Fresh Food T:458-3625, VHF:68,16
Garden, The T:458-3892
Green Boley Boutique T:458-3247, cc:A
Helmsman cc:V
Imperial Drugs T:458 3373
Island Things T:458-3903, cc:V
Knight's T:458-3379,
Local Color T:458-3202, cc:V,A
Lully's Tackle Shop T:458-3008. F:458-3797.
Made in De Shade cc:V
Mauvin's T:458-3669
Melinda T:458-3895, cc:A,V
Noah's Arkade T:458-3424, cc:V,A
Plantation House Boutique T:458-3890, cc:A
S&W T:458-3447

BEQUIA (cont)

Sergeant's T:458-3344
Shoreline T:458-3458 VHF:68
SHOPS (CONT)
Solanas T:458-3554, cc:V,A
Sprotties cc:A,V
Wallace's T:458-3360
Whalebone Boutique T:458-3233, cc:V,A
Wine Rack, (The) T:458 3777, cc:V

RESTAURANTS
Bequia Beach Club T:458-3248, VHF:16, $B-
  C, cc:V,A
Coco's Place T:458-3463, VHF:68
Daphne's T:458-3271, VHF:68, $C
Dawn's Creole T:458 3154, VHF:68, $C
De Reef T:458-3104 VHF:68, $C-D
Frangipani Hotel T:458-3255, $B, cc:A,V
Friendship Bay Resort T:458-3222, F:458
  4380. VHF:68, $A-B, cc:A,V
Gingerbread T:458-3800, VFH:68, $B-C,
  cc:A,V
Green Boley T:458-3247, $D
Julie's Guest House T:458-3304, VHF:68, $C
Keegan's T:458-3530, VHF:68, $D
Le Petit Jardin T:458-3318, VHF:16,68, $B,
  cc:V
Mac's Pizzeria T:458-3474, VHF:68, $C-D
Maranne's Ice Cream, T:458-3041
Old Fig Tree T:458-3201, VHF:68, $C-D
Old Fort, The T:458-3440, VHF:68,73, $A,
  cc:V
Plantation House T:458-3425, f:458-3612,
  VHF:68, $A-B, cc:V,A
Porthole T:458-3458, VHF:68, $C-D
S and W Snack Bar, $D
Schooners T:458-3658, VHF:68, $C
Spring on Bequia T:458-3414, VHF:68, $B,
  cc:A,V
Theresa's T:458 3802, VHF:68, $C
Whaleboner T:458-3233, $C-D, cc:V,A

OTHER
Barclays Bank T:458-3215 is an agent for Visa
Bequia Sailing Club, Box 1, Bequia, welcomes
  visitors to meetings on the last Friday of each
  month (venue on posters).
Federal Express T:458-3553
Grenadine Travel T:458 3795, F:458 3775,
  VHF:16,68, cc:V,A.
Paradise Windsurfing T:457-3142/458-3248
Police T:458-3211

CAR BIKE RENTALS, TAXIS
Gideon Taxi T:458-3760, VHF:68
Handy Andy T:458-3722

MUSTIQUE

The area code is 809
SHOPS
Basil's Boutique T:458-4621, cc:A,V
Treasure T:456-3522, F:456-3607 cc:A,V
Mustiko T:458-4621 ext 522, cc:A,V

RESTAURANTS
Basil's Bar T:458-4621, VHF:68, $A-B,
  cc:A,V
Cotton House T:456-4777, VHF:68, $A,
  cc:A,V

OTHER
Mustique Mechanical Service T:458-4621,
VHF:68
Other places T:458-4621 and ask

SOUTHERN GRENADINES

The area code is 809
MARINAS & SERVICES
Anchorage Yacht Club T:458-8221, T:458-
  8365, VHF:16, 68, cc:V
B and C fuels T:443 9110, VHF:16 "Golf
  Sierra"

RESTAURANTS
Anchor Guest House and Restaurant T:458
  8568, VHF:16, $C
Anchorage Yacht Club T:458-8221, F:458-
  8365, VHF:16, 68, $A-B, cc:V
Boll Head Restaurant and Bar T:458 8657,
  $C-D
Canouan Beach Hotel T:458-8888, VHF:16,
  $A-B
Clifton Beach Hotel T:458-8235, VHF:68,
  $B-C, cc:V,A,Ds
Crystal Sands $B-C
Dennis's Hideaway T&F:458-8594, VHF:68,
  $B-C
Island Paradise T:458 8068, VHF:68, $C
J & C Bar and Restaurant T:458 8558,
  VHF:68,16
Jennifer's T:458-8689, $C-D
Lambi T:458-8549, VHF:68, $C-D
Palm Island (Sunset Bar) T:458-8824, F:458-
  8804, VHF:68, $B-D, cc:V,A
PSV T:458-8801, VHF:16, $A
Salt Whistle Bay Resort T:458-8444,
  VHF:16, 68, $B
Sunny Grenadines T:458-8327, VHF:68, $B-
  C, cc:V
Sydney's Bar and Restaurant T: 458-2965,
  VHF:68, $C-D
T&N T:458-8348, $B-D
The Palm Beach T:443 9103, $C-D

S. GRENADINES (CONT)

SHOPS

Anchorage Boutique T:458-8244, VHF:68, cc:V
Boreal VHF:16
Chic Unique cc:A,V
La Classique T:458-8403,
Palm Island T:458-8824, VHF:68, cc:V,A
Park East VHF:68
PSV T:458-8801, VHF:16
Sandy Feet Boutique T:458-8824, VHF:68, cc:V,A

AIRLINES

LIAT, Air Martinique T:458-8328
Eagle Travel T:458-8179, VHF:68, cc:V,Ds

CARRIACOU

The area code for Carriacou is 809

SERVICES

Carriacou Boatbuilders T:443-7542, VHF:16,09
Dominique Aluminum T:443-8175
Uwe Machine Shop T:445-8572

RESTAURANTS

Callaloo T:443-8004, $C, cc:V,Ds
Cassada Bay Hotel T:443-7494, F:443-7672, VHF:16, $B, cc:V
Constant Spring T:443-7396, $D
Hillsborough Bar T:443-7932, VHF:16, $C-D
L'Aquilone T:445-7197, VHF:16, $C-D,
Liz's Place T:443-7425, $D
Oyster Shell T:443-7454, VHF:16, $C-D
Poivre and Sel T:443 8390, $B-D, VHF:16
Roof Gardens T:443-8919, $D
Scraper's Restaurant and Rum Punch Bar T:443-7403, VHF:16, $C-D
Silver Beach Resort T:443-7337, F:443-7165, VHF:16, $C, cc:V,A
Turtle Dove T:443-7194, VHF:16, $C
Twilight Bar VHF:16, $B

SHOPS

Alexis Supermarket T:443-7179.
Franky's Supermarket T:443-7310, F:443-8107
Twilight Supermarket T:443 8530, cc:V, VHF:16

CAR RENTALS

Alexis T:443-7179
Barba's T:443-7450, VHF:16
Silver Beach Resort T:443-7337, F:443-7165, VHF:16, cc:V,A

GRENADA

The area code for Grenada is 809

MARINAS AND HAUL OUT

Grenada Yacht Services T:440-2508/2883, VHF:16
Secret Harbour Marina T:440-4548/9/4439, F:444-4819, VHF:16/71, cc:V,A
Spice Island Marine T:444-4257/4342, F:444 2816, VHF:16, cc:V

MECHANICS, REFRIGERATION

Albert Lucas Machine Shop T:440-1281
Ben T:440-5360
Lagoon Marine Refrigeration T:440-3381
McIntyre Bros T:440-2044, F:440-4125
Power Tripper T:444-1351, F:444-4638

SAILMAKERS, CANVAS

Jeff Fisher (new sails only) T:440-2556, F:444-4638
Johnny Sails and Canvas T:444-1108, 441-9619, F:444-1108, VHF:16/66
Spice Island Marine T:444-4257/4342, F:444 2816, VHF:16, cc:V
Walker & Sons T:440-1756

SERVICES

CB Stove and Small Engine Repair Shop T:440-9559
Cottle Boat Works F:444-1108/444-2090
Grenada Yacht Club T:440-3050, VHF:6, 16
Henry Safari Tours T:444-5313, VHF:68, SSB:82921
Outfitters International T:440-7949, F:440-6680. In USA:T:474-5780, F:474-5083, Shipping address:6851 S.W. 21st CT., Unit 10, Ft. Lauderdale, FL33317. Mailing:Box 290240 Ft. Lauderdale, FL33329.
Tangey's Laundry and Dry Cleaning Service T:444-4747

SHOPS

Ace Hardware and Napa agent T:440-5265
Arnold John T:440-3412
Best Little Liquor Store in Town T:440-2198/3422, F:440 4179, VHF:16, Rhum Runner Base, cc:A,V
Bon Voyage T:440-4217, cc:A, V, Dn, Ds
Chantilly 444-2554
Essentials T:444-4662, VHF:16
Food Fair T:440-2588, 444-4573
Foodland T:440-1991/4496, VHF:80
Gifts Remembered T:440-2482, cc:A,V
Gittens Duty Free Shop 444-4101, cc:A,V
Hubbard's Home Center T:444-3232
Huggins T:440-2031
Imagine T:444-4028, cc:A,V
Jonas Browne and Hubbards T:440-2087
Marine World T:440-1748

GRENADA (cont.)

Mitchell's Pharmacy T:444-4845
On Site Software Support T:444-3653
Tikal T:440-2310, cc:V,A
Yellow Poui Art Gallery T:440-3878/3001

RESTAURANTS

Aquarium Beach Club T:444-1410, $B-D, cc:A,V,Ds
Beachside Restaurant T:444-4247, $B-D, cc:A, V
Boatyard Restaurant T:444-4662, VHF:68, $B-C, cc:A,V
Calabash T:444-4334, $A, cc:V,A
Canboulay T:444-4401, $A-B, cc:A,V
Coconut Beach French Restaurant T:444-4644, $A-B
Cot Bam T:444-2050, $C-D, cc V,Ds
Delicious Landing T:440-9747, VHF:16, $B-C, cc:V
Gem Holiday Beach Resort T:444-4224/1189, F:440-4124
Horseshoe Beach Hotel T:444-4410/4244, cc:V,A
Indigo's T:444-2000, F:444-1247, $B, cc:A,V
Mamma's T:440-1459, $B-C
Nutmeg T:440-2539, $C-D, cc:V
Portofino T:440-3986, B-D, cc:A,V
Red Crab T:444-4424, $A-B, cc:A,V
Rudolf's T:440-2241, $B-D
Secret Harbour T:440-4548/9/4439, F:444-4981, VHF:71, $A-B, cc:V,A
Tropicana T:440-1586, $C-D, cc:V
Victoria Hotel T:444-9376, $D, cc:A,V

CAR RENTALS/TAXIS

Boatyard Taxi T:444-1703, VHF:16
David's Rent-a-Car T:440 2399/3038, cc:A,V
Funseeker Tours T:444-1342 441-9443, F:444 4847, VHF:16
Jerry's Auto Service T:440-1730, cc:A,V
K&J T:440-4227/9621, VHF:16
Leroy Taxi 440-4803, 444-3640, VHF:16/68
McIntyre Bros T:440-2044, cc:A,V
Rock Taxi Service T:444-5136
Selwyn Maxwell T:444-1653, VHF:68,
Y & R Car Rentals T:444-4448, cc:A,V

AIRLINES, CHARTER, COURIER

American Airlines T:444-2222/2233
BWIA T:440-3818/3819
DHL T:440-5009
Federal Express T:440-2206
LIAT T:440-2796/2904
Point Saline Airport T:440-4101

OTHER

Grenada International Travel T:440-2220/2945 are agents for American Express.

Grenada Bank of Commerce, T:444 4919
Barclays Bank T:440-3232, are agents for Visa
No Problem Apartments T:444-4634

EMERGENCY

Police T:911
Dr Michael Radix, Foodfair Shopping Center T:440-4379/444-4855, emergency:443 5330 General Medicine
Dr Roxanne Nedd, T:444-2273, Marquie Mal Grand Anse, Dentist
General Hospital T:434
St. George's School of Medecine T:444-4271

MAIL DROPS

MARTINIQUE

La Voilerie du Marin, 4, Rue de la Liberte, 97290 Marin, Martinique, FWI
Ship Shop, CarenAntilles, Ancien Usine du Marin, Marin 97290, Martinique, FWI
Ship Shop, Baie de Tourelles, Fort de France, Martinique, FWI (not yet open)

ST. LUCIA

Rodney Bay Marina, P.O. Box 1538, Castries, St. Lucia, W.I.
Outfitters International P.O. Box 928, Castries, St. Lucia, W.I
Marigot Bay Marina, P.O. Box 1538, Castries, St. Lucia, W.I.
The Bistro, Rodney Bay, Castries, St. Lucia, W.I.

BEQUIA

Frangipani Yacht Services, Box 1, Bequia, St. Vincent and the Grenadines, W.I.

UNION ISLAND

Anchorage Yacht Club, Union Island, St. Vincent and the Grenadines, W.I.

GRENADA

Spice Island Marine, P.O. Box 449, St. George's, Grenada, W.I.
Grenada Yacht Services, St. George's, Grenada, W.I.
Grenada Yacht Club, St.George's, Grenada, W.I.
Outfitters International, Box 581, St. George's, Grenada, W.I.
The Moorings, Secret Harbour, P.O. Box 11, St. George's, Grenada WI.

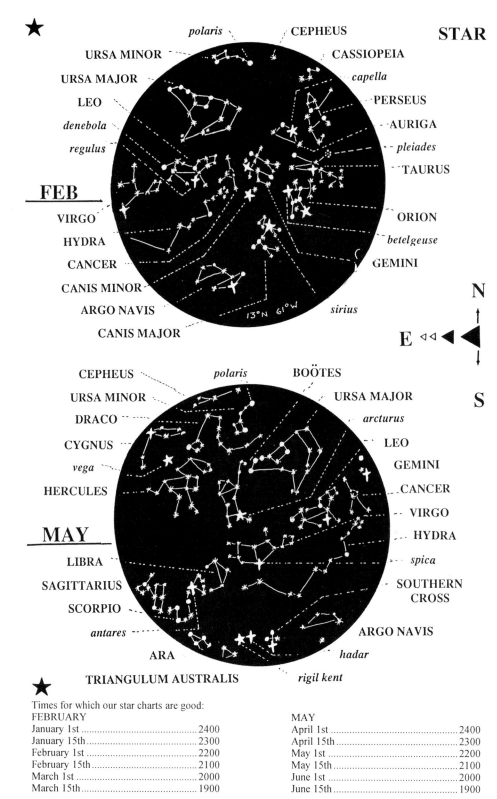

STAR

polaris · CEPHEUS
URSA MINOR · CASSIOPEIA
URSA MAJOR · capella
LEO · PERSEUS
denebola · AURIGA
regulus · pleiades
· TAURUS
FEB
VIRGO · ORION
HYDRA · betelgeuse
CANCER · GEMINI
CANIS MINOR
ARGO NAVIS
CANIS MAJOR
13°N 61°W · sirius

N
E ◁◁ ◀ ◀
S

CEPHEUS · polaris · BOÖTES
URSA MINOR · URSA MAJOR
DRACO · arcturus
CYGNUS · LEO
vega · GEMINI
HERCULES · CANCER
· VIRGO
MAY · HYDRA
LIBRA · spica
SAGITTARIUS · SOUTHERN CROSS
SCORPIO
antares · ARGO NAVIS
ARA · hadar
TRIANGULUM AUSTRALIS · rigil kent

Times for which our star charts are good:

FEBRUARY		MAY	
January 1st	2400	April 1st	2400
January 15th	2300	April 15th	2300
February 1st	2200	May 1st	2200
February 15th	2100	May 15th	2100
March 1st	2000	June 1st	2000
March 15th	1900	June 15th	1900

CHARTS

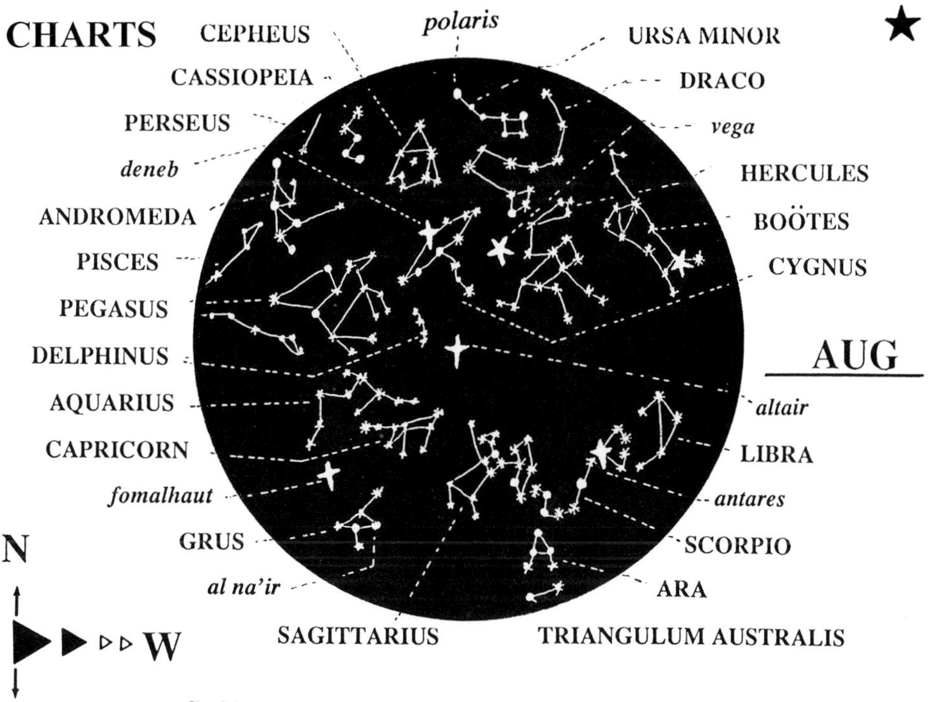

CEPHEUS
polaris
URSA MINOR
CASSIOPEIA
DRACO
PERSEUS
vega
deneb
HERCULES
ANDROMEDA
BOÖTES
PISCES
CYGNUS
PEGASUS
AUG
DELPHINUS
AQUARIUS
altair
CAPRICORN
LIBRA
fomalhaut
antares
N
GRUS
SCORPIO
al na'ir
ARA
W
SAGITTARIUS
TRIANGULUM AUSTRALIS
S

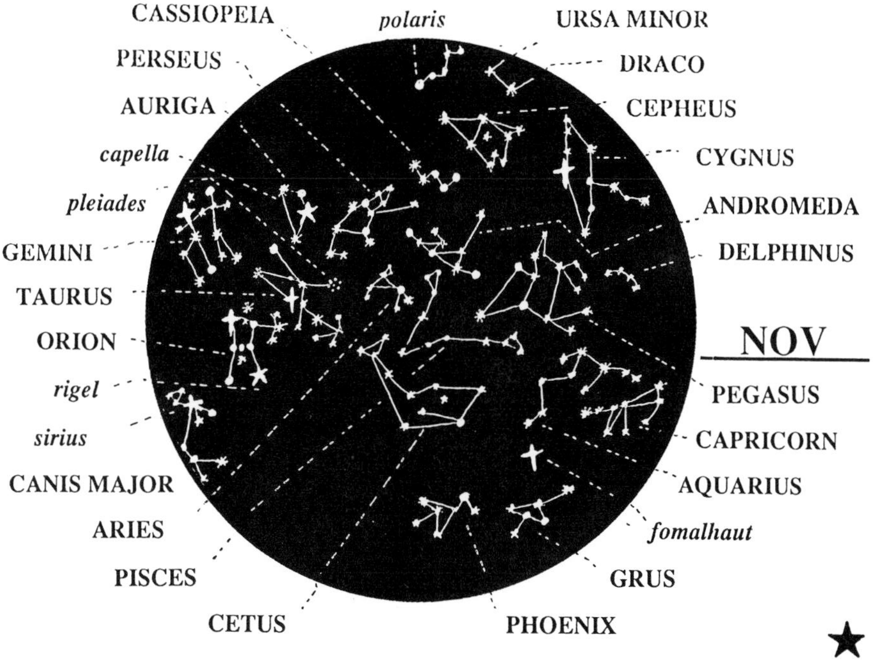

CASSIOPEIA
polaris
URSA MINOR
PERSEUS
DRACO
AURIGA
CEPHEUS
capella
CYGNUS
pleiades
ANDROMEDA
GEMINI
DELPHINUS
TAURUS
ORION
NOV
rigel
PEGASUS
sirius
CAPRICORN
CANIS MAJOR
AQUARIUS
ARIES
fomalhaut
PISCES
GRUS
CETUS
PHOENIX

AUGUST	
July 1st	2400
July 15th	2300
August 1st	2200
August 15th	2100
September 1st	2000
September 15th	1900

NOVEMBER	
October 1st	2400
October 15th	2300
November 1st	2200
November 15th	2100
December 1st	2000
December15th	1900

GENERAL INDEX

ADVERTISERS INDEX